THE
CONFEDERATE
CONSTITUTION
OF 1861

THE CONFEDERATE CONSTITUTION OF 1861

An Inquiry into American Constitutionalism

Marshall L. DeRosa , 1955 -

UNIVERSITY OF MISSOURI PRESS

COLUMBIA AND LONDON

For Americans, North and South, who dutifully participated in the cataclysmic struggle for constitutional government, 1861–1865

Copyright © 1991 by
The Curators of the University of Missouri
University of Missouri Press, Columbia, Missouri 65201
Printed and bound in the United States of America
All rights reserved
5 4 3 2 1   95 94 93 92 91

Library of Congress Cataloging-in-Publication Data

DeRosa, Marshall L., 1955–
    The Confederate Constitution of 1861 : an inquiry into American
constitutionalism / Marshall L. DeRosa.
        p.   cm.
    Includes bibliographical references (p.   ) and index.
    ISBN 0–8262–0806–1 (alk. paper). — ISBN 0–8262–0812–6 (pbk. :
alk. paper)
        1. Confederate States of America—Constitutional law.
    2. Confederate States of America—Constitutional history.
    I. Title
    KFZ9002.D47   1991
    342.75'029—dc20
    [347.50229]   91–23889
                                                           CIP

⊛™ This paper meets the requirements of the
American National Standard for Permanence of Paper
for Printed Library Materials, Z39.48, 1984.

Designer: Kristie Lee
Typesetter: Connell-Zeko Type & Graphics
Printer and binder: Thomson-Shore, Inc.
Typeface: Palatino

Contents

Acknowledgments

Not wanting to draw fire upon colleagues and associates who have assisted me in the course of this research project for any deficiencies found herein, nevertheless I feel obliged to express my sincere thanks to them for their support. Professors Ross M. Lence and Donald S. Lutz at the University of Houston, Professors Ellis Sandoz and René de Visme Williamson at Louisiana State University, Professor M. E. Bradford at the University of Dallas, Ms. Beverly Jarrett, Editor-in-Chief of the University of Missouri Press—all have enhanced the quality of this book beyond what would otherwise have been the case.

I offer special thanks to my dear wife, Mary, who endured much and assisted me greatly in this endeavor; to my parents, Louis and Agnes, for instilling in their children time-tested values; and to my son Elijah, who made the entire endeavor worthwhile.

The present moment discovers a new face in our affairs. Our object has been all along to reform our federal system and to strengthen our governments, to establish peace, order and justice in the community; but a new object now presents. The plan of government now proposed is evidently calculated totally to change, in time, our condition as a people. Instead of being thirteen republics under a federal head, it is clearly designed to make us one consolidated government. . . . This consolidation of the states has been the object of several men in this country for some time past. Whether such a change can ever be effected in any manner, whether it can be effected without convulsions and civil wars, whether such a change will not totally destroy the liberties of this country, time can only determine.

—Richard Henry Lee, 1787

The real revolution in that country was not what is called the Revolution, but is a consequence of the Civil War; after which arose a plutocratic elite; after which the expansion and material development of the country was accelerated; after which was swollen that stream of mixed immigration, bringing (or rather multiplying) the danger of development into a *caste* system which has not yet been quite dispelled. For the sociologist, the evidence from America is not yet ripe.

—T. S. Eliot, 1949

THE
CONFEDERATE
CONSTITUTION
OF 1861

Introduction

The Confederate States of America, politically established in 1861 and militarily extirpated in 1865, was neither simply a historic accident initiated by radicals attempting to prolong the life of an anachronistic system of labor nor the product of "fire-eating" political opportunists seeking personal aggrandizement at the expense of their fellow citizens. These factors had an impact, but in the final analysis the Confederate States of America was the consequence of a constitutional crisis the origins of which could be traced back to the U.S. Constitution of 1789. It was not a crisis for constitutional government per se, but the consequence of an incrementally changing constitutional arrangement increasingly unacceptable to the southern section of the Union. The Southerners did not abandon constitutional government; to the contrary, they reaffirmed their commitment to constitutional government under the auspices of the Confederate Constitution.

From the Southerners' perspective what they abandoned in 1861 was the deterioration of American constitutionalism, a deterioration initiated and sustained by their political rivals in the North. In July of 1861 the moderate Alexander H. Stephens, vice-president of the Confederacy, claimed on behalf of the South that "we simply wish to govern ourselves as we please. We simply stand where our revolutionary fathers stood in '76. We stand upon the great fundamental principle announced on the 4th of July, 1776, and incorporated in the Declaration of Independence—that great principle announced that governments derive their just power from the consent of the governed."[1] The fact that Stephens's sentiments were representative of the South as a whole is evidenced by the second resolution passed by the Confederate Congress. It reads, in part, that

> whereas the United States are waging war against the Confederate States, with the avowed purpose of compelling the latter to reunite with them under the same Constitution and Government; and whereas the waging of war with such an object is in direct opposition to the sound republican maxim, that "all government rest upon the consent of the governed," and can only tend to consolidation in the General Government, and the consequent destruc-

tion of the rights of the States; and whereas the result being attained, the two sections can only exist together in the relation of
the oppressor and oppressed, because of the great preponderance
of power in the Northern section, coupled with dissimilarity of
interest.[2]

Leading Southerners were convinced that the Confederacy, a government premised upon the consent of the citizenry, and its attending
Constitution were essential to the South's political self-determination, convictions most certainly within the tradition of American
constitutionalism.

However, the Southern commitment to constitutional government has been overshadowed by what is generally understood as
the *raison d'être* of the Confederacy: slavery and the economic system it supported. But to focus attention either exclusively or primarily on the slavery issue, thereby casting the Confederate Constitution off as an ill-fated attempt to legitimatize what was for the
most part an anomaly to the civilized world, is to slight a crucial
period of American constitutional development.

It is not by accident that the prevailing view in the academy contends that the Confederate States of America was the product of
"federal dreamers" determined to establish an authoritarian regime
over the South. One leading advocate, *inter alios,* of this school of
thought is Louis Hartz.[3] However, Hartz's position has the support
of substantial precedent, namely the Republican party of Abraham
Lincoln. The party of Lincoln effectively perpetrated a political coup,
the results of which were ingrained into the American political con-
sciousness. Lincoln successfully depicted the struggle between
North and South (i.e., Northern Republican and Southern Demo-
crat) as a contest between republican government and tyranny. In
Lincoln's own words, a Northern victory was imperative so that the
"Government of the people, by the people, and for the people shall
not perish from the earth."[4]

Lincoln's portrayal of the conflict is intelligible in light of the fact
that he was a politician striving for political objectives. But such
portrayals by more recent scholarship are by and large gross over-
simplifications that demonstrate a failure to understand the politics
of antebellum America and the complexities of American constitutional federalism.

The period in which the Confederate Constitution was drafted
marks an important crossroad in American constitutional and political development, the consequences of which are to this day topics
of intense debate—topics such as the nature of American feder-

alism, civil rights and liberties, laissez-faire economics and the scope of governmental power. Accordingly, an analysis of the Confederate Constitution provides useful insight into the substantive and procedural aspects of constitutional development as they pertain to these and other very important constitutional-political issues. As a case in point, much of late has been written regarding the Fourteenth Amendment to the U.S. Constitution. To appreciate the full impact of the Fourteenth Amendment, an understanding of the constitutional debates during the antebellum period is essential, and such an understanding is premised upon, to a significant extent, the Southern (and subsequent Confederate) constitutional principles, many of which the Fourteenth Amendment was designed to constitutionally and politically negate. But that negation has not been finalized, since many of the Confederate principles are indigenous to the American constitutional system of government. Hence, the Confederate Constitution is relevant because it raised, and continues to raise, pertinent questions that cannot be glossed over if American constitutionalism is to be placed on terra firma.

The contemporary relevance of the Confederate Constitution is obvious enough when one considers the partisan furor over the mere symbols of its principles, such as the current drive to remove the Confederate flag from certain southern universities, or more substantive policy issues such as natural rights, federal budget deficits, a presidential line-item veto, and the states' socioeconomic public policy prerogatives, to name a few. The Confederate Constitution has much to contribute toward the articulation of these and other constitutional-political questions.

Unfortunately, the level of analysis regarding the Confederacy has not arrived at what Bernard Bailyn referred to as the tragic stage of historical analysis. Consequently, the contributions the Confederate framers made to past debates and what they have to offer regarding contemporary ones have been neglected. Bailyn provides insight into why this is the case. He delineates three types of historical analysis: heroic, whig, and tragic, with the heroic being the most partisan.

> . . . the earliest historical writings that follow a great and controversial event are still a significant part of the event itself. At that near point in time the outcome is still in some degree in question, the struggle in an extended form is still alive, emotions are still deeply engaged; and because of this immediacy, indeterminacy, and involvement, attempts at explanations of what happened tend to be *heroic* in character. . . . Then in the course of time the

historian's angle of vision shifts. This change in viewpoint is a
logical one, part of an almost inevitable alteration in the historian's
relation to the event. . . . he seeks the seeds of future events,
dwells on cognates and analogues, and strives to show how the
future was implicit in the past. This is the *whig* interpretation. . . .
And then at last there is a final turn in the relation between the
viewer and the event, which leads to a third and, so it seems to
me, an ultimate mode of interpretation. At this point the distance
has become so great, the connections so finely attenuated, that all
of the earlier assumptions of relevance, partisan in their nature,
seem crude, and fall away, and in their place comes a neutrality, a
comprehensiveness, and a breadth of sympathy lacking in earlier
interpretations. . . . Now the historian, in his analysis and de-
scription, is no longer a partisan. He has no stake in the outcome.
He can now embrace the whole of the event, see it from all sides.
What impresses him most are the latent limitations within which
everyone involved was obliged to act; the inescapable boundaries
of action; the blindness of the actors—in a word, the tragedy of the
event.[5]

The level of analysis regarding the Confederacy places contempo-
raries and their predecessors somewhere between the heroic and
whig stages, which to some degree taints constitutional-historio-
graphical scholarship. It is for this reason that the time has arrived
for giving the Confederate Constitution a fair hearing. If its constitutional principles are to be refuted, never again to rise from the
ashes in whatever form, or contrarily, if there is some merit in certain of those principles, scholarship should be willing to confront
that reality. To do otherwise is to implicitly acknowledge the absence of a sound refutation, and in lieu of that a visceral reaction
producing ill-founded political dogma.

Such is the aim of this book: not simply to function as a clarifica-
tion of the constitutional issues that brought this nation to a bloody
civil war but, more important, to reassess those causes and effects
from the perspective of constitutionalism, thereby bringing to light
the connection between the fundamental issues of 1787 and 1861
(issues such as American federalism, fiscal responsibility, and even
republican government itself). As will become evident to the atten-
tive reader, these issues have not been resolved and will not be
resolved until viable alternatives to the current course of constitutional-political development are seriously considered, alternatives
that are consistent with American political principles.

One final prefatory note is in order. The political archaeology this
book undertakes does not pretend to be an exhaustive study of all
the political ramifications of this Southern document. Its aim is

somewhat more modest; to clear away some of the debris that has been heaped upon the constitutional principles of the Confederacy and thus to provide meaningful insight into American constitutionalism, a constitutionalism in which the Confederacy most certainly participated. As will become irresistibly evident, the Confederate States of America was premised upon principles dating back to the American Antifederalists of the constitutional convention. This is to say neither that the Confederate framers were opposed to all aspects of the political doctrine of the Federalists nor that they favored a return to the federal arrangement under the Articles of Confederation. The primary concern of the Confederate framers was the centralization of political power at the national level to the detriment of the states; it was this centralization inherent in the political principles of the Federalists which they rejected. Consequently, their Constitution intentionally reinvigorated the states with the spirit of the Tenth Amendment's reserved-powers provision as interpreted by its Antifederalist sponsors. Such a reinstatement of conservative principles, they were convinced, was necessary to secure "government of, by, and for the people."

Chapter One

Deconstructing the Constitution

The decade preceding the outbreak of the American Civil War presented the spectacle of a developing constitutional crisis, as opposing political forces competed for control of the machinery of government. The contest for control centered on policy objectives of such high conflict and high salience that the period could accurately be described as one of determined political warfare. The linchpin of the conflict was sectionalism, in that political antagonists were coalescing along geographical boundaries that facilitated the formation of sectional political parties (i.e., Northern Republican and Southern Democratic). Public policy issues such as protectionism, federally funded internal improvements, and slavery placed the political combatants on a collision course that went beyond manageable differences of opinion and toward mutually exclusive interpretations regarding key provisions of the U.S. Constitution. This competitive constitutional exegesis strained the tenuous ties that held the American federal system of states together.

American federalism involves many distinct governments—the national and various state governments, each with their respective constitutional powers and obligations. All of these governments are theoretically premised upon the consent of the governed, with sovereignty residing in the people and not in the governments. But the compound republic of America complicates the matter of sovereignty.[1] Within the context of American federalism does sovereignty reside in the people in their national or state capacities? To be more precise, does the U.S. Constitution establish an association of sovereign individuals within their respective states or a national community of sovereign individuals the states notwithstanding? If the former, does a state possess the prerogative to nullify national policies adverse to its interests, nullification being a prerogative of a sovereign state? And if the latter, does the national government have the constitutional authority to enforce its policies over the objections of a state? The answers to these questions have far-reach-

7

ing implications for American federalism, insofar as their resolution will inevitably result in either state or national supremacy, the antebellum Confederate and Republican positions respectively.

But the adherents of each position fluctuated and did not firmly commit to either national or state supremacy until late in the antebellum period. Their circumstantially changing positions reflected their policy objectives depending upon whether national or state supremacy was most conducive to their political needs. For example, some Northerners resorted to state sovereignty in reaction to the 1857 Dred Scott decision as a justification for noncompliance with fugitive slave laws, whereas the South relied upon national supremacy to enforce the same. But when the election of 1860 placed Northern interests in control of the national government, their nationalism and the Southern commitment to state sovereignty crystallized. Such fluctuations between nationalism and state sovereignty certainly had their precedents. The War of 1812 resulted in the Hartford Convention as the New England states threatened to secede from the Union to escape the economic hardships of the war; and New York City considered aligning itself with the Confederacy in 1861 to protect its mercantile interests. But by 1861 the political divisions between North and South regarding constitutional exegesis were so entrenched that the Constitution ceased to be the instrument of a "more perfect Union" and rather served as the vehicle for dissension and separation. It was at this stage of American politics that the inherent cleavages of national and state supremacy were confirmed and the transient fluctuations ceased.

The fact that the U.S. Constitution was the patrimony of North and South did not prevent interpretations of nationalism and state sovereignty that were mutually exclusive and yet mutually plausible. This was due in large measure to the ambiguity of the Constitution regarding federalism. Referring to the complexities involved in the constitutional debates regarding federalism, Publius acknowledged that "there are three sources of vague and incorrect definitions: indistinctness of the object, imperfection of the object of conception, and inadequateness of the vehicle of ideas. Any one of these must produce a certain degree of obscurity. The convention, in delineating the boundary between federal and state jurisdictions, must have experienced the full effect of them all."[2] This was most certainly the case by 1861 as Northerners insisted upon a model of federalism consisting of a national community of individuals, with sovereignty being a national phenomenon—that is, nationalism—whereas Southerners adhered to a model consisting of a community of states, with the citizens in their respective states functioning as the repositories of sovereignty and thereby controlling the bulwarks of their social and economic interests—that is, state sovereignty.

To discern the model of federalism to which Southerners of antebellum America were committed, it is useful to consider the alternative they debated, and ultimately rejected, with their Northern brethren. That debate and rejection unified Southerners to the extent that they were willing to establish their own model of American federalism in the Confederate Constitution of 1861.

New York Senator William H. Seward, the target of the derisive nomenclature "the Wizard of the North" by his Southern congressional colleagues, epitomized the Northern position regarding federalism. Appropriately, attention will be focused on Seward and the responses he evoked from his Southern colleagues. This approach is justified on the grounds that Seward was second to none in articulating the Northern position on the floor of the Senate, thereby serving as a lightning rod for Southern rebuttals that in themselves are manifestations of the Southern position.

The intractable North-South polarization concerning the nature of American federalism was visible in the U.S. Senate during the 1850 senatorial debates on the admission of California into the Union. While most attention has been focused on the forensic skills of Senators John C. Calhoun, Henry Clay, and Daniel Webster, the significant discourse was between Calhoun and Seward—significant in the sense that the positions articulated by them were mutually exclusive and at the heart of the constitutional impasse between North and South.

Making the case for Southern political self-determination, South Carolina Senator John C. Calhoun contended that the Northern states, via the national government, were systematically perpetrating aggressions on Southern interests by cunningly attacking Southern domestic institutions (i.e., slavery) and Southern commercial prosperity (i.e., funding Northern internal improvements through a protectionist policy adverse to Southern economic interests). Calhoun attributed Northern success to the transition from a federal to a consolidated democracy.

> That the Government claims, and practically maintains, the right to decide in the last resort as to the extent of its powers, will scarcely be denied by anyone conversant with the political history of the country. That it also claims the right to resort to force to maintain whatever power she claims, against all opposition, is equally certain. Indeed, it is apparent, from what we daily hear,

that this has become the prevailing fixed opinion of a great majority of the community. Now, I ask, what limitation can possibly be
placed upon the powers of a Government claiming and exercising
such rights? And, if none can be, how can the separate governments of the States maintain and protect the powers reserved to
them, and among others, the sovereign powers by which they ordained and established, not only their separate State constitutions
and governments, but also the Constitution and Government of
the United States? But, if they have no constitutional means of
maintaining them against the right claimed by this Government,
it necessarily follows that they hold them at its pleasure and discretion, and that all the powers of the system are in reality concen-
trated in it. It follows that the character of the Government has
been changed, in consequence, from a Federal Republic, as it
originally came from the hands of its framers, and that it has been
changed into a great national consolidated Democracy.[3]

Led by Calhoun, Southerners maintained that the transition from a
"Federal Republic" to a "great national consolidated Democracy"
placed the exercise of sovereign authority at the national level and
divested the states of the same, particularly the Southern states
because of their national numerical minority status.

According to Calhoun, the transition from a federal republic of
sovereign states to a nationally consolidated democracy was due to
a disequilibrium between the two sections. The South constituted a
minority in both number of states and population, thereby clearing
the way for the political ascendancy of the North. But the constitutional federal republic would have been preserved if (1) revenue
raised in the South had not been disproportionately expended in
the North to establish an economic infrastructure that in turn attracted immigrants en masse who were by and large hostile to
Southern social arrangements, and (2) the South were not prohibited from occupying significant portions of the U.S. territories with
those social arrangements, i.e., the institution of slavery. Had these
two conditions been met, the political equilibrium between the two
sections would have been maintained, and the South could have
remained in the Union with its honor and safety intact. Had the
South not been reduced to a minority status in the House and
Senate, it would have possessed the legislative means to protect its
interests against Northern aggressions.[4]

Seward expressed positions diametrically opposed to those of
Calhoun on two critical points, American federalism and the status
of slavery therein. First, Seward maintained that the U.S. Constitution established a national community of individuals, not a community of states. Responding to Calhoun, Seward contended that "the

States are not parties to the Constitution as States; it is the Constitution of the people of the United States. But even if the States continue as States, they surrendered their equality as States, and submitted themselves to the sway of the numerical majority. . . . the preamble of the Constitution not only asserts the sovereignty to be, not in the States, but in the people, but also promulgates the objects of the Constitution. . . . But for all this, I know only one country and one sovereign—the United States of America and the American people."[5] Accordingly, state minorities are subject to the national numerical majority, due to the absence of state sovereignty and the presence of the nation's only sovereign authority the American people.

And second, Seward attacked the most important of Southern domestic institutions, slavery, on two fronts. First, he argued that the Constitution does not sanction the institution: "I deny that the Constitution recognizes property in man. I submit, on the other hand, most respectfully, that the Constitution not merely does not affirm that principle, but on the contrary, altogether excludes it."[6] If Seward's premises that the states lack sovereignty and the U.S. Constitution does not sanction slavery are accepted, then a national majority could, through statutory laws, not only prohibit slavery in the territories but even nationally emancipate the slaves. Any state constitution that sanctioned slavery would prove to be a minor legal obstacle, due to the subordinate status of state constitutional law in the face of national sovereignty.

Seward's second front for challenging the constitutional legitimacy of slavery is premised on a "higher law" approach; that is, because natural law does not presumably sanction slavery, any positive law that does is in effect null and void as a consequence of the natural law prohibition. A case in point, Article IV, section 2, of the U.S. Constitution, in conjunction with subsequent statutory enactments, provides for the rendition of fugitive slaves. Seward associated compliance with those fugitive slave laws with complicity in upholding slavery and therefore with violating natural laws that should take precedence over the U.S. Constitution in the event of a conflict between the two. Seward argued that "the right of extradition of a fugitive is not admitted by the law of nature and of nations, but rests in voluntary compacts. . . . All these laws must be brought to the standard of the laws of God, and must be tried by that standard, and must stand or fall by it. . . . To conclude on this point: We are not slaveholders. We cannot, in our judgement, be either true Christians or real freemen, if we impose on another a chain that we defy all human power to fasten on ourselves." Seward was implicitly directing his actual and potential constituents toward noncompliance with the laws of the land regarding the rendition of fugitive slaves, by contending that compliance with such laws was unacceptable because they violated the natural rights of the runaway slaves and thereby subverted the higher law component that is implicit in the Constitution. Regarding the extension of slavery into the territories, he proclaimed: "We cannot establish slavery, because there are certain elements of the security, welfare, and greatness of nations, that we all admit, or ought to admit, and recognize as essential; and these are the security of natural rights, the diffusion of knowledge, and the freedom of industry. Slavery is incompatible with all of these, and just in proportion to the extent that it prevails and controls in any republican State, just to that extent it subverts the principle of democracy and converts the State into an aristocracy of despotism."[7]

According to Seward's constitutionalism, the subversion of the U.S. Constitution would result from the violation of the American political axiom that "all men are created equal, and have inalienable rights of life, liberty, and the choice of the pursuit of happiness." However, his "axiom" of American political culture has its premise, not in the U.S. Constitution, but in a simplistic reading of the Declaration of Independence. The Declaration of Independence served a dual purpose for Seward; it asserts the political equality of all men and it functioned as the founding document for the American nation, thereby making its political equality of all men maxim a constitutional responsibility enforceable by the U.S. government. Of course, according to Seward's interpretation of the Declaration, the Southern institution of slavery is incompatible with that maxim.

> But have we come to that stage of demoralization and degeneracy so soon? We, who commenced our political existence and gained the sympathies of the world by proclaiming to other nations that we held "these truths to be self-evident: that all men are created equal, and have certain inalienable rights; and that among these rights are life, liberty, and the pursuit of happiness;" we who, in the spirit of that declaration, have assumed to teach and to illustrate, for the benefit of mankind, a higher and better civilization than they have hitherto known! If the Congress of the United States shall persist in this attempt, then they shall at least allow me to predict its results: Either you will not establish African slavery in Kansas, or you will do it at the cost of the sacrifice of all the existing liberties of the American people.[8]

Seward's elevation of the Declaration of Independence to constitutional status was not alien to American constitutional development.

According to this view, the Declaration of Independence was *the* founding document, established by the sovereign people of America as opposed to being an act of sovereign states. Thus the Declaration supersedes the Articles of Confederation, the state constitutions, and the U.S. Constitution as fundamental law. The significance of Seward's inauspicious utilization of the Declaration of Independence is that it struck at the core of two fundamental assumptions held by Southern statesmen, the sovereignty of the states and the constitutionality of slavery, with the former serving as the bulwark of the latter.[9]

The idea of "higher law" is rooted in a natural law tradition—a tradition full of ambiguity and subject to various interpretations. Due to the universal application of natural law and the extrapolated natural rights therefrom, a political movement that articulates a reasonable political ideology from a natural law basis would, indeed, possess the theoretical wherewithal to effectively challenge conflicting positive laws embodied in a written constitution. A case in point, the self-evident truth that "all men are created equal," is subject to a variety of interpretations. Prima facie, Northern abolitionists who interpreted this self-evident truth to include black and white men would find themselves in the dilemma of mutually exclusive political obligations, as long as the Southern system of slavery was upheld by the common ties of the U.S. Constitution. Southerners responded with a dubious self-evident truth of their own: the natural right Southerners have to their property, including property in men, women, and children of the Negro race. The Southerners, unfortunately, stood on firmer constitutional grounds, because their self-evident truth was also recognized in the U.S. Constitution, as the U.S. Supreme Court reiterated as late as 1857. Thus, in the latter stages of antebellum America, American federalism was a house divided against itself, and the rhetoric of the opposing camps was the wedge splitting the house asunder.[10] Seward and his political allies were aware of this development and with sanctimonious recklessness utilized higher law doctrine as a means to surmount constitutional obstacles to the Republican party's political agenda.

The fugitive slave controversy is a case in point. In the course of the debates concerning the admission of Kansas (1856), Seward's construction techniques reached a new level of sophistication, which if put into effect would nullify what Southerners considered to be the constitutional linchpin of American federalism. He challenged the key provisions of Article IV, the "full faith and credit" and the rendition of fugitive slaves clauses, both of which were inextricably

linked in Southern constitutionalism. Seward challenged these provisions by denying the validity of the law of comity between the
states. The law of comity between the states would oblige the Northern states to respect the legal claims of Southern citizens requesting
the return of fugitive slaves.

In his 1856 annual message to Congress, President Franklin Pierce
stated the standard interpretation of the law of comity.

> Each State expressly stipulated as well for itself as for each and all of
> its citizens, and every citizen of each State became solemnly bound
> by his allegiance to the Constitution, that any person held to service
> or labor in one State escaping into another should not, in conse-
> quence of any law or regulation thereof, be discharged from such
> service or labor, but should be delivered up on claim of the party to
> whom such service or labor might be due by the laws of his State.
> Thus, and thus only, by the reciprocal guarantee of all the rights of
> every State against interference on the part of another, was the
> present form of government established by our fathers and trans-
> mitted to us; and by no other means is it possible for it to exist. If
> one State ceases to respect the rights of another, and obtrusively
> intermeddles with its local interests—if a portion of the States as-
> sume to impose their institutions on the others, or refuse to fulfill
> their obligations to them—we are no longer united friendly States,
> but distracted, hostile ones, with little capacity left of common ad-
> vantage, but abundant means of reciprocal injury and mischief.[11]

In direct response to the president, Seward maintained that because there are no independent states in America, "the supposed
law of comity is not incorporated into the Constitution." Thus, he
rejected the "reciprocal guarantee of all rights" between the states.
Furthermore, if there was no law of comity between the states, the
national government could function as the regulator of interstate
relations, thereby shifting the decision making on the critical issue
of slavery to the national statute-making process and thus effectively subjugating the Southern states to the political will of a hostile
Northern numerical majority, the U.S. Constitution's provisions to
the contrary notwithstanding. Southern legislators were cognizant
of the political implications of Seward's attack on the law of comity.
Senator C. C. Clay of Alabama stated: "The Constitution declares
that the fugitive slave *shall be delivered* on the claim of his master. The
language is plain, unambiguous, and unequivocal. The purpose
and the manner of its execution are beyond doubt, and were never
brought in question until the discovery of that *higher law,* of which
the Senator from New York is a prominent advocate and exponent."[12]

By 1856 the mainstay of Seward's Republican party was its antislavery program. The Republican party platform of the same year explicitly elevated the Declaration of Independence to constitutional status, extended the privileges expressed therein to slaves, and made clear the Republicans' intention not to comply with the rendition of fugitive slaves. Senator Clay voiced the Southern reaction when he stated: "Your platform expressly repudiates the obligations of the Constitution. It is hostile to rights of property existing before the Union in all the States, that formed one of the bases of the Union, and that are better guaranteed by the Constitution than any other property in the Union. Thus the Constitution, that was designed to serve as a shield to protect, is converted into a sword to destroy slave property."[13]

Southern senators discerned a fundamental alteration of American federalism as their Northern counterparts gained political ascendancy at the national level. The Republicans deemphasized their reliance on state tactics, such as personal liberty laws, and posited their disregard for the fugitive slave laws on the elevation of the Declaration of Independence to national constitutional status, thereby transforming the Union from a compact of states to a nationalistic compact of individuals. Due to the Southerners' increasing minority status in the House, Senate, and executive branch, states' rights (a correlative of state sovereignty) became the rallying point of Southern legislators who were convinced that they were not obligated to comply with a national constitution that had been fundamentally altered by the incorporation of a higher law doctrine. Events led to a disruption of Southern states' political obligation to the national government. Referring to the anticipated Republican party electoral victory, Clay reasoned: "When they get control of the Federal Government, which they vauntingly predict, the Southern States must elect between independence out of the Union or subordination within it. The principles of that party are not only hostile to the constitutional rights of those States, but to their political integrity and social organization. They are not only unconstitutional and sectional, but radical and revolutionary." The full impact of Seward's agenda to amend Article IV via congressional construction went beyond the rendition of fugitive slaves; it transformed what Southern legislators contended was the basis of American federalism, state sovereignty, to the Sewardian "one country and one sovereign—the United States of America and the American people."[14] In short, Southern secession was in response to what was perceived to be an advancing and irreversible national supremacy.

Upon the certainty of Republican electoral success in the November, 1860, election, Seward's rhetoric underwent semantical changes. For example, in his conciliatory speech of February 29, 1860, references to free states and slave states were interchanged with labor states and capital states respectively. He thereby placed both systems on a more congruous basis within the context of federalism by deemphasizing moral and ethical aspects and emphasizing economic aspects.[15] The latter were supposedly more negotiable than the former. Furthermore, one is hard-pressed to find a Seward reference to higher law superseding the Constitution at this stage of his rhetorical campaign. Nevertheless, Seward's position regarding the nature of American federalism was in 1861 what it was in 1850, the subordination of the states to the national government. Thus, in 1850, when he contended that the U.S. Constitution incorporated the principles of the Declaration of Independence, and that certain provisions of the Constitution (e.g., Article IV, section 2) and state constitutional guarantees for slavery were contrary to those inalienable rights, he was reinforcing the groundwork for national supremacy. He stated as much on January 12, 1861, as secession was unraveling the Union: "The Constitution of the United States, and the laws made in pursuance thereof, are the supreme law of the land, paramount to all legislation of the States, whether made under their Constitution, or even their organic conventions. The Union cannot be dissolved, not by secession, with or without armed force, but only by the voluntary consent of the people of the United States, collected in the manner prescribed by the Constitution of the United States."[16]

As Seward advanced the doctrine of national supremacy, Southern states withdrew from the Union under the flag of state sovereignty, convinced that continued membership in the Union was a serious threat to their safety and honor. Senator Clay echoed the sentiments of his Southern colleagues on January 21, 1861, in his resignation statement when he posed the following question: "Must we consent to live under a Government that we believe will henceforth be controlled and administered by those who not only deny us justice and equality, and brand us as inferiors, but whose avowed principles and policies must destroy our domestic tranquility, imperil the lives of our wives and our children, degrade and dwarf, and ultimately destroy our State? Must we live by choice or compulsion under those who present us with the dire alternative of an irrepressible conflict?" Following Clay's remarks, Senator Jefferson Davis expressed the expectations of the Confederate convention delegates when he concluded that "secession belongs to a different class of remedies. It is to be justified upon the basis that the States are sovereign. There was a time when none denied it. I hope the time may come again, when a better comprehension of the theory of our Government, and the inalienable rights of the people of the States, will prevent anyone from denying that each State is sovereign, and thus may reclaim the grants that it has made to any agent whomsoever."[17]

The Confederate Constitution of 1861 is the manifestation of the Southerners' better comprehension of the theory of our government. It is, indeed, a reactionary document; a reaction to inevitable changes that political, social, and economic forces were thrusting upon the U.S. Constitution, thereby transforming the community of states into a national community of individuals. The emerging nationalism was not, they alleged, the nation of their mutual fathers of 1787. They feared that Southern rights and interests would be placed in precarious circumstances under the flag of nationalism. As a result, they sought security for those rights and interests in their respective states, and framed a confederate constitution toward that end.

Consequently, the Confederate permanent constitution is a theoretical time capsule that embodies the distinctive principles of republican government to which the South was committed. For the most part postbellum scholarship has been neglectful of Confederate constitutionalism, assuming that the Confederate Constitution was nothing more than an imitation of the U.S. Constitution, lacking substantive differences the status of slavery excepted. For example, according to one notable scholar's comparison of the two documents, both the U.S. and C.S.A. constitutions "have the same number of articles with the subject-matter arranged in the same order of sections and clauses. Only a change in terminology, an addition or omission of a clause, a slight modification of phraseology distinguish the two instruments."[18] Albeit the Confederate framers contended that they were seceding on behalf of the U.S. Constitution, not against it, their understanding of the U.S. Constitution was, in certain significant respects, that of neither the Federalists (e.g., Publius) nor the 1861 Republicans, but rather that of the Antifederalists (e.g., Agrippa) and John C. Calhoun. This distinction is indeed a substantive one, but because constitutional development subsequent to 1789 has been primarily favorable to the Federalists' proclivities, this important fact has been somewhat obscured.

Comparatively analyzing the C.S.A. and U.S. constitutions makes evident the distinctive constitutional principles to which the Confederacy of 1861 was committed and brings to light the conservative nature of those principles and their relevance to American constitutional development.

Chapter Two

John C. Calhoun, the Confederate Phoenix

Aristotle wrote that "a constitution (or polity) may be defined as the organization of a polis, in respect of its offices generally, but especially in respect of that particular office which is sovereign in all issues."[1] The U.S. and C.S.A. constitutions broadly fulfill the general purpose of organizing the offices by establishing the legislative, executive, and judicial branches in Articles I, II, and III, respectively. Yet, in order to discern where sovereignty resides in a federal system consisting of a central and state governments, each with their respective communities and constitutions, one should look not only at the body of the documents but also at the preamble of the national constitution, where the adumbration of the locus of sovereignty is to be found. This does not necessarily mean that the preamble has the force of law, as does, for example, the enumeration of the congressional power to declare war, which is found in Article I, section 8, of the U.S. Constitution. It does mean, however, that the preamble delineates the locus of sovereignty within the federal framework, in conjunction with the institutions established in the body of the document.

The preamble to the U.S. Constitution establishes the locus of sovereignty in the people, a vague establishment to say the least. It is vague because within the federal framework there is not a monolithic people; there exists the people of the United States and the people of the respective states. The peoples of Virginia, New York, Massachusetts, etc., collectively constitute the people of the United States. The phrase "We the People" does not constitute a people separate from the states, for the same reason that the peoples of the respective states do not exist independent of the national community. Within the context of federalism, "the people" is a multifarious designation of those who theoretically could, and historically have, utilized their state governments to exercise sovereignty toward political objectives conducive to and at odds with the national community and its agent the U.S. government.

A historical instance is the tariff controversy of 1832. The U.S. government passed the tariff legislation and South Carolina nullified it on the grounds that it was unconstitutional. In response to South Carolina's nullification, President Andrew Jackson admonished the state while his administration secured passage of the Force Bill in order to coerce South Carolina's compliance with the tariff.[2] Within the federal framework the question arises, were the citizens of South Carolina constitutionally obliged to comply with the national tariff policy or the state nullification policy? The constitutional status of the tariff legislation and South Carolina's subsequent nullification were variously interpreted by officials at both the national and state levels. The assertion that the people are sovereign complicates the matter if two distinct peoples are involved—the American people as represented by President Jackson and the people of South Carolina as represented by their state officials. The U.S. and state officials were in fundamental disagreement as to which policies were constitutional—national or state supremacy. Both sides resorted to the preamble of the U.S. Constitution in an attempt to discern the nature of the relationship between the national and state political communities, as represented by their respective governments. In other words, does the preamble indicate the establishment of a national community of individuals, thereby binding on the citizens of the states, state objections (e.g., nullification) notwithstanding? Or, does it indicate the establishment of a community of states, with the citizens of the states constituting distinct sovereign political communities and with the national community consisting of states first and foremost rather than a nation of individuals, the states notwithstanding? If the latter, the citizens of South Carolina during the tariff controversy would be constitutionally obliged to abide by their state's policy; if the former, as maintained by President Jackson, the national tariff would be the law of the land, militarily enforceable with South Carolinians lacking recourse to the nullification and/or secession from the Union.

In the American federal model, if the national government is invariably at odds with a state (i.e., if the nation's public policy is contrary to a state's public policy preferences), one or the other must eventually prevail, and that which prevails would be, in the final analysis, sovereign, and that which is not sovereign would be subordinate to the other. Coerced state compliance by national authorities indicates the absence of a consensual federal model of politics, a model in which the national government's policy is premised upon the consent of the citizens in their respective states. In the event that the U.S. government's public policies repeatedly prevail over the vehement objections of a state, the people of that state would de facto cease to be sovereign and self-governing.

Because the relationship between the national and state governments is confusing (due to the indeterminacy of the U.S. Constitution regarding the nature of the federal system it established), both the nationalists and the advocates of state sovereignty have historically made compelling arguments in support of their mutually exclusive positions. The C.S.A. framers were determined to avoid ambiguity regarding the status of the states within the Confederacy. Thus they chose for their preamble the words, "We, the People of the *Confederate* States, *each State acting in its sovereign and independent character,*" a notable contrast to "We the People of the United States." Wording was not a new issue. Several leading Antifederalists discerned in the language of the preamble to the U.S. Constitution the spirit "to subvert and abolish all the powers of the State governments" as a consequence of the vague establishment of sovereignty in the people of the Union and not in the several States.[3] The C.S.A. version constitutionally recognizes "the sovereign and independent" status of the states; the U.S. preamble is devoid of such explicit recognition.

The premise of the C.S.A. framers was that sovereign states entered into a federal system to secure their mutual interests, thereby entering into a compact with the other states. The reasons for this union among the states were twofold: first, to deal with foreign threats on the international front, and second, to regulate interstate commerce among the states. The constitutional powers to fulfill these responsibilities were vaguely outlined in the constitutions. But this vagueness should not be equated with incompleteness. The U.S. Constitution is a much more complete document when one realizes that it is supplemental to the state constitutions. That is, for most of the state ratifiers the U.S. Constitution was not intended to supplant the state constitutions; rather, it was designed to enhance them.

In the commercial republics of the U.S. and C.S.A., the central governments have the constitutional mandate, albeit with qualifiers, to regulate and adjudicate conflicting interstate economic interests.[4] This function led Publius to maintain that "the regulation of these various and interfering interests forms the principal task of modern legislation and involves the spirit of party and faction in the necessary and ordinary operations of government."[5] The C.S.A. Constitution is premised upon the same assumption, with two significant differences: wherein sovereignty resides, with the national political community or in the distinct state political communities, and the extent of the regulatory power. Specifically, unlike their Federalist counterparts, the C.S.A. framers were determined to prevent their Confederate government's constitutional mandate to regulate and adjudicate interstate economic interests from taking precedence over the sovereign status of the states. In other words, the states maintained the public policy perimeters of their Confederate government.

The security for the sovereignty of the states was to a significant extent based upon the new language the Confederate framers embodied in their preamble. As one leading participant of the Confederate constitutional convention stated, "The Preamble of the Confederate Constitution holds unmistakable the sovereignty of the states and declares the constitution to be a compact between them."[6] This "unmistakable sovereignty of the States" was the product of a confidence in the states' capacity for self-government, which in turn resulted in a Confederate government constitutionally constrained from interposing in the affairs of a state without the latter's consent.

This Confederate commitment raises an interesting constitutional dilemma: In what manner and to what extent were the Confederate framers willing to permit their commitment to states' rights to take precedence over their simultaneous commitment to an effective central government possessing the capacity to pursue the mutual interests of the states in promoting the development of a commercial republic? The Federalists (and their ideological heirs, the antebellum Republicans) were convinced that the two, states' rights and a nationally thriving commercial republic, were incompatible and that sovereign states would prove to be obstacles to national commercial development and prosperity. The Confederate framers, on the other hand, were convinced that states' rights would actually contribute to the development of a Confederate commercial republic. They held the conviction that the states are more informed as to which public policy is, and which is not, most conducive to their economic, social, and political interests, in contradistinction to the general government, and that the enlightened pursuit of their (i.e., the respective states in the Confederacy) interests would be cumulatively beneficial for the Confederacy as a whole.

Confederate states' rights

The states' rights doctrine pertains to the nature of the relationship between the general and state governments. Essentially, the doctrine establishes that sovereignty resides within the respective states; in the event that a dispute arises between a state and the general government concerning the extent of their constitutional powers, the state is the final arbiter, individually and not necessarily collectively with other states. States' rights may be defined as the prerogative power of a state to exercise its inherent sovereign authority. In the antebellum period, states' rights advocates referred to the Kentucky and Virginia resolutions of 1798 as declaratory of their doctrine.

> Resolved, that the several States composing the United States of America, are not united on the principles of unlimited submission to their General Government; but that by compact under the style and title of a Constitution for the United States and of amendments thereto, they constituted a General Government for special purposes, delegated to that Government certain definite powers, reserving each State to itself, the residuary mass of right to their own self Government; and that whensoever the General Government assumes undelegated powers its acts are unauthoritative, void, and of no force. That to this compact each State accepted as a State, and is an integral party, its co-States forming as to itself, the other party: That the Government created by this compact was not made the exclusive or final judge of the extent of the powers delegated to itself; since that would have made its discretion, and not the Constitution, the measure of its powers; but as in all other cases of compact among parties having no common Judge, each party has an equal right to judge for itself, as well of infractions as of the mode and measure of redress.[7]

To guard against "unlimited submission to the general government" was the primary aim of the C.S.A. framers, and states' rights was the constitutional means to realize that objective, with the expectation that states' rights would not prove to be an insurmountable obstacle to an effective general government. Toward the end of an effective general government, Article VI in both constitutions includes supremacy clauses, to the effect that "the Constitution and the laws made in pursuance thereof, and all treaties, shall be the supreme law of the land; and the Judge in every State shall be bound thereby, anything in the Constitution or laws of any State to the contrary notwithstanding."[8] The important question of who is to decide what laws are and are not made "in pursuance of the Constitution"—the general or state governments—is contingent upon the locus of sovereignty. The Kentucky and Virginia resolutions contended that "each party" (i.e., state) "has an equal right to judge for itself," whereas the nationalists (e.g., Publius and Chief Justice John Marshall) contended the opposite.

Nevertheless, both interpretations are plausible. Sovereignty could reside in the respective states, with state governments functioning as the agents of sovereignty, or in a national political community irrespective of states, with the national government as the agent for exercising the national sovereignty. Apperceptive of the interpretative dilemma that confronted the authors of the Kentucky and Virginia resolutions, the C.S.A. framers committed to the former alternative by semantically modifying their preamble. In the C.S.A. Constitution, language supporting the sovereign status of the states, mutually acting "to form a permanent federal government," replaced the language "a more perfect Union," found in the U.S. Constitution.[9] The phrase "a more permanent federal government" connotes less centralization than the phrase "a more perfect Union"; also take note of the capitalization of "Union" and the noncapitalization of "federal government." When these terminological substitutions are considered in the context of constitutional exegeses—a context in which these lawyer-politicians certainly considered them—it becomes obvious that the Confederate framers were de-emphasizing the stature of the Union vis-à-vis the states.

To explicate the C.S.A.'s simultaneous commitments to states' rights and an effective general government, in contrast to the national supremacy model, the political philosophy of John C. Calhoun, the preeminent states' rights advocate will be contrasted with the political theory of Publius, an advocate of energizing the general government at the expense of state sovereignty. This is justified on the grounds that their positions substantively epitomize the polarized perspectives regarding the ideal status of the states in a federal model of politics. Whereas Calhoun was the spokesman for states' rights, Publius provided an insightful view into the seminal nationalistic tendencies of the U.S. Constitution and the rationale for those tendencies.[10]

Calhoun's theory of states' rights is in certain significant respects comparable to the position of the Whigs of 1787, (pejoratively referred to as the Antifederalists by the Federalists), insofar that they were reluctant to establish and maintain an overbearing central government at the expense of state autonomy.[11] The Antifederalists feared that the general government would eventually dominate the federal system, with a majority of the states, a majority of the national population, or both, thereby negating the consent of a minority of the states or a minority of the national population, respectively. Calhoun, however, extended the principle of state consent to its theoretical limits and attempted to negate the probability of involuntary submission to general government policies on the part of the states. The consent of all significant interests, specifically the states, would be required to place the general government in motion and to sustain it. Within the framework of federalism, states in the minority must possess the constitutional means to protect themselves from arbitrary general government policies contrary to their consent. This flies in the face of Publius's contention that

> to give a minority a negative upon the majority (which is always the case where more than a majority is requisite to a decision) is in its tendency, to subject the sense of the greater number to that of the lesser number. . . . The necessity of unanimity in public bodies, or of something approaching towards it, has been founded upon a supposition that it would contribute to security. But its real operation is to embarrass the administration, to destroy the energy of the government, and to substitute the pleasure, caprice, or artifices of an insignificant, turbulent, or corrupt junto to the regular deliberations and decisions of a respectable majority.[12]

The U.S. Constitution did not establish a unitary model of government in which the states are the mere dependencies of the national government. Indeed, the states make and administrate laws of their own, within the confines of the U.S. and state constitutions, "the great and aggregate interests being referred to the National, and local and particular to the State legislatures." In effect, the model is one in which the national and state governments coexist, each having their respective constitutional responsibilities. However, in the event of a dispute between the national and state governments over constitutional powers, the national government, according to Publius, has the prerogative to resolve the dispute based upon its policy preferences. In support of this nationalistic interpretation of the U.S. Constitution, Publius relied upon the supremacy clause of Article VI which stipulates that laws made pursuant to the Constitution are binding on the states.[13] This tautology on the part of Publius did not firmly establish national supremacy, because it left the question begging. Deciding which laws are and are not pursuant to the Constitution would be the fundamental question at issue between a state (or states) and the U.S. government. The latter's presumed prerogative to decide constitutional questions manifests the type of centralization of power that states' rights advocates found objectionable. Furthermore, the U.S. Constitution, including Article VI, leaves indeterminate the application of the supremacy clause. The language of the second clause of Article VI could be, and was, interpreted to encourage state judges to consider the laws and treaties of the U.S. in their adjudications, and to make such national laws supreme in the event of conflict, state laws to the contrary notwithstanding. But the key qualifier is the word *pursuant*. Who decides what is and is not pursuant to the national Constitution? With the principle of states' rights unmistakably incorporated into their constitution, the Confederate framers left no doubt as to who would decide what was and was not pursuant to the C.S.A. Constitution. The people in their respective states possessed that prerogative.

The important point from a Southern perspective was that a scheme of federalism which secures state sovereignty is neither antidemocratic nor disruptive to "respectable majorities." To the contrary, such state participation was a reaction to what was perceived to be an increasingly authoritarian union of Northern states controlling the national government and thereby incrementally excluding the consent of the states. It was problematical that a state majority could be transformed into a national minority. Accordingly, states' rights was not inherently antimajoritarian because majority rule could function quite well at the state level. Nevertheless, Publius was correct in recognizing the tension between national majority rule and minority consent within the context of federalism. Calhoun's notion of the concurrent majority addressed this tension and provided the Confederate framers with their rationalization of constitutionally mandating states' rights without simultaneously abandoning popular sovereignty.

Concurrent majority

From the Southern point of view, an important tenet of federalism was security from arbitrary national public policies. Southerners acknowledged that the Confederate states required some form of effective general government in order to secure their collective interests without impeding the development of any particular regional or state economy. But they were also convinced that any general government with authority over the states was prone to abuse that authority, thereby posing a threat to the cultural, economic, and/or political interests of the Confederate states. Calhoun's concurrent majority-states' rights was to function as the constitu-

tional mechanism to ensure that the states possessed the wherewithal to secure their own interests within a federal framework. An
analysis of the concurrent majority and the manner in which it is
manifested in the states' rights doctrine delineates a substantive
distinction between U.S. and C.S.A. constitutional arrangements
regarding federal-state relations.

The theoretical substance of the concurrent majority rests upon
four pillars of analysis: the individual, society, government, and
constitutionalism. According to Calhoun, the fundamental component of society is the individual. Without society, however, the individual is merely a brute, because the individual's moral and intellectual development will not occur apart from society.

> In considering this, I assume as an incontestable fact that man is
> so constituted as to be a social being. His inclinations and wants,
> physical and moral, irresistibly impel him to associate with his
> kind, and he has accordingly, never been found, in any age or
> country, in any state other than the social. In no other, indeed,
> could he exist, and in no other—was it possible for him to exist—
> could he attain to a full development of his moral and intellectual
> faculties, or raise himself, in the state of being, much above the
> brute creation. [14]

By stating that the natural condition of man is living in community
with others, Calhoun dismisses the contract theorists' notion of a
state of nature and the corresponding possession of political rights
independent of society. Contrast this to the Aristotelian view of the
individual's relationship to the state:

> We thus see that the polis exists by nature and that it is prior to the
> individual. The proof of both propositions is the fact that the polis
> is a whole, and that individuals are simply its parts. Not being self-
> sufficient when they are isolated, all individuals are so many parts
> all equally depending on the whole (which alone can bring about
> self-sufficiency). The man who is isolated—who is unable to share
> in the benefits of political association, or has no need to share
> because he is already self-sufficient—is no part of the polis, and
> must therefore be either a beast or a god. (Man is thus by nature to
> be part of a political whole, and) there is therefore an immanent
> impulse in all men towards an association of this order. [15]

Similarly, Calhoun reasoned that the state of nature,

> instead of being the natural state of man, it is, of all conceivable
> states, the most opposed to his nature—most repugnant to his
> feelings and most incompatible with his wants. His natural state is
> the social and political—the one for which his Creator made him,
> and the only one in which he can preserve and perfect his race. As,
> then, there never was such a state as the so-called state of nature,

and never can be, it follows that men, instead of being born in it, are born in the social and political state; and of course, instead of being born free and equal, are born subject, not only to paternal authority, but to the laws and institutions of the country where born and under whose protection they draw their first breath.[16]

Hence, individual political rights do not have an existence independent of civil society, excepting the right of self-preservation, "which pervades all that feels, from man down to the lowest and most insignificant reptile or insect." If a conflict arises between individual self-preservation and that of society, the former will not necessarily yield to the latter. The individual's "social feelings may, indeed, in a state of safety and abundance, combined with high intellectual and moral culture, acquire great expansion and force, but not so great to overpower this all-pervading and essential law of animated existence." Furthermore, remove the condition of safety or abundance, or both, which society provides, and the prevalent condition will be "the tendency to a universal state of conflict between individual and individual, accompanied by the connected passions of suspicion, jealousy, anger, and revenge—followed by insolence, fraud, and cruelty," as men pursue their self-preservation unimpeded by governmental restraints.[17]

Society cannot check this "tendency to a universal state of conflict" without the presence of government. Inferentially, as the individual requires society for his self-preservation and perfection, society requires government for its preservation and perfection. Government is the controlling power that maintains society, which in the absence of government would deteriorate into a condition of confusion and universal discord as the pursuit of self-preservation by society's members proceeds uncontrolled. Furthermore, the nature of a society's government, (e.g., tyranny, oligarchy, or democracy) should conform to the character of the people. General characteristics "such as different degrees of intelligence, patriotism, virtue among the mass of the community, and their experience and proficiency in the art of self-government" are instrumental in influencing the type of government that eventually develops.[18] A society predominantly consisting of intelligent, patriotic, and virtuous inhabitants would devise and sustain a government quite dissimilar from a society of ignorant, unpatriotic, vicious inhabitants.

The implications of this Calhounian perspective of the individual's relationship to society and government are significant, especially within the context of a federal system that includes an association of sovereign states with varying cultural, economic, and social characteristics. Calhoun's premise led him to conclude that rights are a product of social circumstances, such as "intelligence, patriotism, virtue, and proficiency in the art of self-government," in contradistinction to the ideal that all men are created equal, circumstances included, and are thus equally entitled to political rights. From this perspective there is no great inconsistency in the association of sovereign states under the auspices of a general government, even if those states significantly differ in their political and social settings. Under such a model the Union could endure half-slave and half-free, and/or one section agricultural and another industrial. Accordingly, the distribution of political rights would be contingent upon the circumstances within the various states and would be determined by the states, not by a general government incompetent to take into account the diverse social and economic circumstances of the states.

Such deference to the states is necessitated because there is not an alternative model of politics for a diverse association of states. To wit:

> Liberty, then, when forced on a people unfit for it, would instead of a blessing, be a curse, as it would in its reaction lead directly to anarchy—the greatest of all curses. No people, indeed, can long enjoy more liberty than that to which their situation and advanced intelligence and morals fairly entitle them. If more than this be allowed, they must soon fall into confusion and disorder—to be followed, if not by anarchy and despotism, by a change to a form of government more simple and absolute, and therefore better suited to their condition.

The above quotation leads to two important deductions. First, political rights are qualified in the sense that one's entitlement to them is contingent upon one's moral and intellectual development. The same holds true for a society in general, in the sense that the nature of its government will be a product of the dominant moral and intellectual characteristics of its people. And second, in the establishment of a government (i.e., the drafting of a constitution and thereby the establishing of sovereignty, a process that Calhoun leaves to speculation), the paramount consideration should be the character of the people. The more congruous the constitution is to the circumstances of society, the greater the stability of the society and its subsequent progressive development.[19] Calhoun concluded that due to the character of the American people, state sovereignty and a consensual model of politics within a federal framework were compatible, providing that the latter included the principle of the concurrent majority.

Just as a society of individuals requires government to prevent a condition of conflict and universal discord, an association of states requires a general government to prevent the same condition between the states. Within the context of American federalism, which could be described as an association (i.e., Union) combining a variety of societies (i.e., states), the primary dilemma was to reconcile the necessity of a general government with the sovereignty of the states. At the heart of the dilemma was the acknowledgment that a general government with the requisite power to secure the collective welfare of all the states could also abusively exercise that power to the detriment of a state. Both Publius and Calhoun were convinced that if this dilemma were properly addressed, there would be beneficent consequences in the form of commercial and social development within the federal framework. They differed, however, about the potential source of the most flagrant abusive use of political power; Publius was apprehensive about the states, whereas Calhoun was anxious about the general government. Because of their concerns, they advocated energizing the one and enervating the other. Publius contended that a "vigorous national government," with weaker state governments, would facilitate the development of a commercial republic to rival the powers of Europe. Calhoun also acknowledged the effects "of an all-pervading commerce, which is daily diffusing over its surface the light and blessings of civilization. . . . But this cannot be unless the ultimate effect of their action, politically, shall be to give ascendancy to that form of government best calculated to fulfill the ends for which government is ordained. For so completely does the well-being of our race depend on good government that it is hardly possible any change, the ultimate effect of which should be otherwise, could prove to be a permanent good."[20]

Nevertheless, good government is difficult to attain, especially good federal government premised upon the consent of all its divergent parts. It "is the most complex and difficult of construction," because of the numerous and competing interests attempting to gain ascendancy and control the government. Furthermore, "self-preservation is the supreme law with communities as well as with individuals," which implies an active and competitive relationship rather than a passive existence, especially in a commercial republic. Calhoun concurred with Publius's observation that "States, like individuals, acquiesce with great reluctance in determinations to their disadvantage."[21] Thus, all advocates of federalism acknowledge that a society of states is subject to the same tendency toward universal conflict as is a society of individuals, and some form of general government is essential to keeping the peace among the states.

Publius was adamant in insisting that anything short of a "consolidation of several smaller States into one great confederacy" (in contrast to two or three confederacies) in which the member states would "be in perfect subordination to the general authority of the union" would be inadequate.[22] "A man must be far gone in Utopian speculations who can seriously doubt that if these States should either be wholly disunited, or only united in partial confederacies, the subdivisions into which they might be thrown would have frequent and violent contests with each other. To presume a want of motives for such contests as an argument against their existence would be to forget that men are ambitious, vindictive, and rapacious." In order to establish an enduring federal system, "a Firm Union will be of the utmost moment to the peace and liberty of the States as a barrier against domestic faction and insurrection." This was to be accomplished by the U.S. Constitution, which established an indissoluble Union (i.e., firm) thereby laying the groundwork for an American empire.[23] Once the Union was established, if a state refused to comply with the policies of the national government, the latter would have the option and, should the need arise, the responsibility to resort to coercion in order to compel state compliance.

> Government implies the power of making laws. It is essential to the idea of a law that it be attended with a sanction; or, in other words, a penalty or punishment for disobedience. If there be no penalty annexed to disobedience, the resolutions or commands which pretend to be laws will, in fact, amount to nothing more than advice or recommendation. This penalty, whatever it may be, can only be inflicted in two ways: by the agency of the courts and ministers of justice, or by military force; by the COERCION of the magistry, or by the COERCION of arms.[24]

Such national-government-applied coercion against individuals and/or states is a constitutional remedy to state noncompliance. Publius wanted to avoid using coercion against a state, which in a federal model could result in war between the state (or states) and the national government, which in turn would be more disruptive and detrimental to commerce than coercion against an individual. To avoid such an inconvenience, "the authority of the Union must extend to the persons of the citizens—the only proper objects of government," rather than exclusively to states, as was the case under the Articles of Confederation. According to Publius, this was the most significant improvement the U.S. Constitution made on the Articles of Confederation.[25]

Publius's acknowledged reliance on compulsion raises the critical issue. If the governed within a state can be compelled to comply, against their will, with national laws, is the consent of the governed then nonexistent? Calhoun argued in the affirmative and articulated the constitutional principle of the concurrent majority as a means to ensure the consent of the governed, insofar as state compliance with national laws is concerned. This is not meant to imply that the bond holding the Union together under the U.S. Constitution is not premised upon the consent of the governed. Both the U.S. and C.S.A. models of federalism are premised upon the consent of the governed, with the qualification that the former allows for the application of coercion when consent between the general and state governments breaks down, whereas the latter does not. Consequently, consent is more pervasive in the C.S.A. model because of the constitutional barriers to applied coercion by the Confederate government upon the states. Once again, a manifestation of the U.S. model's reliance on coercion was the controversy surrounding the tariff of July 14, 1832. On November 24, 1832, South Carolina issued its ordinance of nullification declaring the tariff to be null and void within the state. On December 10, 1832, President Jackson informed the country that the federal laws would be enforced in South Carolina, which was part of an indissoluble nation; this enforcement would be done at the point of a bayonet if necessary. Jackson proclaimed: "Having the fullest confidence in the justness of the legal and constitutional opinion of my duties which has been expressed, I rely with equal confidence on your individual support in my determination to execute the laws, to preserve the Union by all constitutional means, to arrest if possible, by moderate and firm measures the necessity of a recourse to force; and if it be the will of Heaven that the recurrence of its primeval curse on man for the shedding of a brother's blood should fall upon our land, that it be not called down by any offensive act on the part of the United States."[26]

It is very significant that with all the pressures and contingencies of war, Jefferson Davis never declared, not to mention formulated, such Jacksonian "moderate and firm measures." Davis was restrained not only by his personal commitment to states' rights but more significantly by the *modus operandi* of the Confederacy.

The concurrent majority is the constitutional mechanism designed to exclude force from nation-state relations. It is "the principle which makes the constitution in its strict and limited sense." Calhoun reasoned that "power can only be resisted by power, and tendency by tendency. Those who exercise power and those subject to its exercise, the rulers and the ruled, stand in antagonistic relations to each other." The concurrent majority would prevent "any one interest or combination of interests from using the powers of government to aggrandize itself at the expense of the others," thereby securing the self-protection necessary for self-preservation, self-government, and progress within a federal system.[27] Publius concurred. "Ambition must be made to counteract ambition: . . . What is government itself but the greatest reflections on human nature? If men were angels, no government would be necessary. If angels were to govern men, neither external nor internal controls on government would be necessary. In framing a government which is to be administered by men over men, the great difficulty lies in this: you must first enable the government to control the governed; and in the next place oblige it to control itself."[28] However, there were substantive differences in their respective commitments to limited government.

The divergence of the constitutional theories of Calhoun and Publius centers on the matter of protecting the states from abusive use of power by the general government. Calhoun maintained that the U.S. model places too much reliance on the function of suffrage within the context of an extended republic. Suffrage, however well guarded it might be, and however enlightened the people, essentially transfers the execution of the citizens' sovereignty to national government officials who, acting on behalf of the prevailing national political power, will oppress the less powerful subnational states, should a conflict between the two arise. A model such as this, which is primarily premised upon the principle of majority rule, "is but the government of a part over a part, the major over the minor portion." Such a constitutional scheme does not fulfill the purpose of a constitution premised upon popular consent, which is "to resist by its own structure the tendency to abuse power."[29] According to Calhoun, the proper federal constitutional scheme would make certain that all the general government's policies are premised upon the consent of the governed, including subnational majorities within the states as well as national majorities. If such widespread consent is not forthcoming for certain proposed national policies, then those policies are put on hold until, if ever, the requisite consent becomes manifest via the concurrent majority.

Both Publius and Calhoun acknowledged the diversity within the national community and that the constituent parts of majorities and minorities vary. A majority could consist of various property, citizens, and/or states, and a minority could consist of fewer and dissimilar components. A significant difference between their conceptions of majorities and minorities was the former's emphasis on the distribution of property and the latter's on sectional interests. This was a distinction of degrees; in other words, both were concerned with property and regions, but not to the same extent. According to Publius, "The most common and durable source of faction has been the various and unequal distribution of property. Those who hold and those who are without property have ever formed distinct interests in society."[30]

Calhoun went one step beyond Publius's formulation. Unlike Publius, Calhoun did not assume that the rich and poor necessarily form distinct interests. His formulation contended that segments of the rich and poor will form a sectional majority in order to exploit sectional minorities of rich and poor, if suffrage is the primary check on government. If the constitutional system permits, it is in the interest of the rich and poor to form a political alliance within their section in order to exploit their rivals in other sections. In the absence of the proper constitutional safeguards, the prevailing political regional power consisting of rich and poor will determine the distribution of wealth through the government's fiscal policy.

> The two, disbursement and taxation, constitute the fiscal action of the government. What one takes from the community in the name of taxes is transferred to the portion of the community who are the recipients under that of disbursements. . . . The necessary result, then, of the unequal fiscal action of the government is to divide the community into two great classes, one consisting of those who, in reality, pay the taxes and, of course, bear exclusively the burthen of supporting the government; and the other, of those who are then recipients of their proceeds through disbursements, and who are, in fact, supported by the government; or, in fewer words, divide it into tax-payers and tax-consumers.

Calhoun contended that this constitutional flaw (the unwarranted reliance on suffrage as an adequate check on the general government) precipitated the division of the Union along sectional lines, the Southern, Northern, and Western sections, not a national division between capital and labor, or rich and poor. These sections, particularly the Southern and Northern, represented the great interests in the country; the states in their respective sections were the components of each great section.[31]

He maintained that under Publius's model of federalism, national public policy had been formulated through the requisite due process of the legislative system but was nevertheless prejudicial to a particular section of the country, thereby dividing the nation into tax consumers (the Northern states) and taxpayers (the Southern states). Under such a model, legislation could be implemented over the objections of a significant sectional minority, such as was the case during the tariff controversy of 1832. As the dominant section gained control of the national legislature, it could use legislative supremacy to minimize a sectional minority's meaningful participation in the process. This, indeed, was the perception of the Southern section as they seceded from the Union. This is stated clearly in the "Declaration of Causes Which Induced the Secession of South Carolina": "This sectional combination for the subversion of the Constitution has been aided, in some of the States, by elevating to citizenship persons who, by the supreme law of the land, are incapable of becoming citizens; and those votes have been used to inaugurate a new policy, hostile to the South, and destructive of its peace and safety. . . . The Slaveholding States will no longer have the power of self-government, or self-protection, and the Federal Government will have become their enemy."[32] Take note of South Carolina's reference to "the South" and "the Slaveholding States"; evidently, the South perceived the conflict to be a sectional one in which it confronted a hostile U.S. government under the control of Northern interests.

The South's answer to sectional diversity and conflict was recognizing and politically insisting upon states' rights. States' rights advocates maintained that the citizens within their respective states retained sovereignty, with the state governments serving as the agents of that sovereignty. In order for the national government to implement national policy, the consent of the states was essential. This is consensual politics within a federal framework. To consider the national government as something distinct from, independent of, or superior to the states is a misconception. In the words of Calhoun:

> The government of the United States, with all its complication and refinement of organization, is but a part of a system of governments. It is the representative and organ of the States, only to the extent of the powers delegated to it. Beyond this, each State has its own separate government, which is its exclusive representative

and organ, as to all the other powers of government;—or as they are usually called, the reserved powers. However correct, then, our conception of the character of the government of the United States viewed by itself may be, it must be very imperfect, unless viewed at the same time, in connection with the complicated system, of which it forms but a part.[33]

Although the U.S. Constitution is also premised upon the consent of the governed, it is a type of consent significantly different from that of the C.S.A. Publius's *modus operandi* was that the consent of a national majority, as manifested through a system of separation of powers, takes precedence over a subnational majority, i.e., a state. Under national supremacy, political authority resides with the politically predominant citizens in their capacity as members of a national community, in contradistinction to the politically predominant in the state communities first and foremost.

The subtle movement away from a confederation in which states were dominant (as was the case under the Articles of Confederation) to a dominant national government is exemplified by the various plans that were submitted during the 1787 Constitutional Convention.[34] The New Jersey Plan was offered as an alternative to the consolidating impetus advanced by the supporters of the Virginia Plan. For example, the former sustained the sovereignty of the respective states, whereas the latter allowed the national government to veto the laws of the several states.[35] The rationale for diminishing the preponderance of the states was set forward by the Hamilton Plan, which the Federalist rejected, not so much on theoretical grounds, but because of practical politics; it was unacceptable to the smaller states, without whose support ratification would have been improbable. Hamilton's proposed scheme of government resembled that of eighteenth-century Great Britain. It was to consist of a bicameral legislature with three-year terms for the lower chamber, a Senate with legislators serving during good behavior, an executive appointed for life by the legislature, and a judiciary with twelve justices. Thus, the senate, the executive, and the judiciary would consist of officials not subject to periodic elections.[36] Hamilton's objective was to strengthen the central government at the expense of the states. He claimed that the states had become obsolete and that their preponderance over a more efficient and powerful nation could no longer be justified. If the states were "extinguished great economy might be obtained by substituting a general government. . . . They are not necessary for any of the great purposes of commerce, revenue, or agriculture." This rationale is theoretically consistent with Publius's statement that "the prosperity of America depended on its Union."[37]

Calhoun consistently maintained that the U.S. Constitution originally established a federal system in which the states retained their sovereignty. He conceded, however, that the document came from the hands of its framers with considerable uncertainty regarding a crucial constitutional principle.

> The convention which framed it, was divided, as has been stated, into two parties,—one in favor of a *national,* and the other of a *federal* government. The former, consisting for the most part, of the younger and more talented members of the body,—but of the less experienced,—prevailed in the early stages of the proceedings. A negative on the action of the governments of the several States, in some form or other, without a corresponding one, on their part, on the acts of the government about to be formed, was indispensable to the consummation of their plan. They, accordingly, as has been shown, attempted, at every stage of the proceedings of the convention, and in all possible forms, to insert some provision in the Constitution, which would, in effect, vest it with a negative;—but failed in all. The party in favor of a *federal* form, subsequently gained the ascendancy;—the national party acquiesced, but without surrendering their preference for their own favorite plan;—or yielding, entirely, their confidence in the plan adopted,—or the necessity of a negative on the action of the separate governments of the States. They regarded the plan as but an experiment; and determined, as honest men and good patriots, to give it a fair trial. They even assumed the name of Federalists; and two of their most talented leaders, Mr. Hamilton and Mr. Madison, after the adjournment of the convention, and while the ratification of the Constitution was pending, wrote the major part of that celebrated work, *The Federalist;* the object of which was to secure its adoption. It did much to explain and define it, and to secure the object intended; but it shows, at the same time, that its authors had not abandoned their predilection in favor of the national plan.[38]

Thus, according to Calhoun, the original federal system was displaced by a national system. The displacement was by design and by those nationalists who never abandoned their proclivities to subordinate the states to the national government. Such subordination was, according to Calhoun, illegitimate. One should not underestimate the impact of Calhoun's logic on the mind of the South. His indictment of nationalism and support for states' rights provided the South with its justification for secession from the Union.

The central issue of American politics from 1787 through the Civil War period was sovereignty within the context of a federal system. Strengthening the national government at the expense of the states could not be accomplished without affecting sovereignty as it pertained to the national and state levels. Both Publius and Calhoun stipulated that sovereignty is indivisible and must reside at either the national or state level. Referring to the adherents of a confederacy, Publius maintained: "They seem still to aim at things repugnant and irreconcilable; at an augmentation of federal authority without a diminution of State authority; at sovereignty in the Union and complete independence in the members. They still, in fine, seem to cherish with blind devotion the political monster of an *imperium in imperio*." Publius guarded against the "political monster of an *imperium in imperio*" by rhetorically maintaining that sovereignty resided in the people, not in governments, and it was the people who assigned to their national and respective state governments certain functions—the delegated and the reserved powers. Moreover, insofar as the execution of the delegated powers were concerned, sovereignty resided with the people as a whole in the sense of constituting a national community.[39] This is significant, because if sovereignty is indivisible, and the national community is sovereign, the component states would be subordinate to the political will of the national community. Calhoun concurred with Publius's reasoning that "sovereignty is an entire thing, to divide it is to destroy it." But he also charged that this was exactly what Publius was attempting to do: destroy sovereignty at the state level. Referring to the locus of sovereignty within a federal system, Calhoun maintained that it had to be either a national or state phenomenon. He proposed the question,

> . . . How [can] the people of the several States . . . be partly sovereign, and partly not sovereign; sovereign as to the reserved, and not sovereign as to the delegated powers? There is no difficulty in understanding how powers, appertaining to sovereignty, may be divided; and the exercise of one portion delegated to one set of agents, and another portion to another; or how sovereignty may be vested in one man, a few, or many. But how sovereignty itself, the supreme power, can be divided, how the people of the several States can be partly supreme and partly not supreme, it is impossible to conceive.[40]

If sovereignty is indivisible, as Publius and Calhoun acknowledged, then it must be either a national or a state phenomenon. The U.S. Constitution manifests the former, the C.S.A. Constitution the latter. Consequently, two significantly different models of federalism are embodied in each.

Chapter Three

Federalism and Popular Sovereignty

Within the context of American federalism, sovereignty is multidimensional, unlike a unitary model in which sovereignty is a national phenomenon plain and simple. The confusion surrounding American federalism centers on the coexistence of two distinguishable political communities, national and state. Sovereignty resides with the people in their respective states and collectively in the national community. The various state governments and the national government are essentially the agents of the sovereign people. Being the agents of the people, public policies (both national and state) must be premised upon the consent of the governed if the people are to be considered sovereign. If the national agents' policies prevail over the vehement objections of the people within a particular state, and those policies are coercively implemented, then the people within that state will cease to be sovereign and for all intents and purposes subject to an external sovereign authority. Consequently, if the citizens of a state are at odds with national policy and unsuccessfully attempt to negate it by exercising their sovereignty through state nullification, but yet are subject to that national policy against their political will, then the citizens of that state are not sovereign in regard to that policy and are subject to the sovereign authority of the national government. This is especially the case if the people within a particular state lack recourse to secession, that is, withdrawal from the Union. A state's tacit consent to national policies could be deduced from its continual membership in the Union. However, such tacit consent is premised upon the option to secede. The Confederate framers were convinced that such national supremacy can only be realized at the expense of self-governing states, thereby having substantive impact upon popular sovereignty within the context of American federalism.

The Bank of the United States, protectionist tariff, and territorial and slavery controversies of the first half of the nineteenth century convinced many in the Southern states that they were in the process of losing their constitutional place within the federal system and that the public policy preferences of their citizens were increasingly being sacrificed on the altar of nationalism. Accordingly, the framers of the C.S.A. Constitution feared that national supremacy unabated by sovereign states intensified the potential for abuse by national majorities and that, consequently, national public policy would not be securely premised upon the consent of the governed within the respective states, thereby dealing a devastating setback to the principle of popular sovereignty. A state objecting to the policies of the general government would lack recourse to nullification if the states lacked sovereignty distinct from the Confederacy as a whole. In other words, if sovereignty were to be a national phenomenon, the Confederacy would have the prerogative to override the objections of a state, thereby circumventing the political will of the latter's citizenry.

The C.S.A. Constitution inherently checked the emergence of a national sovereign by constitutionally providing for the sovereignty of the states. The objective of this federal arrangement was to ensure that a sovereign state would not have a Confederate superior; hence, compliance with Confederate policies would be at the discretion of the states and not the product of coercion. Four constitutional provisions collectively provided for state sovereignty, in contradistinction to a sovereign Confederacy; they are to be found in Article VI; Article I, section 2; Article V; and the Confederate covenant-compact theory of government.

Article VI

The final two clauses of the C.S.A. Constitution's Article VI correspond to the U.S. Constitution's Ninth and Tenth amendments. They read as follows:

> U.S.: The enumeration in the Constitution, of certain rights, shall not be construed to deny or disparage others retained by the people.

> C.S.A.: The enumeration, in the Constitution, of certain rights, shall not be construed to deny or disparage others retained by the people *of the several States.*

> U.S.: The powers not delegated to the United States by the Constitution, nor prohibited by it to the States, are reserved to the States respectively, or to the people.

> C.S.A.: The powers not delegated to the Confederate States, nor

prohibited by it to the States, are reserved to the States, respectively, or to the *people thereof*.[1]

The C.S.A.'s shift in emphasis from "*the people*" to "*of the several States*" and to "*the people thereof*" (referring to the people in their respective states) is evidence that its general government did not establish a national community of individuals irrespective of the states and constitutionally superior to the states. Indeed, the national community did exist, but only insofar as the delegated powers were concerned—powers that were delegated by the states and for the states, rather than by and for a national community of individuals. Furthermore, the reserved powers were reserved to the states "or to the people thereof," the emphasis being a community of states and not a national community of individuals. In both instances where the U.S. framers referred to "the people," which was subsequently interpreted to indicate the establishment of a national community of individuals irrespective of the states, the Confederate framers referred to "the people of the several States" and "to the people thereof." In the Confederate model an individual was a member of the national community only through his state. The Confederate community was an association of states first and foremost. Thus, the states were given a permanence absent in the U.S. Constitution, since the individual was a citizen of the Confederacy through his state, in contradistinction to membership in a national community distinct from the states.

This is made evident by analyzing the significance of the phrase "several States" from the C.S.A. perspective. According to Calhoun, the "several States" is equivalent to "their people, in their sovereign capacity," with "their" referring to the distinct states.[2] The *Declaration of Causes Which Induced the Secession of South Carolina* acknowledged that the political and constitutional ties between the "several States" resulting from their affiliation under the U.S. Constitution did not detract from state sovereignty, but actually impelled it: "By this Constitution, certain duties were imposed upon the several States, and the exercise of certain of their powers was restrained, which necessarily impelled their continued existence as sovereign states."[3] At the C.S.A. Constitutional Convention, W. Porcher Miles of South Carolina moved to amend the phrase "the enumeration, in the Constitution, of certain rights, shall not be construed to deny or disparage others retained by the people" by adding thereto the words "of the several States."[4] He adamantly took a state's rights position: "I am a state rights person: I am a state-rights man. I do not lay the same stress upon party organization that most politicians in this country do. We assemble here as the representatives of the people of the various sovereign States which compose this Confederacy, and it is our first duty to labor for the best interests of our own immediate people, without doing injustice to the people of any section of the Country."[5] Accordingly, in the scheme of Confederate public policy formulation and implementation, the states had a presence that prevented their respective policy preferences from being set aside by the Confederate government presumably acting on behalf of a national community of individuals, or more specifically the "general welfare," a phrase auspiciously excluded from the C.S.A. Constitution. Hence, the collective interests of the Confederacy could not be justification to override the particular interest of a state in the minority. In an obverse manner, the collective interest of the Confederacy was exactly that, collective and inclusive of all the states.

Publius was opposed to giving the states such a presence and the wherewithal to thwart the political will of a national majority. He maintained that "a unity of commercial, as well as political, interests can only result from a unity of government."[6] A constitutional provision giving the states such permanence would prove to be an obstacle to such unity. For Publius the "general welfare" of all necessitated the establishment of a national community of individuals and the subordination of the states to that community. In reference to Article II of the Articles of Confederation, a provision that mandates state sovereignty,[7] Publius contended:

> The next most palpable defect of the existing Confederation is the total want of SANCTION to its laws. . . . There is no express delegation of authority to them to use force against delinquent members; and if such a right should be ascribed to the federal head, as resulting from the nature of the social compact between the States, it must be by inference and construction in the face of that part of the second article by which it is declared "that each State shall retain every power, jurisdiction, and right, not *expressly* delegated to the United States in Congress assembled." The want of such a right involves, no doubt, a striking absurdity. . . . If we are unwilling to impair the force of this applauded provision, we shall be obliged to conclude that the United States afford the extraordinary spectacle of a government destitute even of the shadow of constitutional power to enforce the execution of its own laws.

Explicit in Publius's "national supremacy" is the contention that the states must be subjected to a dominant national government, and "bound together in a strict and indissoluble Union, . . . in erecting one great American system."[8] Of course, Publius's rationale flies in the face of the C.S.A.'s commitment to prohibit the "use of force against delinquent members" on the part of the Confederate government. This is not surprising in light of the fact that the Federalists were working toward constructing a nationalistic political and economic empire and the Confederates toward constraining one.

Article I, section 2, clause 5

Article I, section 2, clause 5, of the C.S.A. Constitution also secures state sovereignty. It authorizes the states to impeach Confederate officials within their respective borders: "The House of Representatives shall choose their Speaker and other officers; and shall have the sole power of impeachment, except that any judicial or other Federal officer, resident and acting solely within the limits of any State, may be impeached by a vote of two-thirds of both branches of the Legislature thereof." Such impeachment powers provide the states with augmented constitutional means to secure the territorial integrity against perceived encroaching Confederate officials.

The discretionary power this provision extends to the states is contingent upon the C.S.A. Senate, which "shall have the sole power to try all impeachments" when two-thirds of the members present concur (Article I, section 3, clause 6). Nevertheless, providing state legislatures with the opportunity to impeach Confederate officials was designed to make them more accountable to the states. A state could practically as well as constitutionally impact the policies of the Confederate government by impeachment and perhaps removal from office. Keep in mind that senators were elected by the legislatures thereof (Article I, section 3) and were more beholden to their state legislature's directives than are their post-Seventeenth Amendment counterparts. As a result, Confederate officials implementing policies out of step with the policy objectives of a state could be excluded from the jurisdiction of the state, thereby precluding the execution of the unpopular policies. For example, an activist Confederate judge could not act with impunity in a state opposing such activism, because he would be subject to state-initiated impeachment proceedings. In short, Confederate officials were constrained to a greater extent than is the case in the U.S. model to interpret and enforce Confederate laws according to the preferences of the states.

Article V

The amendment process of the C.S.A. Constitution deviates from that of the U.S. Constitution in two important respects. First, a state can with greater ease initiate a constitutional convention. As Article V stipulates, "Upon the demand of any three States, legally assembled in their several conventions, the Congress shall summon a Convention of all the States to take into consideration such amendments to the Constitution as the said States shall concur in suggesting at the time when the said demand is made." Significantly, it is not two-thirds of the states or the Congress, but merely three states, which are requisite to convene a constitutional convention. Because the Confederate framers anticipated the expansion of the Confederacy to include the border states and some western states, the minimum three states, in addition to the exclusion of the congressionally initiated convention, is evidence of the deference to states' rights. Consider for a moment that the same three-state minimum were requisite to convene a constitutional convention to amend the U.S. Constitution. In all probability the constitutional convention would have been regularly called into existence and would have virtually constituted a council of revision addressing perceived inadequacies of the U.S. Constitution.

The second deviation is the substitution of the three-fourths vote with a two-thirds vote as requisite to ratify proposed amendments: "Should any of the proposed amendments to the Constitution be agreed on by the said Convention—voting by States—and the same be ratified by the Legislatures of two-thirds of the several States, or in Conventions in two-thirds thereof—as one or the other mode of ratification may be proposed by the general Convention—they shall thenceforward form a part of this Constitution." Superficially, it seems that rather than reducing the number necessary to ratify, the framers should have increased it so that it might closely approach the unanimity typical of Calhoun's concurrent majority. However, when considered in the contexts of the Confederacy's commitment to state sovereignty and of the national and state governments dichotomy, the streamlined amendment process was a constitutional mechanism at the disposal of the states to check an encroaching nationalism. The two-thirds minimum actually supplemented the status of the states within the federal framework in the event of a constitutional clash between them and the Confederate government.

Even their substitution of "representation" for "suffrage" in the phrase "but no State shall, without its consent, be deprived of its equal *representation* in the Senate" (Article V) reaffirmed their commitment to the states in contradistinction to the Confederacy. The states were being represented in the Senate, rather than the inhabitants of the various states having equal suffrage regardless of population. The distinction is subtle, no doubt, but nevertheless is a manifestation of the framers' preoccupation with centralization and their commitment to the states.

Confederate compact-covenant ideal

The most revealing innovation for securing state sovereignty is to be found in the C.S.A. preamble. As previously mentioned, the constitutional status of preambles is open to debate, but in this case the preamble does delineate the nature of the relationship among the states as they entered into their confederate union.

During the political fire storm of antebellum America, there was an ongoing debate as to whether the U.S. Constitution established a compact among sovereign states, first and foremost, or a national union of sovereign individuals. The Southern states considered the Union to be the product of a compact between the states. To wit, the titles of the ordinances of secession stated that the compact which formed the Union was dissolved by the seceding states. South Carolina's is typical: *An Ordinance to Dissolve the Union between the State of South Carolina and the Other States United with Her under the Compact Entitled "The Constitution of the United States of America."*[9] This concurs with Calhoun's position: "Having ratified and adopted it [the U.S. Constitution], by mutual agreement, they stand in relation of parties to a constitutional compact; and, of course, it is binding between them as a compact, and not on, or over them, as a constitution. . . . the people of the several States, in their sovereign capacity, agreed to unite themselves together, in the closest possible connection that could be formed, without merging their respective sovereignties into one common sovereignty."[10]

The Confederate framers were determined to remove ambiguity as to the nature of their federal arrangement. Whereas the U.S. preamble's first fifteen words are "We the People of the United States, in order to form a more perfect Union," the C.S.A. preamble explicitly refers to the "sovereign and independent character" of the states that are parties to the compact. It reads: "We, the people of the Confederate States, each State acting in its sovereign and independent character, in order to form a permanent Federal Government."[11] It is also significant that the phrase "to form a more perfect Union" was replaced with "to form a permanent Federal Government." The phrase "permanent Federal Government" does not connote the consolidation associated with "a more perfect Union" as that phrase was being interpreted by Republican nationalists. The C.S.A. framers were determined to establish a compact among member states patterned after their understanding of the U.S. Constitution, and in their understanding they did not equate union with consolidation.

Throughout the C.S.A.'s Constitutional Convention, the delegates stipulated that their constitution was to be patterned after the U.S. Constitution, which, following Calhoun's lead, they alleged was a compact of sovereign states, rather than a consolidation of the states into a union of individuals. The South Carolina secession declaration articulates the meaning of "compact" from the Southern perspective. "We maintain that in every compact between two or more parties, the obligation is mutual; that the failure of one of the contracting parties to perform a material part of the agreement, entirely releases the obligation of the other; and that, when no arbiter is provided, each party is remitted to his own judgement to determine the fact of failure, with all its consequences."[12] The "parties" to the compact would be the state governments; the Confederate government would be their common agent, with each state reserving the prerogative to make the final determination as to whether or not the compact had been breached. According to Publius, such a compact would defeat the purpose of government: "In fine, the world would have seen for the first time, a system of government founded on an inversion of the fundamental principles of all government; it would have seen the authority of the whole society everywhere subordinate to the authority of the parts; it would have seen a monster, in which the head was under the direction of the members."[13] It was at this type of subordination of the whole society to the authority of the parts that the C.S.A. compact theory of government aimed. This constitutional arrangement was to be ensured by making the policies of the Confederacy contingent upon the consent of the states. Such was the nature of the C.S.A. framers' version of federalism—a version Publius described as monstrous.

To discern how this compact theory of government would safeguard the consent of the governed within a federal framework, it is necessary to delineate the procedural aspects of the concurrent majority and to contrast those with the internal and external checks of the U.S. Constitution. The concurrent majority is a constitutional mechanism designed to facilitate compromise and thereby ensure the consent of the governed. It would function by providing sovereign political bodies, in this case states, with the constitutional means to resist the usurpations of the general government.[14] In the event of a nation-state constitutional crisis, who should judge which laws are in pursuance of the constitutional compact? The states should judge, that is, the sovereign power within each state. Theoretically, in the absence of the states, the concurrent majority could be premised upon economic, ideological, cultural, and/or religious categories, provided they were prominent interests within the national community. Nevertheless, there is an underlying assumption that the prominent interests or parts (i.e., the states) are diverse but have enough in common for consent to be a meaningful and workable basis for an effective central government; accordingly, the principle does have practical application, providing the states are directed by rational men. "In coming to this conclusion I have assumed the organism to be perfect and the different interests, portions, or classes of the community to be sufficiently enlightened to understand its character and object, and to exercise, with due intelligence, the right of suffrage. To the effect that either may be defective, to the same extent the government would fall short of fulfilling its end. But this does not impeach the truth of the principles on which it rests."[15] Obviously Calhoun acknowledged that such a system of government requires an advanced stage of enlightened self-interest on the part of the electorate and elected public officials.

Within the context of American federalism, the practical application of the concurrent majority corresponds to the community being the equivalent of the nation and the significant interests being the states. The states constitute the portions of the larger community, and these portions are communities in their own right. Thus the units of analysis are twofold, the general and state governments. The function of the concurrent majority is to protect the diversity of interests of the several states from national public policies adverse to their interests; in other words, the cultural, social, political, and economic development of the states is in the public policy domain of the states, and not of the central government. This scheme of government is in contrast to the U.S. model, in which the consent of a national majority (of either states, citizens, or both) is sufficient to initiate government action over the objections of a state, or states, which constitute a national minority. For states in the minority such a model would be absolute, because its consent would be lacking. "Hence the great and broad distinction between governments is not that of the one, the few, or the many, but of the constitutional and absolute," with constitutional federal government being that in which the consent of the states is requisite to the implementation of national policies within their jurisdiction, and absolute government being that which does not require such consent.[16]

Calhoun's analysis questioned two basic Publian tenets: the reliance on the extended republic and institutional separation of powers. According to Calhoun, without the concurrent majority, these Publian tenets were significantly insufficient in maintaining a national government premised upon the consent of the governed. Publius maintained that to minimize the probability that the national government would be unconstitutionally utilized by national majorities, the scope of the republic must be extended to include a wide variety of economic and social factions, thereby ensuring popular consent throughout the national community by minimizing the likelihood of an overbearing national majority coalescing. The formation of such a majority would be minimized because of the diversity of the factions and the corresponding inherent competitive nature of their relations. However, and most important, this scheme of popular consent does not mandate the consent of all the states.[17] Nevertheless, popular consent premised upon majority rule would be forthcoming: in such a pluralistic setting, no one faction or coalition of factions would dominate the policymaking process indefinitely, because alliances would fluctuate and new coalitions would be organized to displace those in power.

> The smaller the society the fewer will probably be the distinct parties and interests composing it; the fewer the distinct parties and interests, the more frequently will a majority be found of the same party; and the smaller the number of individuals composing a majority, and the smaller the compass within which they are placed, the more easily they will concert and execute their plans of oppression. Extend the sphere and you take in a greater variety of parties and interests; you make it less probable that a majority of the whole will have a common motive to invade the rights of other citizens.

Calhoun contended the opposite. Concerning the consequences of the extended republic, and the centralization of political power at the national level, he reasoned that

> The more extensive and populous the country, the more diversified the condition and pursuits of its population; the richer, the more luxurious, and dissimilar the people, the more difficult it is

to equalize the action of the government, and the more easy for
one portion of the community to pervert its powers to oppress and
plunder the other.[18]

Publius's explanation of the beneficial aspects of an extended
republic centered on the presumption that the components of a
national majority will occasionally change as the various factions
organize and compete for political power against one another, thereby functioning as an internal check against oppressive majorities.
Calhoun maintained that indeed a national majority will material-
ize, but it will be a sectional majority, sustaining its solidarity in
opposition to a sectional minority. The end result will be a division
of the community "into two great parties, a major and a minor,
between which there will be incessant struggles on the one side to
retain, and on the other to obtain the majority and, thereby, control
the government and the advantages it confers." Because a state is
more homogeneous than the nation, and homogeneity of interests
is more conducive to a government premised upon the consent of
the governed than is the case with a heterogeneous community, the
less extensive republic (the state) will be less oppressive than an
extended republic (the Nation), because of the absence of intensely
rival parties, political or otherwise, maintaining control of the government and pursuing policies adverse to the parochial interests of
the states. This being the case, the states should be paramount to the
national government in order to ensure a greater degree of consent
throughout the federal system.[19]

This does not mean that Publius placed inordinate confidence in
the electoral process as the means for a national majority to ensure
the consent of the governed. Both Publius and Calhoun maintained
that the electoral process by itself is inadequate, because it subjects
the minority to majority tyranny. According to Publius, "When a
majority is included in a faction, the form of popular government,
on the other hand, enables it to sacrifice to its ruling passion or
interest both the public good and the rights of other citizens." Calhoun concurred: "The numerical majority, instead of being the people, is only a portion of them, such a government, instead of being a
true and perfect model of the people's government, that is a people
self-governed, is but the government of a part over a part, the major
over the minor portion."[20]

As a remedy to the problem of majority tyranny, Publius relied
upon a scheme of external and internal checks and balances, as did
Calhoun, but with the qualification of states' rights. According to
Publius, within a federal framework a significant aspect of the exter-

nal checks is the restriction on governmental power that the national and state governments place on each other. The national government with its delegated powers and the states with their reserved powers will keep each other within their respective constitutional spheres. "The powers delegated by the proposed Constitution to the federal government are few and defined. Those which are to remain in the State governments are numerous and indefinite. . . . The operations of the federal government will be most extensive and important in times of war and danger; those of the States in times of peace and security."[21]

Should a conflict arise between the national and state governments concerning the extent of their delegated and reserved powers, which is to serve as the final adjudicator? The final adjudicator would be, in the final analysis, sovereign. There are, of course, two mutually exclusive alternatives: national or state sovereignty. Publius, while advocating the supremacy of national laws over state laws, rationalized on behalf of national supremacy. "If a number of political societies enter into a larger political society, the laws which the latter may enact, pursuant to the powers entrusted to it by its constitution, must necessarily be supreme over those societies and the individuals of whom they are composed. It would otherwise be a mere treaty, dependent on the good faith of the parties, and not a government, which is only another word for POLITICAL POWER AND SUPREMACY."[22] Calhoun vigorously contested Publius's interpretation of federalism, maintaining that the essence of American federalism is the sovereignty of the states: "Nothing short of a negative, absolute or in effect, on the part of the government of a State, can possibly protect it against the encroachments of the government of the United States whenever their powers come in conflict."[23] The states, acting individually or in unison, are to function as the final adjudicators in the event of a constitutional conflict between them and the national government.

The C.S.A. Constitution's utilization of internal institutional checks and balances is similar to that of the U.S. Constitution, the former being patterned after the latter. However, the two are dissimilar in the extent of their reliance on internal checks to ensure the consent of the governed. The C.S.A. framers had little confidence in the internal checks without state rights. In both constitutions the scheme of internal checks is mechanistic; the legislative, executive, and judicial branches have specific constitutional functions to write, enforce, and adjudicate the laws. Each branch's functional integrity is to be secured from usurpation by the other branches by providing

the officials of each branch—the congressmen, president, and justices—with institutional arrangements in which the pursuit of their
personal and political interests coincided with the functional integrity of their respective departments. According to Publius, "The
great security against a gradual concentration of the several powers
in the same department consists in giving to those who administer
each department the necessary constitutional means and personal
motives to resist encroachments of the others. The provision for
defense must in this, as in all other cases, be made commensurate to
the danger of attack. Ambition must be made to counteract ambition. The interest of the man must be connected with the constitutional rights of the place."[24]

Thus the Constitution established the governing institutions with
the expectation that they would be utilized by officials attempting to
promote their particular interests, in contradistinction to the pursuit of the common good. Publius contended that "as long as the
reason of man continues fallible, and he is at liberty to exercise it,
different opinions will be formed. As long as the connection sub-
sists between his reason and his self-love, his opinions and passions will have a reciprocal influence on each other," resulting in the
division of society into various factions competing for political power.
Indeed, "what are the different classes of legislators but advocates
and parties to the causes which they determine."[25] In the policymaking process, the common good is not the primary policy objective of public officials. Instead, the common good is the by-product
of the competition for power between public officials pursuing pref-
erential treatment for the factions to which they are accountable.[26]
What supposedly prevents a dominant faction or coalition of factions from permanently controlling the governmental apparatus,
thereby negating meaningful participation by other factions, are the
electoral process, the dispersion of political power among the various institutions, and the multitude of factions innately competing
against one another for political power. Accordingly, "the regulation of these various and interfering interests forms the principal
task of modern legislation and involves the spirit of party and faction in the necessary and ordinary operations of government."[27]

Calhoun insisted that Publius's reasoning was flawed, primarily
because of the failure to anticipate the emergence of a two-party
system. He maintained that the various factions would coalesce into
a numerical majority and minority, facilitated by political parties.
The end result would be that instead of a multiplicity of factions
competing against one another, thereby ubiquitously distributing

political power throughout the political system, there would exist two dominant factions, the major and minor sectional political parties. Subsequently, constitutional restrictions on legislative, executive, and judicial functions would be meaningless; the Constitution notwithstanding, the major political party would accrue all political power to itself and control the government.

> A written constitution certainly has many considerable advantages, but it is a great mistake to suppose that the mere insertion of provisions to restrict and limit the powers of the government, without investing those for whose protection they are inserted with the means of enforcing their observance, will be sufficient to prevent the major and dominant party from abusing its powers. Being the party in the possession of the government, they will, from the same constitution of man which makes government necessary to protect society, be in favor of the powers granted by the constitution and opposed to the restrictions intended to limit them. As the major and dominant parties, they will have no need of these restrictions for their protection. The ballot box, of itself, would be ample protection for them. Needing no other, they would come, in time, to regard these limitations as unnecessary and improper restraints and endeavor to elude them with the view of increasing their power and influence.[28]

It was this concern with centralization of political power at the national level, facilitated by a political party, that led Calhoun and, in 1861, the South, not to rely solely on the external and internal checks on government. Hence, they placed their hopes on states' rights, a manifestation of the concurrent majority, on the grounds that the states would serve as guarantors for the sectional minority interests contesting the policies of the general government under the control of the sectional majority political party. Such a reliance would ensure the consent of the majority and minority interests prior to putting the central government into action. If consent was not forthcoming, a state could exercise its right of noncompliance or, if necessary, its right of secession from the federal compact, thereby excluding itself from the jurisdiction of national policy. For example, suppose that in 1861 a Northern political party hostile to Southern interests gained control of the national executive branch, two-thirds of the Senate and House, and a majority on the Supreme Court. Under such circumstances the internal and external checks of the U.S. Constitution would be inadequate in protecting the Southern states from hostile national legislation. On the other hand, if national legislation could only be implemented with the states' consent, the South would indeed be secure. It was such a scenario that led the South to endorse states' rights so adamantly in the later stages of the antebellum period.

The right of secession from a federal compact depends upon the status of sovereignty. As was mentioned above, the U.S. Constitution is ambiguous concerning state sovereignty, whereas the C.S.A. Constitution's preamble recognizes the "sovereign and independent character of each State." Reproaching the secessionists in his first inaugural address, President Lincoln maintained "that no State, upon its own mere motion, can lawfully get out of the Union; that resolves and ordinances to that effect, are legally void; and that acts of violence within any State or States against the authority of the United States, are insurrectionary or revolutionary, according to circumstance."[29] The South, meanwhile, maintained that "the whole question is whether or not the State can release her citizens from their obligations to the federal authority, and protect them under the sufficient shield of her own sovereign authority! . . . Hapless would be the condition of these States if their only alternative lay between submission to a government of self-construed, or, in other words, unlimited powers, and the certainty of coercion, in case of withdrawal, by force of arms. The way of escape from both extremes is the acknowledged *right of secession.*"[30]

The question naturally comes to mind, if the C.S.A. was committed to a states' rights doctrine, especially in light of the historical developments of the antebellum period, why did the states not expressly constitutionally mandate a state's right of secession? The answer to this question is threefold. First, the framers of the C.S.A. Constitution contended that they were seceding on behalf of the U.S. Constitution, and not because they were opposed to its principles. The claim was consistently reiterated that because of this commitment to the principles embodied in the U.S. Constitution, the C.S.A. Constitution was to be patterned after it. With the exception of Florida, six of the original states forming the Confederacy directed their delegates to draft a constitution that adhered to the principles of the U.S. document. Mississippi's directive to its delegates is typical: "That the people of the State of Mississippi hereby consent to form a federal union with such States as have seceded, or may secede, from the Union of the United States of America, upon the basis of the present Constitution of the said United States."[31] Their affinity for the U.S. Constitution included the understanding that it did not deny the right of secession but implicitly protected that right as a prerogative of state sovereignty. They claimed that it was fallacious construction that had cast doubts on the right of secession. To draft their Confederate Constitution with the expressed right of secession would, it was claimed, be yielding to the Northern interpretation of the U.S. Constitution that if such a right is not expressly granted, it does not constitutionally exist. This they were not about to do.

Second, the seven Southern states that had initially seceded from the Union had the practical problem of attracting the variable border states into the Confederacy. Virginia was especially reluctant to join a confederacy lacking a viable central government. To mandate constitutionally the right of secession would give the appearance of a loose league of disparate states held together by a feeble central government, not destined to endure. In reference to the U.S. Constitution, Jefferson Davis made a similar deduction. "The simple truth is, that it would have been a very extraordinary thing to incorporate into the Constitution any express provision for the secession of the States and the dissolution of the Union. Its founders undoubtedly desired and hoped that it would be perpetual; against the proposition for power to coerce a State, the argument was that it would be a means, not of preserving, but of destroying the Union. It was not for them to make arrangements for its termination—a calamity which there was no occasion to provide for in advance. . . . It was not necessary in the Constitution to affirm the right of secession, because it was an attribute of sovereignty, and the States had reserved all they had not delegated."[32] Consequently, the C.S.A. framers decided to make the right of secession constitutionally implicit by explicitly recognizing the "sovereign and independent character of the States," thereby providing the central government with the appearance of viability that otherwise might be lacking.

And third, and most importantly, the C.S.A. Constitution has a covenant component, establishing a central government held together by the consent and good faith of its members, not by coercion. In other words, it is a voluntary association grounded in a transcendental order. In this context, "a covenant differs from a compact in that its moral dimensions take precedence over its legal dimensions. In its heart of hearts, a covenant is an agreement in which a higher moral force, traditionally God, is either a direct party to or guarantor of a particular relationship. Whereas, when the term compact is used, moral force is only indirectly involved. A compact, based as it is on mutual pledges rather than guarantees by or before a higher authority, rests more heavily on a legal though still ethical grounding for its politics. In other words, compact is a secular phenomenon."[33] This is not meant to imply that the U.S.

Constitution is exclusively a secular document lacking elements of a covenant tradition. Rather, what is asserted is that the C.S.A. Constitution explicitly invokes "the favor and guidance of Almighty God" in its preamble, thereby making the Supreme Being a guarantor of the Constitution. This led Thomas R. R. Cobb to conclude that the C.S.A. Constitution "acknowledged the overruling providence of God."[34] The U.S. Constitution lacks such a reference, so to that extent it is a secular document.

The precedence of the legal over the moral dimension in the U.S. Constitution is made evident by Publius's analysis of the role of religion in the American political process. Concurring with David Hume and John Locke, the contention was that religion poses a threat to civil stability. Religious groups (factions) of different persuasions will attempt to gain preeminence over rivals by accruing political power.[35] To reduce the probability of instability and oppression at the hands of religious sects, the number of competing sects must be increased so that the principle of the extended republic is applicable to the distribution of political power among the sects. According to Publius, "In free government the security of civil rights must be the same as that for religious rights. It consists in the one case in the multiplicity of interests, and in the other in the multiplicity of sects. The degree of security in both cases will depend on the number of interests and the number of sects." Religion was not intrinsically viewed as a means to worship and serve the Supreme Being, but rather it was viewed as another category of faction, "actuated by some common impulse of passion, or of interest, adverse to the rights of other citizens, or to the permanent and aggregate interests of the community."[36] From this viewpoint, religion was problematic, to be dealt with on a technical basis, whereas for the Confederates, Almighty God was a source of "favor and guidance," invoked in their preamble.

The Confederacy did not dismiss the notion that a multiplicity of sects is preferable to a few dominant sects competing for political power. However, it did not relegate religion to the arena of competing factions. The South was experiencing a "great revival" of religious fundamentalism, which was influencing the direction of political events.[37] Repeatedly the South justified its political actions by claiming divine sanction. Following are a few typical eulogies of the period by influential Southern statesmen:

> An all wise God has controlled our destinies and made the wrath of man to praise Him. To Him let our hearts turn in humble thankfulness as we say: "Not unto us, not unto us, but unto Thy name

Oh Lord, be all the praise and the glory." . . . Today, with purblind eyes, Europe is awakening to behold us as we are, not semi-barbarians relapsing into savage life, but a people with the most liberal political institutions, and most patriarchal and perfect social polity, and the most pure unadulterated, simple Christian Faith, that the world now contains.[38]

I think you will agree with me in pronouncing our constitution a great improvement upon the constitution of the U.S. in all the amendments we have made. Our people are not only content but joyous and happy, and blessed beyond all calculation with prosperity in every department of business. Providence has smiled upon us, and with grateful hearts we go on our way rejoicing.[39]

I enter upon the duties of the office to which I have been chosen with the hope that the beginning of our career, as a Confederacy may not be obstructed by hostile opposition to our enjoyment of the separate existence and independence we have asserted, and which, with the blessing of Providence, we intend to maintain. . . . But if this be denied to us, and the integrity of our territory and jurisdiction be assailed, it will but remain for us with firm resolve to appeal to arms and invoke the blessing of Providence on a just cause. . . . Obstacles may retard, but they cannot long prevent, the progress of a movement sanctified by its justice and sustained by a virtuous people. Reverently let us invoke the God of our fathers to guide and protect us in our efforts to perpetuate the principles which by his blessing they were able to vindicate, establish, and transmit to their prosperity. With the continuance of His favor ever gratefully acknowledged, we may hopefully look forward to success, to peace, and to prosperity.[40]

This great revival and the application of biblical teachings to political questions were provoked by the Southern attempt to defend the institution of slavery against Northern declamations that it was immoral and contrary to Christian standards. Consequently, this revival influenced the Confederates to view the establishment of their national community as sanctioned by God.[41]

The C.S.A. Constitution, with its covenantal qualities, associated the distinct sovereign states into a community of states. This community of states was to be held together by a moral force willingly complied to, with secession serving as a constitutional exit for a member state in which this moral force was lacking. The binding moral force was either there or it was absent. In the latter case, a state would cease to be a member of the community de facto. Thus, to mandate constitutionally the right of secession would have been superfluous because of the consensus that the Confederacy was a voluntary association of sovereign states, contingent upon the goodwill of its members. The covenantal dimension of the C.S.A.

Constitution is in response to the Publian maxim, and subsequent national policy, that the national supremacy of the U.S. Constitution is based upon political power and not on the good faith of the parties, or states.[42]

Two important constitutional principles have been analyzed: First, the C.S.A. Constitution is committed to a states' rights doctrine in which sovereignty is a state phenomenon, whereas the U.S. Constitution inherently treats sovereignty as a national one; and, second, this states' rights doctrine is premised upon a consensual model politics within a federal framework in which no state can be constitutionally coerced into compliance with Confederate public policies. Consequently, Confederate public policies would be premised upon the consent of the states, whereas under the U.S. Constitution the consent of the states is not necessarily requisite to the implementation of U.S. public policies.

Does this mean that consent is more pervasive in the C.S.A. model than in the U.S.? Within the confines of federalism, that is, national-state relations, one must answer in the affirmative. Moreover, insofar as the people within their respective states were capable of sustaining republican government, the Confederacy was closer to the Revolutionary ideal of premising the government upon the consent of the governed. This ideal was in contradistinction to the emerging nationalistic political order that was embodied in the U.S. Constitution, cultivated by Publius, and harvested by the Lincoln Republicans.

Chapter Four

The Bill of Rights

A bill of rights is essentially a constitutional declaration of privileges retained by the people—privileges which the sovereign authority is obligated to recognize as inviolable and from which ema-
nate security for denoted civil liberties and rights of the people.
Both the U.S and C.S.A. constitutions contain such declarations.
However, there are two important distinctions between the two
documents' declarations. First, some of the more important declarations of rights in the U.S. Constitution are in the form of amendments, whereas the C.S.A. Constitution has its declarations of
rights in the body of the text; and, second, there are significant
terminological differences.

Initially, the first distinction could be dismissed as a result of the
Confederate framers' merely copying the U.S. Constitution in its
totality as of 1861, including the first twelve amendments, as one
complete text. As a result, the need for amendments to include a bill
of rights was obviated. But when one takes into consideration the
debate that led to the inclusion of a U.S. Bill of Rights, and the
placement of those rights in the C.S.A. Constitution, it becomes
clear that the distinction involves a fundamental constitutional disparity, especially when the terminological differences are considered.

To delineate the nature of this disparity, it is necessary to analyze
the Antifederalist-Federalist debate that resulted in the inclusion of
a bill of rights in the U.S. Constitution. The analysis will make
evident the intent of the U.S. framers, which in turn will be contrasted with the intent of their Confederate counterparts.

The Federalists were not opposed to a declaration of rights within
a constitutional context; they drafted and supported a document
that contained many such rights. Examples are: constitutional prohibitions against bills of attainder, *ex post facto* laws, the conviction
of a citizen for treason on the testimony of only one witness, corruption of blood, the denial of trial by jury in criminal cases, the
unwarrantable suspension of habeas corpus, religious tests as a

precondition to a position of public trust, and others.[1] But they were opposed to a declaration of rights that would make the constitutional prohibitions exclusively applicable to the national government. With the exception of Rhode Island,[2] all the state constitutions in effect during the 1787 convention contained a declaration of rights in one form or another, and four states ratified the U.S. Constitution on the condition that it would be subsequently amended to include an analogous declaration of rights.[3] The states' declarations of rights were for the most part in the form of self-contained enumerations, rather than being intermixed throughout the documents. Such enumerations, it was hoped, increased the validity of the rights by giving them an explicit constitutional status, especially when the enumeration was designated "Declaration of Rights" (as was the case in Maryland, Massachusetts, North Carolina, Pennsylvania, and Vermont) or "Bill of Rights" (as was the case in New Hampshire and Virginia). New Jersey utilized the title "Rights and Privileges." So the idea of limiting government with a bill of rights was not alien to American constitutionalism.

Virginia's Declaration of Rights, mostly the work of George Mason (who later refused to sign the completed U.S. document of the 1787 convention), served as the model for subsequent constitutions. Its sixteen sections, in essence, are as follows: (1) citizens have the natural rights of life, liberty, property, and happiness; (2) all power is derived from the people, and magistrates are their trustees and servants; (3) government ought to be instituted for the common benefit, and if it is not so constituted, the people have the right to alter or abolish it; (4) emoluments and privileges are forthcoming from the community for public services only; (5) the legislative and executive powers of the state should be separate and distinct from the judiciary; (6) there exists the right of suffrage; (7) the suspension of the laws is to be on the consent of the representatives of the people; (8) there exists the right of habeas corpus and the right of the accused to confront witnesses; (9) there shall be prohibitions against excessive bail, fines, and cruel and unusual punishment; (10) search and arrest warrants are to be supported by evidence; (11) trial by jury ought to be held sacred; (12) there shall be freedom of the press; (13) standing armies in times of peace ought to be avoided and the military should be under civil authority; (14) the people have the right to a uniform government; (15) there exists the right to frequent recurrence to fundamental principles; and (16) the free exercise of religion is protected.[4]

Some of the above stated rights, which were typical in one form or another in state constitutions, were initially included in the U.S. Constitution; others were subsequently added as a result of the amendment process. It is this latter class that is of interest, because the Federalists argued against including these in the U.S. Constitution. Publius maintained that such a declaration of rights in the U.S. Constitution was unnecessary and dangerous. It was unnecessary because the government being instituted was to be premised upon the consent of the governed and the common-law tradition of the British Constitution, which adequately secured the rights of citizens without constitutionally delineating the rights and privileges retained by the people. A declaration of rights would be dangerous because it could not possibly be exhaustive, and those rights not included in the declaration could be assumed to be violable by the government. Furthermore, those rights included could be used as a pretext by the government as justification for jurisdiction over those rights. According to Publius, bills of rights have

> no application to constitutions professedly founded upon the power of the people and executed by their immediate representatives and servants. . . . I go further and affirm that bills of rights, in the sense and to the extent in which they are contended for, are not only unnecessary in the proposed Constitution but would even be dangerous. They would contain various exceptions to powers which are not granted; and, on this very account, would afford a colorable pretext to claim more than were granted. For why declare that things shall not be done which there is not power to do? Why, for instance, should it be said that the liberty of the press shall not be restrained, when no power is given by which restrictions may be imposed? I will not contend that such a provision would confer a regulating power; but it is evident that it would furnish, to men disposed to usurp, a plausible pretense for claiming that power.[5]

Publius's reasoning contains significant inconsistency. Initially, he surmises that the people have nothing to fear from a government elected by them and serving at their pleasure, or from laws and judicial processes constrained by the common-law tradition of the British Constitution. After maintaining that the people have nothing to fear from a government so constrained, Publius sets these constraints aside and argues that the inclusion of a declaration of rights could serve as a pretext for jurisdiction over those very rights included in the declaration (or those rights not included, or both), and such a pretext could be used to violate the rights of the people. In other words, to constitutionally stipulate "liberty of the press" would open the way for the government to limit other types of expression, such as oral political expression. This qualification calls into question the initial assumption that a government premised upon the consent of the governed and the common-law tradition of the British Constitution poses no serious threat to the citizens' political and civil rights, the absence of a bill of rights notwithstanding. This specious argument calls into question the sincerity of Publius's commitment to consent as an effective basis of American federalism and the actual rationale behind his opposition to an inclusion of a bill of rights to the U.S. Constitution. One should not assume that the caliber of minds that produced *The Federalist Papers* would mistakenly include such an inconsistency.

The Antifederalists were aware of the inconsistency but had difficulty articulating a theoretical justification for a declaration of rights at the national level. To insist on a national declaration of rights was perhaps to concede that the national government would have jurisdiction over individuals. This would be a more drastic modification of the federal arrangement established under the Articles of Confederation than many Antifederalists were prepared or authorized to make. They suspected that a national bill of rights would be unnecessary if the states were not placed in a subordinate position to the national government, primarily because the citizens within their respective states could be protected from arbitrary government power by the various states' bills of rights. The Antifederalist predicament is typified by the dissenting members of the Pennsylvania delegation to the 1787 convention:

> The new Constitution, consistently with the plan of consolidation, contains no reservation of the rights and privileges of the state governments, which was made in the confederation of the year 1781, by article two, viz., "That each state retains its sovereignty, freedom, and independence, and every power, jurisdiction and right, which is not by this confederation expressly delegated to the United States in Congress assemble." . . . the omission of a BILL OF RIGHTS, ascertaining and fundamentally establishing those unalienable and personal rights of men without the full, free, and secure enjoyment of which there can be no liberty, and over which it is not necessary for a good government to have control [would be detrimental to the federal system] . . . . The stipulations heretofore made in favor of them in the state constitutions are entirely superseded by this constitution.[6]

Antifederalist demands for a national declaration of rights, enforceable by a national government, were inconsistent with their support for state sovereignty. To prevent the subordination of the states to the national government, the states must be sovereign within their respective spheres; that is, they must be sovereign in regard to the reserved powers. But how is a national declaration of rights over individuals to be reconciled with state sovereignty?

The Antifederalists formulated a tentative solution. There would, indeed, be a national declaration of rights designed to constrain the national government vis-à-vis the states, the enforcement of which would be primarily the responsibility of the states, if necessitated by circumstances. Consequently, the declaration of rights insisted upon by the Antifederalists was designed to secure states' rights. Various ratification-related documents reiterate this concern for the status of the states vis-à-vis the national government:

> That the sovereignty, freedom, and independency of the several states shall be retained, and every power, jurisdiction, and right which is not by this constitution expressly delegated to the United States in Congress assembled.

> Nothing in this constitution shall deprive a citizen of any state of the benefit of the bill of rights established by the constitution of the state in which he shall reside, and such bills of rights shall be considered as valid in any court of the United States where they shall be pleaded.[7]

> That the rights of the states respectively to nominate and appoint all state officers, and every other power, jurisdiction, and right, which is not by the said Constitution clearly delegated to the Congress of the United States, or to the departments of government thereof, remain to the people of the several states, or their respective state governments, to whom they may have granted the same.[8]

> That the senators and representatives, and all executive and judicial officers of the United States, shall be bound by oath or affirmation not to infringe or violate the constitutions or rights of the respective states.

> That it be explicitly declared that all powers not expressly delegated by the aforesaid Constitution are reserved to the several states, to be by them exercised.[9]

The above quotations typify the Antifederalist design to utilize the Bill of Rights as a legal weapon to keep the national government within its specified sphere of constitutional trust. Had their design been adopted, a state would have been more secure in the event of a constitutional contest between itself and the national government. Madison was aware of this and as a result managed to push through the First Congress a declaration of rights package contrary to the Antifederalist intentions.

Madison's proposal for a declaration of rights was designed to limit both the national and state governments, with the former as the enforcing agent. In the course of the debate concerning a declaration of rights in the House of Representatives, Madison made the following statement about governmental authority:

> I think there is more danger of those powers being abused by the State Governments than by the Government of the United States. The same may be said of other powers they may possess, if not controlled by the general principle, that laws are unconstitutional which infringe the rights of the community. I should therefore wish to extend this interdiction, and add, as I have stated in the 5th resolution, that no State shall violate the equal right of conscience, freedom of the press, or trial by jury in criminal cases; because it is proper that every Government should be disarmed of powers which entrench upon those particular rights. I know, in some of the State constitutions, the power of the Government is controlled by such a declaration; but others are not. I cannot see any reason against obtaining even a double security on those points; and nothing can give a more sincere proof of the attachment of those who oppose this constitution to these great and important rights, than to see them join in obtaining the security I have now proposed; because it must be admitted, on all hands, that the State Governments are as liable to attack these invaluable privileges as the General Government is, and therefore ought to be cautiously guarded against. [10]

A declaration of rights premised accordingly would necessitate the subjection of the states to national authority simply as a matter of enforcement, or "interdiction," to use Madison's terminology. National interdiction to protect citizens from state governments violating their rights would have unambiguously established national supremacy in the areas of civil and political rights. [11]

Thus the declaration of rights to limit the national government, which the Antifederalists insisted upon, was utilized by the Federalists as a means to limit all government, with the national government as the ultimate enforcer. The essence of the Antifederalist response to this Federalist maneuver is typified by Representative Thomas Tudor Tucker during the same House debates. "It seemed to him [Tucker] as if there was a strong propensity in this Government to take upon themselves the guidance of the State Governments, which to his mind implied a doubt of their capacity to govern themselves; now his judgement was convinced that the particular State Governments could take care of themselves, and deserved more to be trusted than this did, because the right of the citizen was more secure under it." [12]

Madison did, indeed, doubt the state governments' capacities for judicious self-government, meaning limited government that respects the fundamental rights (i.e., property rights) of the governed. [13] For this reason Madison insisted that if a bill of rights were to be included in the U.S. Constitution, its application should extend to the states. A proposed Federalist amendment (which was passed in the House but defeated in the Senate) stated that "in article 1st, section 10, between clauses 1 and 2, be inserted this clause, to wit: No State shall violate the equal rights of conscience, or freedom of the press, or the trial by jury in criminal cases." And echoing the logic of Publius, Madison expressed his distrust of state governments in the Virginia ratifying convention in the course of a discussion concerning religious freedom. "It is better that his [citizen's] security should be depended upon from the general legislature, than from one particular state. A particular state may concur in one religious project. But the United States abound in such a variety of sects, that it is a strong security against religious persecution; and it is sufficient to authorize a conclusion, that no one sect will ever be able to outnumber or depress the rest."[14] Hence, the declaration of rights in the United States should be uniform, with the national government as the guardian of those liberties.

The C.S.A. framers did not adhere to this "uniformity" of liberty and the distrust of a state government's ability or willingness to secure fundamental liberties. This is reflected in their rewrite of the ninth article of the U.S. Bill of Rights:

> Article Nine, U.S. Bill of Rights: The enumeration in the Constitution, of certain rights, shall not be construed to deny or disparage others retained by the people.

> Article Six, clause 5, of the C.S.A. Constitution: The enumeration, in the Constitution, of certain rights, shall not be construed to deny or disparage others retained by the people of the several States.

As discussed in Chapter Three, rights "retained by the people" is general, in the sense that the phrase refers to a national community, whereas those "retained by the people of the several States" is particular, in the sense that the phrase refers to the people in their respective states. The declaration of rights in the C.S.A. Constitution was strictly applicable to the Confederate government (unless explicitly stated otherwise, e.g., Article I, section 10), leaving the state constitutions as the guarantors for those fundamental rights retained by the people within their respective states.

The fact that the C.S.A. framers intended that their bill of rights be applied to the Confederate government is evidenced by their placement of most of the reserved rights in Article I, section 9, where the list of what the Congress shall not do is to be found. Counterparts of the U.S. Constitution's first eight amendments were all incorporated into Article I, section 9. Of course the list is not exhaustive; the rights of Amendment Nine are unenumerated. But those gaps are filled in by the state constitutions. The Confederate government shall not infringe upon those rights retained by the people "of the several States," providing those states' rights do not conflict with Confederate laws pursuant to the Confederate Constitution (the supremacy clause of Article VI). Under the C.S.A. federal arrangement, a state would have dominion in those areas of constitutional rights not enumerated in the Confederate Constitution. So Utah, for instance, could constitutionally permit polygamy because the Confederate Constitution is silent about that. It is silent, as well, about a wide range of issues such as the status of slavery within a state. In short, the C.S.A. Constitution restricts the Confederate government, not the states, unless it explicitly states otherwise, as it does regarding bills of attainder, *ex post facto* laws, the impairing of the obligation of contracts, and titles of nobility (Article I, section 10).

This constitutional arrangement was necessary because of the retention by the Confederate states of their sovereignty. It was the states that delimited the fundamental liberties of their citizens, and liberties might vary from state to state. Theoretically, this concurred with the Calhounian dictum "that it is a great and dangerous error to suppose that all people are equally entitled to liberty. It is a reward to be earned."[15] The sovereign within the respective states would determine who merited which liberties based upon circumstances within the respective states. Accordingly, a state and a confederacy, half-free and half-slave, could be, depending on circumstances, a viable constitutional arrangement. The Confederate defense of slavery brought to light this anomalous interpretation of civil liberties—that is, anomalous from the perspective of twentieth-century America.

To reconcile their commitment to a government based upon the consent of the governed, while simultaneously upholding the institution of slavery, the Confederate framers articulated a classical republicanism rather than a republicanism premised upon the contract theorist's notion of natural rights. Edmund Ruffin's rationale was typical of the Confederate position.

> The most injurious, in their consequences, of such erroneous deductions from the true principles and sound propositions, are to be found in the now generally received doctrines of natural rights,

and political rights, of all the male citizens or members of a free or Republican Government—or that every man has or ought to have, the right to exercise an equal influence in the direction of all public affairs, and of the government of the country. . . . Among the false and dangerous, but yet legitimate deductions from the broad doctrine of the equal natural rights of man, there subsequently was started the then novel claim of freedom for the negro slaves."[16]

Drawing on the ideas of the eighteenth-century Antifederalists and the nineteenth century Calhounian theory of rights, they integrated the liberties of the individual with the welfare of the community, making the former contingent upon the latter. This, of course, facilitated the sanctioning of slavery, which, in the Southern mind, was not only in the interest of the community at large but also in the interest of the slave. And it was the responsibility of the citizens within their states, in contradistinction to the national community, to determine which rights were compatible with the interest of the state community.

A tract written in 1860 by Albert Taylor Bledsoe, delineates the Confederate systematic view. According to Bledsoe, "the institution of slavery, as it exists among us at the South, is founded in political justice, is in accordance with the will of God and the designs of his providence, and is conducive to the highest, purest, and best interests of mankind."[17] The C.S.A. Constitution reflects Bledsoe's sentiments. Contrast the U.S. Constitution's omission of the terms "slaves" and "slavery" from its text with the C.S.A. Constitution's explicit mention of them. Article I, section 9, reads: "The importation of negroes of the African race, from any foreign country other than the slaveholding States or Territories of the United States of America, is hereby forbidden; and Congress is required to pass such laws as shall effectually prevent the same. Congress shall also have power to prohibit the introduction of slaves from any State not a member of, or Territory not belonging to, this Confederacy. . . . No bill of attainder; ex post facto law, or law denying or impairing the right of property in Negro slaves shall be passed."

It is important to keep in mind that the prohibition against passing a law "denying or impairing the right of property in Negro slaves" applied to the C.S.A. Congress and not to the states. Nevertheless, the Confederate framers pointed to such linguistic explicitness in their Constitution as evidence of their affirmation of the institution of slavery. Robert H. Smith of Alabama, an influential member on the Permanent Constitution Committee, maintained:

> We have dissolved the late Union chiefly because of the negro quarrel. Now, is there any man who wished to reproduce that strife among ourselves? And yet does not he, who wished the slave trade left for the action of Congress, see that he proposed to open a Pandora's box among us and to cause our political arena again to resound with this discussion. Had we left the question unsettled, we should, in my opinion, have sown broadcast the seeds of discord and death in our Constitution. I congratulate the country that the strife has been put to rest forever, and that American slavery is to stand before the world as it is, and on its own merits. We have now placed our domestic institution, and secured its rights unmistakably, in the Constitution; we have sought by no euphony to hide its name—we have called our negroes "slaves," and we have recognized and protected them as persons and our rights to them as property.[18]

It should come as no surprise that the Confederates dismissed admonitions of a conflict between the "peculiar institution" and republicanism, just as their Northern counterparts failed to choke on a conflict between republicanism and exclusive male suffrage.

As a case in point, the Calhounian position that slavery was a positive good was contingent upon what was understood to be in the interests of African-Americans and Southern communities. A sort of mutually beneficial relationship supposedly existed between slaves and whites. However, as social circumstances necessitated, the status of African-Americans in Southern communities must also change. In the world of practical politics, both President Davis and a majority of the C.S.A. Congress acknowledged as much when they supported legislation to impress the slaves and to anticipate their incorporation into Southern society on terms distinct from slavery. In a November, 1864, address to Congress, albeit in response to military necessity, Davis made the following recommendations regarding the arming of slaves:

> Viewed merely as property, and therefore as the subject of impressment, the service or labor of the slave has been frequently claimed for short periods in the construction of defensive work. The slave, however, bears another relation to the State—that of a person. . . . Whenever the entire property in the service of the slave is thus acquired by the Government, the question is presented by what tenure should he be held. Should he be retained in servitude, or should his emancipation be held out to him as a reward for faithful service, or should it be granted at once on the promise of such service; and if emancipated, what action should be taken to secure for the freedman the permission of the State from which he was drawn to reside within its limits after the close of public service? . . . The policy of engaging to liberate the negro

on the discharge after service faithfully rendered seems to me preferable to that of granting immediate manumission, or that of retaining him in servitude.[19]

This legislation did not infringe upon a state's prerogative to regulate the institution of slavery within its jurisdiction, that is, upon the determination of the status of slavery along the lines of popular sovereignty within a sovereign state, which is to be distinguished from a territory. Rather, the legislation impressed persons into the service of the Confederacy, provided the slave owner with "just compensation," and then offered freedom to those slaves who as a consequence of impressment would be the property of the C.S.A. In essence, the institution of slavery remained intact, while the legislation recognized the fitness of some slaves for freedom and provided them with an opportunity to secure it.

Following Calhoun's lead in the attempt to substantiate the "political justness" of such a constitutional arrangement, the Confederates were obliged to devise some means of refuting the Lockean basis of civil society. Bledsoe made such an attempt; he acknowledged that "it seems to have become a political maxim that civil society is no other than a certain portion of our natural liberty, which has been carved therefrom, and secured to us by the protection of laws." Bledsoe was questioning the assumption that individuals possess certain rights independent of civil society and that they consent to concede some rights to civil society in return for the liberty to exercise those rights they retain. Bledsoe's primary objection to this Lockean scheme was that individuals do not possess rights distinct from civil society. In the Aristotelian and Calhounian tradition, the individual and civil society coexist, and individual liberties should be concordant with the state of civil society.

> Herein, then, consists the true relation between the natural and the social states. Civil society does not abridge our natural rights, but secures and protects them. She does not assume the right of self-defense, she simply discharges the duty imposed by God to defend us. The original right is in those who compose the body politic, and not in any individual. Hence, civil society does not impair our natural liberty, as actually existing in a state of nature, or as it might therein exist; for, in such a state, there would be no real liberty, no real enjoyment of natural rights.

On these grounds, the contract theorists' state of nature is erroneous. Concurring with Calhoun, Bledsoe maintained that "God himself has laid the foundations of civil society deep in the nature of man. . . . It is not a thing of compacts, bound together by promises and paper, but is itself a law of nature as irreversible as any other. Compacts may give it one form or another, but in one form or another it must exist."[20]

Accordingly, neither the freeman nor the slave enters into civil society with established rights guaranteed as a precondition to compliance with civil laws. Such rights are to be determined by the transmutable sovereign authority, whose determinations are supposedly designed to secure the public good of the state first and foremost, and through the public good the good of the individual. But the basis of the sovereign's determinations (in this case the citizens of a state constitute the sovereign) must be the principles of justice.

> One thing seems to be clear and fixed; and that is, that the rights of the individual are subordinate to those of the community. An inalienable right is a right coupled with a duty; a duty with which no other obligation can interfere. But, as we have seen, it is the duty, and consequently, the right, of society to make such laws as the general good demands. This unalienable right is conferred, and its exercise enjoined, by the Creator and Governor of the universe. All individual rights are subordinate to this inherent, universal, and unalienable right. It should be observed, however, that in the exercise of this paramount right, this supreme authority, no society possesses the power to contravene the principles of justice. In other words, it should be observed that no unjust law can ever promote the public good. Every law, then, which is not unjust, and which the public good demands, should be enacted by society.[21]

The rights of the people in their community, the state, are contingent upon the interest of the community. In other words, the public good should dictate individual rights. Of course, Southern spokesmen maintained that under current circumstances, the institution of slavery was in the interests of their respective communities, including the interests of the slaves themselves, and by necessity the "peculiar institution" did not contravene republican principles, but rather it secured them.

Acknowledging that changing social circumstances necessitate alterations in the political order, many Southerners were prepared to alter the status of the slaves within their states. Because most Southerners recognized the humanity of slaves, such alterations were not insurmountable. Unless one accepts the Marxist interpretation of religion, how else does one explain the sincere efforts at Christianizing slaves; if slaves were regarded as subhuman, such efforts would have been an absurdity. A willingness to accept such alterations is exemplified in President Davis's 1864 inaugural address, in which he submitted for congressional consideration the proposal to impress slaves into the Confederate ranks. Encouraged by General Robert E. Lee's policy initiative to provide slaves the opportunity to earn their freedom by serving in the Confederate army, Davis reasoned that the status of slaves was a social and political question to be resolved by the states.

> If the subject involved no other consideration than the mere right of property, sacrifices heretofore made by our people have been such to permit no doubt of their readiness to surrender every possession in order to secure their independence. But the social and political question, which is exclusively under the control of the several States, has a far wider and more enduring importance than that of pecuniary interest. In its manifold phases it embraces the stability of our republican institutions, resting on the actual political equality of all its citizens, and includes the fulfillment of the task which has been so happily begun—that of Christianizing and improving the condition of the Africans who have, by the will of Providence, been placed in our charge. . . . the people of the several States of the Confederacy have abundant reason to be satisfied with the past, and will use the greatest circumspection in determining their course.[22]

Davis's address reveals that the relationship between the political community and slaves was susceptible to change and that Confederate social arrangements regarding the "peculiar institution" were not to be static. Furthermore, if a particular state within the Confederacy determined that manumission should be a precondition for service in the military, then that state was within its rights to make such changes as its interests dictated, even if such changes included the collective state action elevating the former slaves to the status of citizenship.[23]

As Article IV of the U.S. and C.S.A. constitutions guarantees to each state a republican form of government, each state is ensured some model of government premised upon the consent of the governed. The theoretical underpinning of the C.S.A. Constitution was that state civil authorities, chosen according to republican principles, had the responsibility to determine the nature and extent of state citizens' rights. This legitimatized a type of majority rule about which Publius was very apprehensive. The concern was understandable. For example, if an entire class of people could be denied their most fundamental rights, then how secure were other minorities, such as economic, religious, cultural, ethnic, and so on? The answer to this question is contingent upon one's confidence in the majority's willingness to adhere to the "principles of justice." Regarding state majorities Publius had little confidence. Due to the absence of a diversity of factions at the state level—a diversity that would prevent the formation of a monolithic oppressive majority—the state minorities would be continuously exposed to majority tyranny. Conversely, the Confederates placed their concern for majority tyranny at the national level, confident that the citizens within their respective states were more competent of judicious and effective government.

Evidence of the Confederate Constitution's deference toward the states' capacities for self-government is the absence of a Confederacy-wide policy on the status of slavery. Even though the Confederate framers were convinced that slavery was a positive good for all concerned in the South, they did not include in the C.S.A. Constitution a stipulation that all the states must maintain slavery. The C.S.A. Constitution does prohibit the Confederate general government from abolishing slavery (Article I, section 9), but not the states. Article IV, section 3, of the C.S.A. Constitution mandates that in Confederate territory "the institution of negro slavery, as it now exists in the Confederate States, shall be recognized and protected by Congress and by the territorial government." The significance of this section is that it reflects the policy Southern legislators were advocating in the U.S. Congress during the territorial disputes. But significantly, by omission the C.S.A. Constitution does not mandate that every state in the Confederacy recognize the right of its citizens to own slaves, which means that if the sovereign authority in a state so desired, slavery could be prohibited. As a matter of fact, Article IV, section 2, is anticipatory of the inclusion of free states in the Confederacy: "The citizens of each State . . . shall have the right of transit and sojourn in any State of this Confederacy, with their slaves and other property; and the right of property in said slaves shall not be thereby impaired." This is not to imply that the C.S.A. framers endorsed manumission; but it does indicate the Confederate commitment to state sovereignty in the domain of civil liberties, and not to a declaration of rights uniformly applicable to all the states.

Furthermore, the constitutional stipulation that slavery be recognized in the Confederate territories does not disclaim the commitment to state sovereignty. Confederate territory was considered to be the common property of the Confederacy (as Southern congressmen maintained was the case in the U.S. territories) and therefore lacked sovereignty. In an 1860 U.S. Senate debate, Jefferson Davis articulated the Southern position.

> I do not admit that sovereignty necessarily exists in the Federal
> Government or in a territorial government. I deny the proposi-
> tion, which is broadly laid down, of the necessity which must exist
> for it in the one place or the other. I hold that sovereignty exists
> only in a State, or in the United States in their associated capacity,
> to whom sovereignty may be transferred, but that their agent is
> incapable of receiving it, and, consequently, incapable of transfer-
> ring it to Territory inhabitants.

In the same speech Davis approvingly referred to Calhoun's position on the subject, quoting from Calhoun's speech on the bill to
admit California into statehood.

> In claiming the right for inhabitants, instead of Congress to legis-
> late for the Territories, the executive proviso assumes that the
> sovereignty over the Territories is vested in the former, or to ex-
> press it in the language used in a resolution offered by one of the
> Senators from Texas, (General Houston, now absent) they have
> "the same inherent right of self-government as the people in the
> States." The assumption is utterly unfounded, unconstitutional,
> without example, and contrary to the entire practice of the Gov-
> ernment, from its commencement to the present time.[24]

Davis acknowledged that a sovereign power (a state) may prohibit
slavery, but a territorial government may not, unless the prohibition
is mandated in the national constitution.[25] Accordingly, the C.S.A.
Constitution's stipulation that slavery be recognized in the territories is compatible with the doctrine of state sovereignty, due to the
fact that territories are not states but are the common property of all
the states and therefore lack sovereignty.

Nevertheless, there were several attempts made during the C.S.A.
Constitutional Convention to require all states in the Confederacy
constitutionally to recognize slavery. T.R.R. Cobb of Georgia offered such a proposal: "But no State shall be admitted which, by its
constitution or laws, denies the right of property in negro slaves."[26]
Such proposals were not adopted, and the Convention finally settled on the following: "Other States may be admitted into this Confederacy by a vote of two-thirds of the Senate, the Senate voting by
States."[27] Thus slavery was not a constitutional prerequisite for
admission, and once admitted, a state could either recognize or
prohibit the institution. Senator Albert G. Brown of Mississippi
stated the Southern consensus on this issue when he maintained
that "each State is sovereign within its own limits; and that each for
itself can abolish or establish slavery for itself."[28]

This flexibility toward the slavery issue was due in part to the
practical consideration of instituting a constitutional arrangement

conducive to the establishment of a commercial republic not restricted to the Southern section. It was anticipated that states, free and slave, in the Midwest, Northwest, and West would eventually join the Confederacy in order to benefit from the anticipated commercial prosperity. Commenting on the admission policy of the Confederacy, Robert H. Smith asserted:

> I justify the catholicism of the above provision on higher ground, and throwing aside the feelings which the irritation of the moment creates and looking to the future with full confidence that our domestic policy will justify itself and long outlive the puny assaults of maddened fanaticism, led on by ambitious politicians. I earnestly hope that not only will the kindred States join us, but abide in confidence that some of the great Northwestern States, watered by the Mississippi, will be drawn by the strong current of that mighty river and by the laws of trade, to swell the number and power of this Confederation; and that we shall receive them on such terms of their organic law as we ourselves may prescribe; and in doing so, grasp the power of empire on this continent and announce to the startled North that it has reached its western limit, and must spread if spread it can, towards the frozen sea.

In short, the Confederate framers did not want to restrict the expansion of the Confederacy by limiting admission to slave states. As Smith pointed out, "sentiment in nations never long rules master of interest."[29]

This concession to the admission of free states was not an indication of diminishing Confederate support for slavery. Southerners continued, with increasing intensity, to eulogize the political and moral consequences of slavery, regarding it "as the most safe and stable basis for free institutions."[30] Using ancient Rome and Athens as their models, the Southern apologists for slavery defended it as a means to control the politically obtuse portion of society, without which free institutions would be subsequently undone. Senator James Henry Hammond articulated the Southern rationale in no uncertain terms.

> No society has ever yet existed . . . without a natural variety of classes. The most marked of these must, in a country like ours, be the rich and the poor, the educated and the ignorant. It will be scarcely disputed that the poor have less leisure to prepare themselves for the proper discharge of public duties than the rich; and that the ignorant are wholly unfit for them at all. . . . Though intelligence and wealth have great influence here, as everywhere, in keeping in check restless and unenlightened numbers, yet it is evident to close observers, if not to all, that these are rapidly usurping all power in the nonslave holding States, and threaten a

fearful crisis in republican institutions there at no remote period. In the slaveholding States, however, nearly one-half of the whole population, and those the poorest and most ignorant, have no political influence whatever, because they are slaves. Of the other half, a large proportion are both educated and independent in their circumstances, while those who are unfortunately not so, being still elevated far above the mass, are higher toned and more deeply interested in preserving a stable and well-ordered government, than the same class in any other country. Hence, slavery is truly the "cornerstone" and foundation of every welldesigned and durable "republican edifice."[31]

Hammond contends that slavery was beneficial toward republican governments because it provided the ruling segments of society with an essential resource, the necessary leisure time to be politically active, and it prohibited the ignorant segment from meaningful political participation. This Aristotelian social structure[32] was given added validity in the South by the 1857 *Dred Scott* v. *John Sandford* Supreme Court decision, which in effect declared slaves as noncitizens and the natural and legal property of their masters.[33] For the Confederates this decision reconciled what appeared to many in the North as irreconcilable: a republican form of government actively condoning a policy of subjugating a significant portion of its population.

This logic was applied not only to slaves but also to foreigners making their way into the Confederacy. The naturalization process was made the responsibility of the Confederacy, in order to make the standards for citizenship uniform throughout the Confederacy. The Confederate framers were convinced that under the U.S. Constitution the right of voting (the highest political right ever given to a people) was too universal.[34] It permitted anti-Southern political parties to extend the franchise to immigrants, who, lacking an understanding of the American political process, became the means of party aggrandizement by Northern political machines. Thus the national political process was corrupted to the disadvantage of the South.

The C.S.A. framers, in the attempt to limit political participation to citizens capable of meaningful participation, reformulated Article I, section 8, clause 4, from "to establish an uniform Rule of naturalization" to "establish uniform laws of naturalization." The change from "Rule" to "laws" was designed to remove the ambiguity as to which level of government confers citizenship, an issue that was the center of controversy in the 1857 Dred Scott decision. The C.S.A. framers favored having the Confederate government make the determination. This constitutional arrangement divested the states of a fundamental prerogative of sovereignty: the definition of citizenship.[35] However, its impact on state sovereignty appears to have been negligible, especially when balanced against Article IV, section 2, which stipulates, "The citizens of each State shall be entitled to all the privileges and immunities of citizens of the several States." Chief Justice Roger B. Taney articulated the Southern position when he was confronted with the naturalization issue in *Dred Scott* v. *Sandford*.

> For, when they gave to the citizens of each State the privileges and immunities of citizens of the several States, they at the same time took from the several States the power of naturalization, and confined that power exclusively to the Federal Government. No State was willing to permit another State to determine who should or who should not be admitted as one of its citizens, and entitled to demand equal rights and privileges with their own people, within their own territories. The right of naturalization was therefore, with one accord, surrendered by the States, and confined to the Federal Government.[36]

The Northern contention that the U.S. Constitution's stipulation that the Congress shall have the power to "establish an uniform Rule of naturalization" merely set guidelines to be followed by the states, thereby permitting the Northern states to elevate to citizenship immigrants and manumitted slaves, who in turn would be entitled to all the privileges and immunities in the Southern states (Article IV, section 2). The Confederacy specifically delegated to the C.S.A. government that high responsibility in order to allow all the states a say in the matter of who would be entitled to those "privileges and immunities" within their respective jurisdictions.

Furthermore, Article I, section 2, of the C.S.A. Constitution states that "the electors in each State shall be citizens of the Confederates States, . . . but no person of foreign birth, not a citizen of the Confederate States, shall be allowed to vote for any officer, civil or political, State or Federal." Hence, the C.S.A. Constitution precluded newly arrived immigrants from voting. Obviously, this Confederate power could have served as a pretext to negate the intent of the reserved powers clause of Article VI of the C.S.A. Constitution. The distinction they made between citizen and noncitizen is significant, and was a consequence of their commitment to the Calhounian dictum that liberty and political participation should be sagaciously conferred.[37]

The acknowledged intent of the Confederate framers was to make the transition to citizenship dilatory and uniform, as is evidenced by their declamations of the Northern states' practice of elevating non-English-speaking immigrants to the rank of citizenship and thereby increasing Northern states' representation in the U.S. House. In reference to the naturalization process, Robert Smith reasoned: "The simple rule is that whatever probation is necessary to fit a man for the rank of citizen is essential to his wisely exercising the high privilege of a voter. Wishing to see no proscription of any, but desiring that our land may remain the asylum of all freemen, yet I hope and believe that Congress while giving facility to naturalization, will place such safeguards around its attainment, that it will be felt to be a high boon to be admitted to participation in control of this Republic."[38] There was an apparent anxiety on the part of the Confederates that if foreigners and Negroes were numerously and expeditiously elevated to citizenship, the demise of the Southern political system would result. This Southern concern had been expressed by Calhoun some twenty years earlier and more recently by his home state South Carolina in its *Declaration of Causes:* "This sectional combination for the subversion of the (U.S.) Constitution has been aided, in some of the States, by elevating to citizenship persons who, by the supreme law of the land, are incapable of becoming citizens; and their votes have been used to inaugurate a new policy, hostile to the South, and destructive of its peace and safety."[39] The concern about the foreigner was similar to that about the Negro, albeit to a different extent. That is, in the South there were many more Negroes than there were foreigners; however, due to the anticipated influx of Northerners, at the time considered to be foreigners pursuing the expected Confederate economic boom, it was thought that the Confederacy was better positioned to deal with the subsequent problems of a rapidly increasing population than were the states individually.

In the public policy area of constitutional rights, the relationship between the Confederacy and the states was tenuous, primarily because of the ongoing war and the centralization necessitated by the Confederate war effort. For example, the Confederate government's conscription policy, the suspension of habeas corpus in designated areas, and the management of the Confederate economy were all necessitated by the war and were considered by Confederate and state officials to be a temporary adjustment of federal relations. A case in point is the Conscription Act of 1862. Acknowledging the necessity of a centralized conscription policy while simultaneously addressing the sensibilities of states' rights advocates, President Davis informed the Senate that the cooperation of the Confederate and state governments was essential and that the public defense must be reconciled "with a proper deference for the most scrupulous susceptibilities of the State authorities."[40]

The military and administrative centralization did indeed respect the sovereign status of the states. The various jurisdictional disputes between the Confederate and state governments were always resolved with state sovereignty as the guiding principle. C.S.A. Attorney General Thomas Hill Watts opined that "the laws of the several States, as State laws, cannot be legally and constitutionally enforced by either the Civil or Military Courts of the Confederate States: As well might the Civil or Military Courts of the Confederate States undertake to enforce the Laws of Great Britain or France. The jurisdictions are separate and distinct."[41] And when the Confederate and state jurisdictions are muddled, the latter determines which has what jurisdiction.

> Our complicated system of Government makes it difficult, sometimes, to separate, with distinctness the boundaries between the State and Confederate jurisdiction. I do not agree with Judge Taney, in thinking that the U.S. Government possessed sovereign powers: it does not in my opinion possess them. Nevertheless, the delegated powers given by the Constitution to the Confederate Government, when exercised, become the supreme law of the land, within their legitimate sphere of action. When, therefore, it is ascertained, in the proceedings under the writ of habeas corpus issued by a State Judge or State Court, that the prisoner is held by a Confederate Officer, under authority of the Confederate States, for any matter over which the Confederate laws operate, the State Judge or the State Court can proceed no longer.

It is significant that it was the responsibility of state courts to "ascertain whether or not the Confederate Government is exercising powers within their legitimate sphere of action," because "the Court or Judge of a State has the clear right to inquire in this mode of proceeding for what cause, and by what authority the prisoner is confined within the territorial limits of the State Sovereignty."[42]

Such deference to state authorities to adjudicate jurisdictional disputes was reiterated by C.S.A. Attorney General George Davis as late as 1864. The C.S.A. Congress authorized the surgeon general to establish urgently needed distilleries for military and medicinal purposes. The state of Virginia, where such a distillery was to be placed, prohibited distillation within the state. Concerning this controversy Davis held:

In regard to the course to be pursued by the Government, upon which I am requested to advise you, as a conflict of force with the Authorities of a State ought only to be resorted to in case of extreme emergency, if ever; there is but one remedy left, and that is to defend the suits in the Court below, and if necessary take them by appeal to the highest tribunal in the State. I have every confidence that they will be adjudicated by that tribunal with due regard to the constitutional rights of the Confederate States, as well as to those of the State of Virginia.

As the Surgeon-General intimates that delay may be injurious, and as the Legislature of Virginia is soon to assemble I respectfully suggest that the matter be laid before the Governor, with a request that he will call it to the attention of the Legislature, and thus give them an occasion, of which I doubt not they will readily avail themselves, so to modify their legislators as not to interfere with the exercise of the just powers of the Confederate States.[43]

Had the C.S.A. Supreme Court been organized, such deference to the state courts and legislatures might not have been so readily invoked, thereby placing the states in a subordinate position to the Confederacy. But it was because of this concern that the C.S.A. Supreme Court was not organized, making evident the states' unwillingness to acquiesce to such domination. In response to a bill introduced in the C.S.A. Senate to organize the Supreme Court, William Yancey of Alabama remarked in no uncertain terms that "when we decide that the state courts are of inferior dignity to this Court, we have sapped the main pillars of this Confederacy." And as one notable scholar put it, "The fear of centralizing tendencies, past experiences under the Federal Supreme Court, and a desire to protect states' rights led to the failure to establish a Confederate Supreme Court."[44]

In the final analysis, impeaching Confederate officials from the state (Article I, section 2 of the C.S.A. Constitution) and the implied right of secession were the ultimate guarantees of state sovereignty in the constitutional areas of civil liberties and rights, because in the event that federal relations went sour in these areas, a state (or states) could impeach over-zealous Confederate officials, for example, activist Confederate judges, or withdraw from the Confederacy altogether.[45] For example, if Attorney Generals Watts and Davis decided to show no deference to the states, perhaps rationalizing that the contingencies of war necessitated a dominant Confederate government at the expense of state sovereignty, a state could constitutionally negate the policies of the C.S.A. government by exercising its sovereignty through one of several options. Any state could initiate the impeachment of pertinent Confederate officials within its jurisdiction: any three states could initiate a constitutional convention; and any state could secede from the Confederacy. None of these options would have been unconstitutional remedies.

Without question, the C.S.A. Constitution, especially Article VI, clauses 5 and 6, defers to the states the defining and defense of the civil liberties and rights of their respective citizens. Furthermore, the C.S.A. declaration of rights is applicable to the Confederate government rather than to Confederate and state governments (unless specifically stated); the states delimit the rights and liberties of their inhabitants respectively, an important function of a sovereign state and consistent with the Confederate commitment that the states constitute distinct sovereign entities capable of judicious government.

Chapter Five

Institutional Innovations

The Confederate system of separation of powers is recognizably American, and cursorily the similarities between it and the U.S. system far outweigh the differences. Both are structured in such a way that the powers of government are limited and premised upon the consent of the governed. This is no small acknowledgment in light of the numerous theses contending that the Confederate model is premised upon a landed slavocracy. Such a slavocracy was not provided constitutional status, misinformed perceptions to the contrary notwithstanding. Nevertheless, the scope of the limited government as established distinguishes the Confederate separation of powers from the U.S. model. What at first view appears to be minor institutional innovations, significant procedural and substantive distinctions become manifest upon closer scrutiny. With the benefit of historical experience as their guide, the Confederate framers devised a type of federalism in which their national institutions were constitutionally and operationally constrained from usurping the prerogatives of popular sovereignty to a far greater extent than is the case with the U.S. model.[1] This augmented constraint was to be achieved by five constitutional innovations: executive branch representation in the Confederate Congress, an executive line-item veto, modifications pertaining to political economy, a non-reeligible six-year presidential term, and the abrogation of the nationalistic "general welfare" mandate.

Taken selectively, these innovations could, and in all probability would, strengthen the national government and pose more of a threat to state sovereignty. But collectively, they intensified the institutional checks at the national level, thereby diminishing the capacity of the national government to divest the states of their constitutional prerogatives. The political effects of these constitutional innovations were twofold: first, the decision-making process was more rational, and second, the public policy prerogatives of the Confederate government were lessened. The end result was a Confederate government subject to increased limitations on the exercise of power and constrained to function within those limitations to a greater extent than was the case with the U.S. model.

Executive branch representation

A rational decision-making process is one in which the deliberations include all relevant aspects of public policy issues and the selection of the best courses of action for meeting public policy objectives. For example, if the deliberative process reveals that the consequence of a policy X is the promotion of economic growth, and if policy X is implemented for that reason and policies Y and Z are avoided because of their negative effects, then the process is rational. On the other hand, assume that the process is dominated by a particular faction whose members have unmatched influence and that they anticipate benefiting politically and economically from policy Z, neither concerned with nor realizing the full implications of implementing policy Z and forgoing policy X, then the process is considered to be irrational, not necessarily for the members of the faction but for the body politic that tolerates such a process.

In an American-styled representative democracy, increasing the rationality of the central government pertains to the procedures utilized by the legislative and executive branches to formulate public policy. A rational procedure is one characterized "by the power of hearing the reasons of others, and comparing them quietly with one's own reasons, and then being guided by the result."[2] The aim of the Confederate framers was to facilitate the discussion of issues by intensifying communication between the legislative and executive branches. The intensification of institutional communication would result from an increased number of participants discussing public policy issues in the legislative forum, which in turn would expose lawmakers to a wider range of policy options. This was to be accomplished by providing executive officers with the opportunity to participate in congressional debates by actually assigning them seats in the Confederate Congress.

Article I, section 6, clause 2, of the C.S.A. Constitution provides that "Congress may, by law, grant to the principal officer in each of the executive departments a seat upon the floor of either House, with the privilege of discussing any measures appertaining to his department." Although the required enabling legislation to put this provision into effect was never passed, the Confederate framers did attempt to imbue the legislative process with an executive influence over and beyond the legislative committee conduit. According to Robert H. Smith, "The want of facility of communication between the Executive and Legislature, has, it is believed, been a serious impediment to the easy and harmonious working of the Government. Experience has shown that our Fathers, by refusing the executive the right to be heard through his constitutional advisers on the floor of the Legislature, had interposed barriers to that free intercourse between the two departments which was essential to the wise and healthy action of each."[3]

The C.S.A. presumption was that this constitutional innovation was proximate to the British cabinet model of government. To a certain extent the contention was accurate. The British cabinet system combines the lawmaking function with the law-executing function.[4] This combination (or more precisely, connection) was to be established by the presence of executive department heads on the floors of the Confederate Congress. But in the British cabinet system the cabinet ministers are not independent of the House of Commons, whereas in the Confederate system the executive department heads are independent of Congress, once confirmed by the Senate (Article II, section 2, clause 2), impeachment proceedings notwithstanding. Furthermore, to protect the executive branch's independence and control over the cabinet and the attendant bureaucracy, the C.S.A. chief executive had the explicit constitutional authority to remove from office department heads detrimental to the president's policy agenda. Article II, section 2, clause 3, of the C.S.A. Constitution stipulates that "the principal officer in each of the executive departments, and all persons connected with the diplomatic service, may be removed from office at the pleasure of the President. All other civil officers of the executive departments may be removed at any time by the President, or other appointing power, when their services are unnecessary, or for dishonesty, incapacity, inefficiency, misconduct, or neglect of duty; and, when so removed, the removal shall be reported to the Senate, together with the reasons therefor." This presidential power of removal facilitated the independence of the executive branch from the Congress by providing the former with greater control over the Confederate bureaucracy. The policy triangles between Congressional committees, interest groups, and bureaucracies, which have been so pervasive in American legislative processes, could more readily be disrupted through the Confederate president's power of removing troublesome bureaucrats. Because this enhanced executive-branch independence was at Congress's expense, the Confederate model of checks and balances was more similar to a presidential system than to a cabinet system of government. Walter Bagehot noted the fundamental distinction between the two systems.

> This fusion of the legislative and executive functions may, to those who have not much considered it seem but a dry and small matter, to be the latent essence and effectual secret of the English Constitution; but we can only judge of its real importance by looking at a few of its principal effects, and contrasting it very shortly with its great competitor, which seems likely, unless care be taken, to outstrip it in the progress of the world. That competitor is the Presidential system. The characteristic of it is that the President is elected from the people by one process, and the House of Representatives by another. The independence of the legislative and executive powers is the specific quality of Presidential Government, just as their fusion and combination is the precise principle of Cabinet Government.[5]

Hence, regarding the rationality of the Confederate legislative process, there was more of a fusion of the two branches because of the discretionary presence of executive department heads on the floors of Congress participating in the deliberative process in the attempt to represent the administration's policy positions. Conversely, the independence of the executive branch from the legislative was enhanced because of the president's augmented prerogative to replace appointed officials within the executive branch. The former characteristic typifies cabinet government, the latter does not. The intended result was a more independent executive branch participating in a more rational process.

Executive line-item veto

Both the U.S. and C.S.A. constitutions provide their respective executives with the prerogative to veto legislation that has passed the Congress, such vetoes being subject to a congressional override if at least two-thirds of the membership concur. To supplement this presidential prerogative, the C.S.A. Constitution provides that the president may veto portions of an appropriations bill while accepting others. Article I, section 7, clause 2, declares that "the President may approve any appropriation and disapprove any other appropriation in the same bill. In such case he shall, in signing the bill, designate the appropriations disapproved; and shall return a copy of such appropriations, with his objections, to the House in which the bill shall have originated; and the same proceeding shall then be had as in case of other bills disapproved by the President." This supplemental line-item veto prerogative was designed to impede a spendthrifty Congress to a greater extent than does the veto power in the U.S. Constitution. This seminal issue of "the power of the purse" has deep roots in American constitutional development, and its relevance becomes evident by analyzing the debate concerning the veto during the 1787 convention, which instituted the veto power to serve as a check on congressional power. Although the line-item veto prerogative of appropriations was not at issue during the 1787 convention, the veto power of the president in general was. The three alternatives seriously considered were an absolute veto, the prohibition of an executive veto, and an executive veto subject to a congressional override.

Delegates who supported an absolute veto power reasoned that it should be the responsibility of the executive to check an irresponsible Congress. The assumption that the Congress would act irresponsibly was at the core of the justification for the absolute veto. For example, James Wilson of Pennsylvania and Alexander Hamilton of New York agreed that "the Executive ought to have an absolute negative. Without such a self-defense the Legislature can at any moment sink it into non-existence. . . . [and] There was no danger of it being too much exercised."[6] This position was obviously based upon a lack of confidence in the legislature's willingness to responsibly exercise its power of the purse. This was consistently the Federalists' position as they witnessed state legislatures enervate state executives and proceed to wreak havoc on their own state economies.

The delegates opposed to an executive veto, such as Elbridge Gerry of Massachusetts and Roger Sherman of Connecticut, attested that there was "no necessity for so great a control over the legislature as the best men in the community would be comprised in the two branches of it." Furthermore, "no one man could be found so far above all the rest in wisdom." Concurring with Gerry and Sherman, Gunning Bedford of Delaware added that "the Representatives of the people were the best judges of what was in their interests, and ought to be under no external control within the Legislature itself."[7] This consistently was the Antifederalist position, due to their distrust of the executive branch, which during colonial times was by and large under the control of the crown; the legislatures, however, were seen as the "people's" branch, opposing the fiscal policies (mercantilism) of the mother country.

Because neither the Federalists nor the Antifederalists were willing to abandon their fundamental principles regarding which branch posed the greatest threat to the people's liberties, both proposals were defeated, resulting in the passage of a compromise measure giving the president veto power but subjecting it to a two-thirds override vote of Congress.[8] Publius articulated the intent of the convention.

> The propriety of the thing does not turn upon the supposition of superior wisdom or virtue in the executive, but upon the supposition that the legislature will not be infallible; that love of power may sometimes betray it into a disposition to encroach upon the rights of other members of the government; that a spirit of faction may sometimes pervert its deliberations; that impressions of the moment may sometimes hurry it into measures which itself, on maturer reflection, would condemn. The primary inducement of conferring the power in question upon the executive is to enable him to defend himself; the secondary one is to increase the chances in favor of the community against the passing of bad laws, through haste, inadvertence, or design. The oftener the measure is brought under examination, the greater the diversity in the situation of those who are to examine it, the less must be the danger of those errors which flow from want of due deliberation, or of those mis-steps which proceed from the contagion of some common passion or interest.

The "qualified" veto was preferred to the absolute veto because "in the proportion it would be less apt to offend, it would be more apt to be exercised; and for this very reason it may in practice be found more effectual."[9] In short, the prerogative of vetoing congressional proposals was designed, first, to secure the constitutional integrity of the executive branch against legislative usurpations and, second, to protect the community from defective legislation by subjecting the latter to additional checks by supplementing the rationality of the process.

The line-item veto expanded the rationality of the process beyond the simple veto because, at the discretion of the president, portions of legislation could be selectively returned to the Congress for further deliberations and subject to two-thirds approval. Even the possibility of the line-item veto would modify the legislative behavior regarding pork-barrel bills, as the legislators would be obliged to consult with the executive branch in advance, thereby facilitating dialogue between the two branches.

The Confederate framers concurred with Publius that certain checks must be placed on the legislature by the executive, especially regarding fiscal policy. The constitutional innovations that the Confederates devised in order to alter the relationship between the legislative and executive branches in favor of the latter were a consequence of what they perceived to be legislative abuses of the appropriations process. The line-item veto was such an innovation. They contended that the U.S. Congress had become too unscrupulous as a result of its power of the purse, and they intended to save their Confederate Congress from a similar fate. Referring to the line-item veto, Robert H. Smith wrote,

> Of this character is the power given the President to arrest corrupt or illegitimate expenditures, by vetoing particular clauses in an appropriation bill, and at the same time approving other parts of the bill. There is hardly a more flagrant abuse of its power, by the Congress of the United States than the habitual practice of loading bills, which are necessary for governmental operations with reprehensible, not to say venal dispositions of the public money, and which only obtain favor by a system of combinations among members interested in similar abuses upon the treasury.[10]

Of course, from the Southern perspective the U.S. Congress's "flagrant abuse of its powers" had a disproportionate regional impact. Northern congressmen supported the extension of the national government's spending prerogatives for the purpose of funding northern internal improvements at the South's expense. The Confederate presidential model, it was hoped, would bring some balance to regional differences; the line-item veto and the two-thirds requisite to override would negate some of the influence regional numerical majorities could exercise over their minority counterparts.

Political economy

A concurring check on the C.S.A. Congress along the same lines as the line-item veto is in Article I, section 9, clause 9, which places the appropriations initiative in the hands of the executive.

> Congress shall appropriate no money from the treasury except by a vote of two-thirds of both Houses, taken by yeas and nays, unless it be asked and estimated for by some one of the heads of departments, and submitted to the Congress by the President; or for the purpose of paying its own expenses and contingencies; or for payment of claims against the Confederate States, the justice of which shall have been judiciously declared by a tribunal for the investigation of claims against the Government, which it is hereby the duty of Congress to establish.

This provision marked a significant shift in the balance of power from the legislature to the executive concerning the fiscal policy of

the central government. It "proceeds upon the idea that the chief
Executive as the head of the country and his cabinet should understand the pecuniary needs of the Confederacy, and should be an-
swerable for an economical administration of public affairs, and at
the same time should be enabled and required to call for whatever
sums may be necessary to accomplish the purposes of Government."[11] Constitutionally, the C.S.A. president, not the C.S.A.
Congress, headed the branch of government primarily responsible
for the fiscal policy of the Confederate States of America.

The intent of the Confederate framers was not to negate the legislature's meaningful participation in the formation of fiscal policy;
the process continued to be subject to their approval. But under the
Confederate model, the executive was at a distinct advantage as the
initiator of fiscal policy, unless two-thirds of the legislature were to
vote against the policy. This constitutional arrangement was an
attempt to address another perceived inadequacy of the U.S. model.
The Confederate framers were convinced that in the U.S. system a
disequilibrium of power developed between the executive and legislative branches, in favor of the latter. Article I, sections 7 and 9,
were designed to define the balance of power between the two
branches, the end result being a more deliberative process with
greater consensus being requisite to the passage of the Confederacy's fiscal policies—policies such as internal improvements and
tariffs, which were so contentious in antebellum politics.

Moreover, the rationality of the legislative process was to be facilitated by Article I, section 9, clause 20, which stipulates that "every
law, or resolution having the force of law, shall relate to but one
subject, and that shall be expressed in the title." This provision in
effect discontinued the practice of attaching riders to bills. Under
the U.S. Constitution it is not only possible, but highly probable,
for a proposal to continue through the legislative process as a result
of the merits of another legislative proposal besides its own. The
C.S.A. Constitution requires all proposals, instead of one resolution consisting of a collection of proposals, to be singularly approved or disapproved by the legislative and executive branches
(unless the Congress exercises its veto-override prerogative, thereby surmounting executive objections). Imagine the U.S. Congress
operating under this provision, in which all legislative riders, ger-
mane and nongermane, had to stand on their own merits and be
voted up or down accordingly. Such a modification would certainly
substantively alter the legislative process by making it more rational
and would be in accordance with the Calhounian dictum that the

more checks there are on the legislative process, the more popular the basis of government. For example, a law passed by two-thirds of the legislature would have a broader base of support than one approved by a simple majority. Likewise, subjecting legislative proposals to increased scrutiny (i.e., by eliminating riders) and to a more readily available presidential line-item veto would require a broader base of support for legislative programs than would a process not subject to such checks. Hence, the "principle in constitutional governments is compromise," which in lieu of widespread consensus, the government would, indeed, be very limited.[12] Even though the Confederate president would be presiding over a more limited government, he would also be participating in a more rational process, generating public policy premised upon a broader base of support.

Presidential tenure

The primary institutional innovation affecting the power of the executive branch is the single six-year term. Article II, section 1, clause 1, stipulates that "the executive power shall be vested in a President of the Confederate States of America. He and the Vice President shall hold their offices for the term of six years; but the President shall not be re-eligible."

Reelection and duration of the presidential term were important issues in 1787 and 1861. In the 1787 convention, the proposals considered ranged from life tenure to subjecting the president to annual elections. Of course, the convention eventually agreed to reeligible four-year terms. (Theoretically, had President George Washington not initiated the two-term precedent, chief executives could have been successively elected to what in effect was life tenure.) According to Publius, this arrangement had five basic advantages. First, it provided the "personal firmness of the executive magistrate in the employment of his constitutional powers, and to the stability of the system of administration which may have been adopted under his auspices." Second, a term of less duration (e.g., two years) would make the president too dependent upon public sentiment.

> The republican principle demands that the deliberate sense of the community should govern the conduct of those to whom they entrust the management of their affairs; but it does not require an unqualified complaisance to every sudden breeze of passion, or to every transient impulse which the people may receive from the arts of men, who flatter their prejudices to betray their inter-

> ests. . . . When occasions present themselves in which the inter-
> ests of the people are at variance with their inclinations, it is the
> duty of the persons whom they have appointed to be the guard-
> ians of those interests to withstand the temporary delusions in
> order to give them time and opportunity for more cool and sedate
> reflection.[13]

Instead of shorter terms and more frequent elections, the successive reelection of four-year terms would facilitate the president's
function as a check on precipitous democratic tendencies inherent
in the people and manifested in their agents in the U.S. Congress.

Third, to deny reeligibility would remove an important induce-
ment to the faithful execution of constitutional responsibilities.

> There are few men who would not feel much less zeal in the
> discharge of a duty when they were conscious that the advantage
> of the station with which it was connected must be relinquished at
> a determinate period, than when they were permitted to entertain
> a hope of obtaining, by meriting, a continuance of them. This
> position will not be disputed so long as it is admitted that the
> desire of reward is one of the strongest incentives of human con-
> duct; or that the best security for the fidelity of mankind is to make
> their interests coincide with their duty.

In other words, the effects of the lame duck syndrome would be
minimized, and the executive branch would be energized. Fourth,
to deny reeligibility would be "depriving the community of the
advantage of the experience gained by the Chief Magistrate in the
exercise of his office."[14]

It was the fifth advantage with which the Confederate framers
took issue. Publius contended that limiting the president to one
term would "operate as a constitutional interdiction of stability in
the administration. By necessitating a change of men, in the first
office of the nation, it would necessitate a mutability of measures."
However, the Confederate framers questioned whether the continuity of measures would be adversely affected, and regardless, they
preferred a mutable chief executive to an overly assertive and entrenched one. They aimed at establishing a custodial executive who
would obstruct congressional excesses, would not pit the general
government against the state governments, and would use the executive branch to secure the common interests of the states as collectively defined by the latter. Thus, the energy (i.e., power) of the
general government would be kept in check by disrupting its stability (i.e., continuity). The stability Publius aimed for "requires
that the hands in which power is lodged should continue for a
length of time the same. A frequent change of men will result from a

frequent return of elections; and a frequent change of measures from a frequent change of men: whilst energy in government requires not only a certain duration of power, but the execution of it by a single hand."[15] It was just this type of powerful executive that concerned the Confederates.

Without specified limits, a president repeatedly reelected to successive terms would eventually resemble an elected monarch, serving, essentially, a life term contingent upon good behavior as defined by the prevailing public opinion. Such an arrangement would indeed prove to be energetic and stable. The patronage at the disposal of the Publian president would be phenomenal, providing the opportunity for a successively elected president of four terms to entrench the bureaucracy with his own "placemen." Such a tactic was very effectively used by British monarchs in their contest for power with the parliament.[16] For the Confederate framers, energy and stability in the administration of the general government, to the extent that Publius advocated, presented a serious threat to judicious federal government. The Confederates concluded that an energetic and stable general government was an important factor contributing to political strife between the general and state governments, because the acquisition of political power by the national government was inevitably at the states' expense. As the interests of those in control of the general government clashed with various state interests, which according to Calhoun was inevitable, the latter would prove to be no match for the former.[17] With the president leading the way in the pursuit of the political power by the general government, the prerogatives of obstructing states would be overwhelmed by the rising nationalism. To protect the states from such a tendency, the C.S.A. framers diminished the power of the Confederate executive by constitutionally mandating a changing of the guard every six years, thereby destabilizing and subsequently de-energizing it.

Every six years the Confederacy would have a new executive branch of government, thereby offsetting the advantages of incumbency not only of the President but also that of the entrenched national bureaucracy whose interests are so closely linked to an ever-expanding national government.

General welfare

The fourth category of institutional innovations designed to limit the powers of the central government vis-à-vis the states pertains to the "general welfare" provision. This is not an institutional innovation in itself, but it was certainly designed to fundamentally affect the institution of the C.S.A. Congress. The C.S.A. Constitution omitted the constitutional mandate to "promote the general welfare"—a mandate conferred upon the U.S. government in its constitution's preamble and Article I, section 8.

The South's consternation with the U.S. government's constitutional prerogative to "promote the general Welfare" was articulated by Calhoun.

> It is a bold and unauthorized assumption, that Congress has the power to pronounce what objects belong, and what do not belong to the general welfare; and to appropriate money, at its discretion, to such as it may deem to belong to it. No such power is delegated to it; nor is any such power necessary and proper to carry into execution those which are delegated. On the contrary, to pronounce on the general welfare of the States is a high constitutional power, appertaining not to Congress, but to the people of the several States, acting in their sovereign capacity. . . . To prove, then, that any particular object belongs to the general welfare of the States of the Union, it is necessary to show that it is included in some one of the delegated powers, or is necessary and proper to carry some of them into effect, before a tax can be laid or money appropriated to effect it. For Congress, then, to undertake to pronounce what does, or what does not belong to the general welfare, without regard to the extent of the delegated powers, is to usurp the highest authority; one belonging exclusively to the people of the several States in their sovereign capacity. And yet, on this assumption, thus boldly put forth, in defiance of a fundamental principle of the federal system of government, most onerous duties have been laid on imports, and vast amounts of money appropriated, to objects not named among the delegated powers, and not necessary or proper to carry any one of them into execution; to the great impoverishment of one portion of the country, and the corresponding aggrandizement of the other.[18]

Unequivocally concurring with Calhoun that the "general welfare" mandate resulted in the usurpation of state prerogatives, the Confederate framers excluded general welfare language from their constitution's preamble and Article I, section 8. This omission in the C.S.A. Constitution implicitly made the promoting of the general welfare a function of the several states. The exclusion of general welfare clauses reduced the probability of the Confederate Congress supporting questionable public policies premised upon the Confederacy's pursuit of some vague definition of the general welfare.

For the Confederate framers, the arbitrariness of the U.S. Congress was most obvious in its exercise of the residuary clause (i.e., the constitutional stipulation "to make all laws which shall be necessary and proper for carrying into execution the foregoing powers, and all other powers vested by this Constitution"). According to Publius, "Had the Constitution been silent on this head, there can be no doubt that all the particular powers requisite as means of executing the general powers would have resulted to the government by unavoidable implication. No axiom is more clearly established in law, or in reason, than that wherever the end is required, the means are authorized; wherever a general power to do a thing is given, every particular power for doing it is included." Publius's interpretation of this provision provided the U.S. government with the discretionary powers to pursue policies not specifically delegated. The C.S.A. Constitution also stipulates the obligation to exercise residuary powers.[19] However, the Confederates claimed that the U.S. Congress exercised its residuary powers in conjunction with a nationalist interpretation of the general welfare clause, thereby contravening popular sovereignty within the several states and extending their powers beyond the limits delegated in the Constitution. The end result of this freewheeling application of the general welfare clause was unconstitutional interference by the U.S. government into the affairs of the Southern states, inhibiting the latter's exercise of their own discretionary powers as sovereign entities while the national government assumed the responsibility for the general welfare of all Americans.

The C.S.A. framers attempted to reconcile their apprehensions of residuary powers with the acknowledged need for such powers but within specified constraints. The reconciliation was premised upon the inclusion of residuary powers and constitutional prohibitions of what were considered to be the most egregious abuses of such powers under the U.S. Constitution. The declared abuses centered on the fiscal policies of the U.S. government; as a result, the C.S.A. prohibitions placed new constraints on the fiscal policies of the Confederate government, beyond the procedural ones between the C.S.A. Congress and president, discussed above.

These C.S.A. constitutional prohibitions were calculated to prevent the C.S.A. government from implementing the type of allegedly inequitable fiscal policies of the U.S. government that Calhoun so vehemently railed against. Such policies "divide the community into two great classes; one consisting of those who, in reality, pay the taxes and, of course, bear exclusively the burthen of supporting the government; and the other, of those who are the recipients of their proceeds through disbursements, and who are, in fact, supported by the government."[20] The embryonic Southern position concerning the inequitable fiscal action of the U.S. government was succinctly stated by Calhoun in his 1831 Fort Hill address:

> If there be any point on which the (I was going to say, southern section, but to avoid as far as possible, the painful feelings such discussions are calculated to excite, I shall say) weaker of the two sections is unanimous, it is that its prosperity depends, in a great measure, on free trade, light taxes, economical, and as far as possible, equal disbursements of the public revenue, and unshackled industry, leaving them to pursue whatever may appear most advantageous to their interests. From the Potomac to the Mississippi, there are few, indeed, however divided on other points, who would not, if dependent on their volition, and if they regarded the interest of their particular section only, remove from commerce and industry every shackle, reduce the revenue to the lowest point that the wants of the government fairly required, and restrict the appropriations to the most moderate scale consistent with the peace, the security, and the engagements of the public; and who do not believe that the opposite system is calculated to throw on them an unequal burden, to repress their prosperity, and to encroach on their enjoyment.[21]

The "shackles" on commerce and industry to which the antebellum South took particular exception were the protectionist tariff and the internal improvement policies of the U.S. government. Calhoun and his kindred-spirit Confederates adhered to a national political economy of minimal interference with market forces.

Southerners bemoaned the utilization of such interfering policies, maintaining that they promoted Northern interests at the expense of Southern. This Southern attitude permeated national politics, for example, in 1857, in the midst of the Congressional debate over the extension of slavery into the territories, when the U.S. Treasury announced an expected $77 million deficit for fiscal year 1858. To remedy the deficit, Northern legislators proposed a revision of the 1842 tariff, increasing the level of duties to be paid, thereby making it more protectionist. The Southern legislators advocated the issuance of U.S. Treasury notes, redeemable subsequent to the eradication of the deficit. Southern legislators argued that the deficit would be eliminated, not by raising duties, but only as a consequence of free trade and the retrenchment of the national government's role in the economy, especially insofar as that role had been prejudicial to Southern interests. To follow are four typical Southern declamations concerning protectionism versus free trade, in reference to the 1858 fiscal deficit:

We have education, skill, experience, capital, labor, food, and raw materials lying all around, and millions of acting, producing consumers, and free Government. These are the imperishable elements of our material prosperity. Strike down your custom's duties tomorrow, and you will not thereby extinguish your furnace fires, nor shut up your factories or workshops, but they would survive it, and still flourish, perhaps all the better, for standing on industry rather than fluctuating legislative enactments.

Suppose the agriculturalists of my State, when cotton falls from fourteen to eight cents, and the wheat and wool growers of the West, when their productions fall in like proportion, should claim from the other classes, and especially from the manufacturing class, a bounty sufficient to make up the deficit: what a yell and howl of rage would we hear coming from that quarter now so clamorous for plunder! And this reminds me of a remark which I once heard made, characterizing these two interests. It was, that the agricultural interest was like a flock of sheep, which may be shorn of its fleece without evincing the least resistance, or giving forth the faintest bleat of distress; and that the manufacturing class was like a drove of hogs; you cannot pull the bristles of a single one without throwing the whole heard into commotion.

And despite the ingenious theories of politicians, as to an enlightened public opinion having settled it this way or that, I will venture to say there is not a civilized nation or community now on earth, where the manufacturing interest is dominant, what does not seek protection for its workshops at the expense of its fields, and *vice versa*. This, sir, is another reason why I am opposed to a tariff for protection—that it would build up northern manufactures at the expense of southern agriculturalists. We need no protection for that which we raise for market; and that which we buy, we want the free markets of the world to choose from.

I ask the people of the South if they would not prefer to see this Union dissevered than endure the operation of a system which is to transfer, as I have shown, one fourth of the net proceeds of their labor to northern capitalists annually. I repeat, Mr. Chairman, this is a contest between capital and labor, a contest of power against weakness; a contest in which the pride of the freemen of this country is to be humbled and their spirits broken, until they will consent to any degradation, even serfdom; and from this, Mr. Chairman, if our people desire to escape, they must stand by the Democratic organization, and thereby perpetuate the great doctrine of limitation on the powers of the Federal Government, and the absolute right of the States to legislate alone upon subjects which concern their domestic and civil rights; doctrines which leave the people of each State with the full and undivided right to pass for themselves laws suited to their climate, soil, and industrial pursuits.[22]

The *Congressional Globe* is replete with Southern denouncements of what they considered to be the Northern practice of rationalizing nationalistic policies favorable to their parochial interests under the guise of the general welfare.

The Confederate commitment to market forces, in contradistinction to a federally managed economy in pursuit of the general welfare, did not go unnoticed in the North. For example, in 1863 J. T. Headley, who at the time wrote what was considered to be the definitive Northern account of the Civil War, maintained that Calhoun and his successors wanted to take the South out of the Union in order to secure free trade. Headley asserted that free trade was the primary factor threatening the Union in 1831 and an important contributing factor of the 1861 crisis.[23]

This free-trade sentiment is eminent in the C.S.A. Constitution, specifically in its prohibition against protectionist legislation. To wit, Article I, section 8, clause 1, stipulates that "the Congress shall have power to lay and collect taxes, imposts, and excises, for revenue necessary to pay the debts, provide for the common defence, and carry on the Government of the Confederate States; but no bounties shall be granted from the Treasury; nor shall any duties or taxes on importations from foreign nations be laid to promote or foster any branch of industry; and all duties, imposts, and excises shall be uniform throughout the Confederate States."

Furthermore, to secure the Confederacy against sectional legislation and a burgeoning central administration, the C.S.A. Constitution placed significant limitations on centrally funded internal improvements. Article I, section 8, clause 3, stipulates that

> the Congress shall have the power to regulate commerce with foreign nations, and among the several States, and with Indian tribes; but neither this, nor any other clause contained in the Constitution, shall ever be construed to delegate power to the Congress to appropriate money for any internal improvement intended to facilitate commerce: except for the purpose for furnishing lights, beacons, and buoys, and other aid to navigation upon the coasts, and the improvement of harbors and the removing of obstructions in river navigation, in all which cases, such duties shall be laid on the navigation facilitated thereby, as may be necessary to pay the costs and expenses thereof.

The Confederate framers were convinced that internal improvements should be a state function. Accordingly, they constitutionally recognized internal improvements as a state prerogative. Article I, section 10, clause 3, provides that "no State shall, without the consent of Congress, lay any duty on tonnage, except on sea-going vessels, for the improvement of its rivers and harbors navigated by the said vessels; but such duties shall not conflict with any treaties of the Confederate States with foreign nations; and any surplus revenue thus derived, shall, after making such improvements, be paid into the common treasury. . . . *but when any river divides or flows through two or more States, they may enter into compacts with each other to improve the navigation thereof"* (emphasis added). Its U.S. counterpart stipulates that "no State shall, without the consent of Congress, lay any Duty of Tonnage, keep Troops, or Ships of War in time of Peace, enter into any Agreement of Compact with another State, or with a foreign Power, or engage in War, unless actually invaded, or in such immenent Danger as will not admit of delay" (Article I, section 10, clause 3). The C.S.A. version obviously places new emphasis at the state level for internal improvements. Robert H. Smith articulated the implications of these constitutional provisions.

> Holding steadily in view the principle that the great object of the Federal Government is to perform national functions and not to aggrandize or depress sectional, or local, or individual interests, and adhering to and enforcing the doctrine that a people should be left to pursue and develop their individual thrift without direct aids or drawbacks from Government, and that internal improvements are best judged of, and more wisely and economically directed by the localities desiring them, . . . the Constitution denies to Congress the right to make appropriations for any internal improvement.[24]

These restrictions on the prerogative of the Confederate government (i.e., prohibitions against protectionism and carte blanche internal improvement agendas), and the constitutional recognition of the states' responsibilities for their respective intrastate economic infrastructures, ran counter to the prevailing tendencies of the U.S. Constitution.

Auspiciously, this debate of antebellum America was also an issue in the 1787 convention. Northern and Southern economic interests were at that time coalescing along sectional lines. Some Southern delegates anticipated the emergence of a Northern majority that would take control of the national government, thereby enabling it to sacrifice Southern economic interests for Northern. For example, Colonel George Mason of Virginia declared that "if the Government is to be lasting, it must be founded in the confidence and affections of the people, and must be so constructed as to obtain these. The **Majority** will be governed by their interests. The Southern States are the minority in both Houses. It is to be expected that they will deliver themselves bound hand and foot to the Eastern States, and enable them to exclaim, in the words of Cromwell on a certain occasion—*the Lord hath delivered them into our hands.*"[25]

Mason's remarks were in support of a motion which stipulated that "no act of the Legislature for the purpose of regulating the commerce of the United States be passed without the consent of two thirds of the members of each House." Madison opposed the motion, on the grounds that the institutional checks and balances would serve as an adequate check against the abusive exercise of the power to regulate commerce. Furthermore, Madison reasoned that North ern and Southern commercial interests were inextricably connected, and that the prosperity of the former would inevitably benefit the latter, provided that the regulation of commerce was made to be a national function.[26] Accordingly, Madison was not satisfied with the compromise provision that permitted the states to participate in the regulation of commerce with Congressional consent.[27] He moved to make the prohibition on state participation in the regulation of commerce absolute; he reasoned that otherwise the mischiefs experienced under the Articles of Confederation would continue.[28] Publius concurred and articulated the cause and nature of the mischiefs resulting from a lack of national authority to regulate the significant aspects of commerce.

> Competitions of commerce would be another fruitful source of contention. The States less favorably circumstanced would be desirous of escaping from the disadvantages of local situation, and in sharing in the advantages of their more fortunate neighbors. Each State, or separate confederacy, would pursue a system of commercial policy peculiar to itself. This would occasion distinctions, preferences, and exclusions, which would beget discontent. The habits of intercourse, on the basis of equal privileges, to which we have been accustomed since the earliest settlement of the country would give a keener edge to those causes of circumstance. We should be ready to denominate injuries those things which were in reality justifiable acts of independent sovereignties consulting a distinct interest. The spirit of enterprise, which characterizes the commercial part of America, has left no occasion of displaying itself unimproved. It is not at all probable that this unbridled spirit would pay much respect to those regulations of trade by which particular States might endeavor to secure exclusive benefits to their own citizens. The infractions of these regulations, on the one side, the efforts to prevent and repel them, on the other, would naturally lead to outrages, and these to reprisals and wars.[29]

Hence, state sovereignty, or, more specifically, too much discretion on the part of a state in determining its commercial relations with other states, would be an obstacle to the development of a national commercial empire because of the inevitable contentions and wars between the states vying to maximize their own prosperity. To avoid such discord, commercial policy must be made uniform throughout the country, with the national government functioning as the formulator and enforcer thereof. There is no room for state sovereignty in such a model.

In sharp contrast, the C.S.A. framers minimized the Confederate government's role in the economy, placing the emphasis on market forces within and among the states. The organization of the C.S.A. Postal Service embodied the Confederate *modus operandi* with regard to the role of the Confederate government in the economy. Premising the postal service's continued operation on market forces rather than on government subsidies was the result of a laissez faire point of view. Article I, section 8, clause 7, stipulates "that the Congress shall have the power to establish post offices and post routes; but the expenses of the Post-Office Department, after the first day of March, in the year of our Lord eighteen hundred and sixty-three, shall be paid out of its own revenues." The rationale leading to this provision was expressed in 1859 by Senator Robert Toombs of Georgia and Representative William W. Boyce of South Carolina. Toombs contended: "You need not talk to me, then, about a deficiency of $10,000,000 in your Post Office Department for the next fiscal year. I will not vote for it, I will not provide for it, and, without that single item, we need no increases of taxes. Make those who use the Post Office pay for their own business, and you have no need to levy a single shilling out of labor for the next year. . . . We must alter our system, bring down this Department to the wants of the country to be tested by what those who use it are willing to pay for it."[30] And, according to Boyce: "That the Department should be self-sustaining, I assume as an axiom; for, why should one man be taxed to carry the letters of another? There is no justice in it. Let those who send letters pay for them. It is very convenient, doubtless, for the merchants, literary men, and professional men, to have the hard-working masses pay for their letters; but it is not right. . . . Let letters, like merchandise, be carried by private enterprise. The service, I have no doubt, would be well and cheaply done, for private enterprise is always more efficient than Government action. Indeed, when I consider the immense patronage of this Department, as a State-rights man, opposed to too strong a Federal Government, I see great advantage in getting rid of this patronage, and thus simplifying the Government."[31] This Southern rhetoric marks a significant deviation from Publius's contention that "nothing which tends to facilitate the intercourse between the States can be deemed unworthy of the public care."[32] In other words, a national postal service, to which Publius was referring, would facilitate intercourse between the states and therefore was entitled to the nation's financial support.

Thus, whereas the U.S. Constitution embodies the advancement of national economy, being the product of national public policy— for example, protectionism and internal improvement policies—the C.S.A. Constitution reserves to the states the management of their respective economies within the framework of free trade.

The South's commitment to free trade was an important dimension of their political culture. Moreover, the Southern ideal regarding the type and scope of government involvement in the economy was distinct from that of the North. From the tariff controversies of the 1820s through the antebellum period, Southerners held local, state, and regional commercial conventions, the purpose of which, as stated by Calhoun, was to secure the commercial, industrial, and financial independence of the South from the North. One Southern patriot stated Southern motivations thus: "Free trade with all the world, untrammeled by legislative restrictions was their motto; and they opposed an absorbing centralism in commerce, just as they fought centralization in government."[33] These commercial conventions set the stage for Southern political independence, because the Southern merchants-politicians who sought to secure Southern financial independence would naturally turn to political means. Because of the perception that Northern interests were utilizing the national government to subjugate the South economically and that the South constituted a minority interest in national politics, secession was concomitant to Southern economic self-determination.[34]

Indeed, for the states to control their own "political destinies," the Confederacy would have to be limited and thereby prevented from unwarranted or unwanted interference in the affairs of the states. The C.S.A.'s constitutional innovations were designed to prevent such interference by intensifying the checks and balances on the Confederate government. The anticipated result was prospering sovereign states associated within a federal framework. As stated by Robert H. Smith, in his closing remarks on the C.S.A. Constitution: "Having taken our political destinies into our own hands, let us not, in the moment of exultation, forget the duties that devolve upon us, and let us remember that, however wise and beneficent

may be the working of the General Government, it is to State action
we must mainly look for the advancement which shall secure high
civilization; for the enactment and enforcement of laws, which shall
give security to life, liberty, and property; for that intellectual and
moral culture which shall enable us wisely to govern men and guide
the State."[35]

Chapter Six

Judicial Review

Due to the American tradition of deference toward the judiciary for expounding what is or shall be constitutional law, an analysis of judicial activity in the political process reveals much about constitutional law as understood by the political community. In the event that a judicial tribunal is out of step with the nonjudicial consensus regarding the meaning of the constitution, corrective measures would be forthcoming in order to make constitutional law consistent with the policy preferences of the community. Such measures include proposing an amendment to rectify an unpopular judicial interpretation of the constitution, disregarding the court decision, and making personnel changes within the court. The mere presence of these measures impacts judicial behavior by putting judges on notice that their decisions can be modified. Such modifications are evidence of the fact that American high courts, state and national, do not operate in political vacuums. This is especially the case with state high court judges, whose tenures are closely tied to electoral processes. Thus, when a judge expounds the meaning of a constitution, and when amendments, disregard, or personnel changes are not directed toward the judge's court, one can be somewhat confident that the decision, even if unpopular, is within the perimeters of acceptable construction from the perspective of the community at large. In other words, the constitution has been satisfactorily construed. This was especially the case in the Confederate state high courts, in contradistinction to the U.S. Supreme Court, because the state judges were subject to an electoral process which necessitated that they defer to the political, social, and cultural preferences of their constituents; otherwise they could be voted out of office, whereas Supreme Court justices, nominated by the president and confirmed by the Senate for life, were protected from such electoral pressures.

With this in mind, it is useful to analyze Confederate and state judicial activity in light of the application of constitutional law to political affairs, thereby providing insight into the Confederates' understanding of their constitution and their commitment to popular control of constitutional exegeses. The analysis is threefold: first, the *de jure* and *de facto* textual innovations of the Confederate judicial process in contradistinction to that of the U.S., especially in regard to Article III of the respective constitutions; second, the concurrent jurisdiction between the Confederate and state high courts, which in reality was deference to the state high courts' supremacy over their Confederate counterparts; and third, the judicial adjudication of several controversial constitutional issues that confronted the Confederacy. Inherent in the legal controversies that confronted the Confederacy was the Publian "political monster *imperium in imperio*" as the various state high courts adjudicated national controversies. However, a review of these high court decisions reveals not only the stabilizing influence of the judiciary in the Confederate political process but also a functional Confederate application of federalism.

Textual innovations

Article III of the C.S.A. Constitution textually deviates from its U.S. counterpart in three instances. The changes were designed to modernize provisions in Article III of the U.S. Constitution, which had already been or were in the process of being incorporated into the U.S. legal system. First, the judicial power of the C.S.A. extended simply "to all cases arising under this Constitution," whereas the judicial power of the U.S. extended specifically "to all cases in Law and Equity" (Article III, section 2). This C.S.A. innovation was designed to place into effect procedural reforms supported by the legal community in the antebellum period. The state of New York implemented such reforms in the 1840s as did the U.S. Supreme Court in the first half of the twentieth century.[1] Essentially, the reforms combined law and equity rules of procedure. Within the Confederacy this combined rule of procedure was compatible with states' rights, particularly regarding Texas and Louisiana, where single jurisdictions prevailed. Accordingly, the enforcement of legal rights and the pursuit of equitable remedies were to be statutorily established, providing the Confederate courts greater flexibility in coping with the various forms of action.[2] This is not to suggest that the dual forms of action were not addressed in the U.S. For example, in 1792, Congress gave the Supreme Court the power to adopt rules of equity, which the Court did in 1822 and 1842.[3] The Confederate framers, most of whom were at one time or another in the legal profession, were responding to an emerging trend regarding the law and equity forms of procedure.

In the course of the ratification debates of 1787 through 1789, it was acknowledged that the removal of equity jurisdiction from the U.S. Supreme Court would mitigate the discretionary powers of federal judges by constraining them to function within a more rigid system of constitutional and statutory laws, in contradistinction to a common law or natural rights premised upon equity. Publius conceded that "there is hardly a subject of litigation between individuals which may not involve those ingredients of *fraud, accident, trust, or hardship,* which would render the matter an object of equitable rather than legal jurisdiction, as the distinction is known and established in several of the States."[4] Consequently, Publius maintained, many equitable cases will of necessity arise under the U.S. Constitution, making Article III, section 2, indispensable for the federal judiciary to fulfill its appellate responsibilities.

The Antifederalists voiced concerns about the nature and scope of jurisdiction conferred upon the federal courts, equitable relief included. One such Antifederalist, writing under the pseudonym Brutus, was convinced that extending the Supreme Court's jurisdiction to state cases of equity significantly contributed to the irresistible expansion of power of the national government at the expense of the states. He reasoned that "every adjudication of the supreme court, on any question that may arise upon the nature and extent of the general government, will effect the limits of state jurisdiction. In proportion as the former enlarge the exercise of their powers, will that of the latter be restricted. That the judicial power of the United States, will lean strongly in favour of the general government, and will give such an explanation to the constitution, as will favour an extension of its jurisdiction, is very evident from a variety of considerations."[5]

Based upon the common-law tradition, equity does provide the judges with ample discretionary powers. According to the English jurist Sir William Blackstone, "The liberty of considering all cases in an equitable light must not be indulged too far, lest thereby we destroy all law, and leave the decision of every question entirely in the breast of the judge. And law, without equity, though hard and disagreeable, is much more desirable for the public good than equity without law; which would make every judge a legislator, and introduce most infinite confusion."[6] Partial to Blackstone's view on legislative judges, the Confederate framers were not averse to curtailing the discretionary powers of Confederate judges and justices operating under the guise of equity. To be sure, under the C.S.A. Constitution, "the judicial power shall extend to all cases arising under this Constitution" (Article III, section 2), but it is an open question as whether the state courts of equity were to be considered as "cases" under this modified language of the C.S.A. Constitution.[7] In one of the more determined attempts to pass the enabling legislation establishing the C.S.A. Supreme Court, the legislative language specifically extended the Court's jurisdiction to "cases in law and equity." Presumably the jurisdiction of Confederate courts could be statutorily extended to equity cases, as well as statutorily excluded from them. The important point is that equity jurisdiction was not constitutionally mandated, but rather it was subject to congressional regulation. Congressional exclusion of equity jurisdiction would be to the advantage of the state courts, their equity cases then not being susceptible to direct appeal to Confederate courts.

Second, the judicial power of the C.S.A. did not extend to cases between a state and citizens of another state, unless the state was the plaintiff, whereas originally under the U.S. model the judicial power extended to cases between a "State and citizens of another State" (Article III, section 2), which jurisdiction was later qualified to exclude suits in law and equity initiated by "citizens of another State or by citizens or subjects of any foreign State" (Eleventh Amendment).

Third, and closely related to the second innovation, the Confederate framers added the prohibition that "no State shall be sued by a citizen or subject of any foreign State" (Article III, section 2). The first innovation was designed to bolster the states' "sovereign immunity" to the extent that a state could not be brought before a federal tribunal without its consent. Its consent would be implicit if it initiated a suit in which constitutionally the defendant could appeal to the federal courts. The U.S. Constitution provides the states with the same type of sovereign immunity in the Eleventh Amendment. The Eleventh Amendment resulted from the controversial Supreme Court decision *Chisholm* v. *Georgia* (1793). It was unpopular in the sense that it ran counter to the widely held belief that the states had such sovereign immunity.[8] However, within the context of federalism, the Confederate prohibition that "no State shall be sued by a citizen or subject of any foreign state" goes beyond the protection of the Eleventh Amendment by prohibiting suits by foreigners against the states. The U.S. Constitution does not prohibit such suits; it simply limits the U.S. judiciary jurisdiction over such matters if they are not commenced by a state. It should be kept in mind that foreigners included U.S. citizens, and the C.S.A. framers were placing a constitutional barrier between the Confederate states and the anticipated multitudinous lawsuits headed their way as a consequence of secession's economic disintegration between North and South.

The three innovations mentioned above can be described as *de jure* innovations because they found their way into fundamental law. More significant for the Confederate judiciary were the *de facto* innovations, those innovations that pressingly emanated from the political perimeters of states' rights. The most important of these was the prevailing political determination to leave the C.S.A. Supreme Court unorganized.

With governmental centralization being the concomitant of war (concomitant in the sense that a centralized decision-making process is more efficient in maximizing the utilization of resources than a decentralized one), it is significant that the Confederate Congress chose to functionally decentralize the judiciary. This Confederate decentralization resulted in a democratization of judicial processes in contradistinction to the U.S. judiciary, which is dominated by Supreme Court justices not subject to elections. In the state judiciaries of the Confederacy, most of the judges were placed on the bench through elections, and if elections meant anything the elected were accountable to the electors.[9] Because the C.S.A. Supreme Court was not organized, the states' highest courts were *de facto* supreme within the respective states and the Confederacy at large. It is significant that the judges of the various high courts were held accountable by an electoral process. This repudiates the Publian maxims that judges should hold their offices during good behavior and that there should be a national judicial review superior to the state courts.[10] This fundamental innovation was consistent with the C.S.A. version of limited national government and state sovereignty. Within the Confederacy, there would be no "national supremacy" dictum imposed upon unwilling states, because there was no Confederate Supreme Court from which the dictum could be issued.

Article III of the C.S.A. Constitution provides for a Supreme Court, so why did the Confederate Congress fail to pass the enabling legislation? The failure to pass such legislation cannot simply be dismissed as a consequence of the contingencies of national security.[11] The Confederate Congress addressed all types of legislative proposals, including the matter of the Supreme Court. Indeed, the Confederate district courts were organized and operational. If anything, the contingencies of the war favored the establishment of a Supreme Court capable of overruling recalcitrant state judges and thereby facilitating the enforcement of C.S.A. policies over the objections of state officials.

The major obstacle to the C.S.A. Supreme Court's organization was the commitment to states' rights. This same commitment minimized the role of the C.S.A. district courts and subordinated them to the state courts. As explained by A. B. Moore, "(1) The State courts were naturally more popular with those who had grievances against the Confederate Government; (2) the fact that the organization of the Confederate court system was never completed impaired the dignity of the district courts and neutralized the influence they might otherwise have had; (3) they had no appellate jurisdiction over the State courts; and (4) the Government usually prosecuted in the State courts, because it was thought that their opinions would be respected more than those of the Confederate courts."[12]

Moreover, the need for the establishment of an operational system of Confederate courts was minimized because "the principle of State sovereignty apparently never established itself as firmly on the bench as it did in the councils of state and in the norms of political philosophy"; being less committed to states' rights, the state courts were less obstructive toward Confederate policies.[13] This is manifested in their legal opinions, in which the vast majority of state high court judges supported the Confederate position, in contradistinction to the radical states' rights positions, which were more prevalent in the state executive and legislative bodies. The support by state courts for C.S.A. policies mitigated the urgency for an alternative to obstructionist state court decisions. That alternative, of course, would have been the establishment of the C.S.A. Supreme Court, which would have provided an expedient avenue for overturning troublesome state court decisions. Their deference to the Confederate legal positions notwithstanding, state high court judges consistently maintained the supremacy of their courts over the Confederate courts, a fact not taken lightly by congressional supporters and opponents of legislation to organize the Supreme Court.

Southern apprehension about the centralizing tendencies of a national supreme court had ample precedent, most notably *McCulloch* v. *Maryland* (1819).[14] The Provisional Constitution had stipulated in Article III, section 1, that the C.S.A. Supreme Court would consist of district judges, with a quorum being a majority. That Court became obsolete when the Permanent Constitution was ratified a few weeks later. But this short-lived stipulation does indicate support for radical modifications to the federal judiciary. Curiously, it was the unicameral Congress, sitting under the Provisional Constitution, that passed the Act of March 16, 1861, which established the Confederate Supreme Court and its relationship to the state courts. It was the jurisdictional relationship between the C.S.A. Supreme Court and the state courts, as set forth in section 45 in the legislation, which proved to be the Court's undoing. Adhering to statutory and legal precedent established in section 25 of the 1789 Judiciary Act[15] and the Supreme Court decisions *Fletcher* v. *Peck* (1810) and *Martin* v. *Hunter's Lessee* (1816),[16] section 45 gave the C.S.A. Supreme Court appellate jurisdiction over the state courts. The significant clauses stipulate

> that a final judgment or decree in any suit, in the highest court of law or equity of a State in which a decision in the suit could be had, where is drawn in question the validity of a treaty or statute of, or an authority exercised under the Confederate States:
>
> Or where is drawn in question the validity of a statute of, or an authority exercised under any State, on the ground of their being repugnant to the Constitution, treaty or laws of the Confederate States:
>
> Or where is drawn in question the construction of any clause of the Constitution, or of a treaty, or statute or commission held under the Confederate States:
>
> In each of these causes, the decision may be re-examined, and reversed or affirmed in the Supreme Court of the Confederate States, upon a writ of error, the citation being signed by any judge of the said Supreme Court, in the same manner and under the same regulations, and with the like effect as if the judgment or decree complained of had been rendered or passed in a district court of the Confederate States; and the proceeding upon reversal shall be the same, except that the Supreme Court, instead of remanding the cause for a final decision, may at their discretion, if the cause shall have once been remanded before, proceed to a final decision of the same and award execution. But no other error shall be assigned or regarded as a ground of reversal in any such case as aforesaid than such as appears in the face of the record, and immediately respects the beforementioned question of validity or construction of the said Constitution, treaties, statutes, commissions, or authorities in dispute.[17]

Several congressional resolutions to repeal the controversial section 45 were introduced in the attempt to appease the states' rights element that found such an appellate process inconsistent with state sovereignty. But because section 45 openly represented all the centralizing tendencies of the U.S. Supreme Court, these resolutions failed to achieve bicameral support. The section proved to be a rallying point for advocates of state judicial supremacy; and as long as the controversial section remained part of the C.S.A. Supreme Court's enabling legislation, there was little chance of it passing both chambers of the Confederate Congress, thereby precluding the C.S.A. Supreme Court even the opportunity to challenge the supremacy of the state courts. As William Yancey of Alabama maintained, "When we decide that the state courts are of inferior dignity to this Court, we have sapped the main pillar of this Confederacy."[18] On another occasion Senator Clement C. Clay of Alabama offered an amendment to repeal section 45 of the provisional Congress's "Act to Establish the Judicial Courts of the C.S.A." In response Senator James Phelan of Mississippi, who supported the establishment of a Confederate Supreme Court with appellate jurisdiction over the states, cautioned that "if each State was entitled to its own construction of what laws were constitutional, the Confederate Government was at an end."[19]

Between the polarized positions there seemed to be no middle ground. Either the Confederate court or the state courts would reign supreme. As the congressional debates about the issue make clear, if section 45 were repealed, the Supreme Court would be divested of its appellate jurisdiction over the state courts, and if not repealed, the requisite votes for passing the enabling legislation to organize the Supreme Court would not be forthcoming. Either alternative was to the advantage of the state judiciaries. In response to Senator Phelan, Senator Yancey articulated the rationale behind the anti-Supreme Court sentiment when he stated on the floor of the Senate that

> the State rights majority will alone preserve this Government. This Government can be preserved only by executing no power that is not delegated. The powers of the Government must not be strained against the sovereign States, and no jealousies and animosities will be produced. But when you strain the powers of the Government against the States you will have a war of intellect, which will soon become a moral war, the flashing of judgements will soon become a flashing of swords. . . . In accordance with the new order of things we should endeavour to have the Constitution administered so as not to give rise to future troubles.[20]

Yancey and like-minded Confederates, rejecting the "national supremacy" reasoning of Publius, John Marshall, and James Kent, contended that political stability in the C.S.A. was contingent upon state judicial supremacy, which in turn was an integral component of states' rights.

On March 18, 1863, the C.S.A. Senate finally voted, 16 yeas to 6 nays, to repeal section 45, thereby denying the Supreme Court appellate jurisdiction over the states. Immediately thereafter, they voted 14 to 8 to organize the C.S.A. Supreme Court, consisting of five justices, with three constituting a quorum, lacking appellate jurisdiction over the state courts. In the C.S.A. House of Representatives, the enabling legislation for the Supreme Court was obstructed at every turn. Henry S. Foote of Tennessee spoke for the obstructionists on December 16, 1863, when he argued that

> the establishment of the court, with appellate power over the supreme courts of the States would be utterly subversive of States' rights and state sovereignty; and instead of securing the desired harmony between the Confederate Government and the Governments of the States, would tend to bring them immediately into conflict. No reasonable person could expect that the supreme judicial tribunals of the States would submit to the exercise of appellate power on the part of the supreme court of the Confederate States upon constitutional questions. No, sir, the establishment of the court would have the inevitable effect of bringing the sovereign States of our system in dire conflict with the central government here.[21]

With this type of attitude prevailing in the House, the Supreme Court was destined to oblivion or, if subsequently organized, obscurity within Confederacy.

The final outcome was that the linchpin of the federal judicial system was never put into place, and after much legislative debate, the state courts reigned supreme within their respective spheres. Thus, state judicial supremacy was neither accidental nor unintended but was the result of the Congress intentionally deferring to the prevalent states' rights position.

Concurrent jurisdiction

The Confederate framers were confronted with an extremely complicated constitutional and political issue. In the American federal system, judicial jurisdiction is complicated by the coexistence of two governments within the same geographical boundaries. As one antebellum legal scholar noted, "*Jurisdiction* is a term signifying the authority of law over a certain territory, or over certain persons; but since the actions of persons must always be the essential object of all laws, the jurisdiction of laws over a certain territory means over all persons within that territory."[22] Obviously, all the states are within the territory of the national government, and the national government has a presence within the states. Concurrent jurisdiction consists of the two levels of government simultaneously having authority over the same people.

Because the national and state governments have jurisdiction over the same people, their respective court systems share jurisdictions. Such concurrent jurisdiction was gradually established in American constitutional law. As a consequence of the legal reasoning of Chief Justice John Marshall, a hierarchy of courts was established in which appeals from the state courts to the federal courts placed the former in a subordinate position to the latter—subordinate in the sense that the federal courts possess the prerogative to make final authoritative decisions in cases. Publius encouraged this hierarchical arrangement on the grounds that it promoted procedural and substantive efficiency and uniformity.[23] Chancellor Kent, commenting along those same lines on the concurrent power of the states "in matters of judicial cognizance," concluded that

> a concurrent jurisdiction in the state courts was admitted, in all except those enumerated cases; but this doctrine was only applicable to those descriptions of causes of which the state courts had previous cognizance, and it was not equally evident in cases which grew out of the Constitution. Congress in the course of legislation, might commit the decision of causes arising upon their laws, to the federal courts exclusively; but unless the state courts were expressly excluded by the acts of Congress, they would of course take concurrent cognizance of the causes to which those acts might give birth, subject to the exceptions which have been stated. In all cases of concurrent jurisdiction, appeal would lie from the state courts to the Supreme Court of the United States; and without such right of appeal, the concurrent jurisdiction of the state courts, in matters of national concern, would be inadmissible; because, in that case, it would be inconsistent with the authority and efficiency of the general government.[24]

Reiterating Publius's appellate structure, Kent's nationalistic interpretation of concurrent jurisdiction was authoritative. The states shared jurisdiction with the U.S. courts in those areas neither constitutionally nor statutorily prohibited, with the qualification that the state proceedings were subject to review by U.S. courts. In short, the state courts were subordinate procedurally to the U.S. courts.

The prevailing national-court supremacy view did not go unchallenged, and the support for a states' rights version of concurrent jurisdiction among the States of the Confederacy was not without precedence in antebellum America. For example, in the early 1820s the state of Virginia contended that concurrent jurisdiction was sanctioned by the U.S. Constitution. Virginia's contention, however, was repudiated by the centralizing policies of the U.S. Supreme Court. Nevertheless, repudiation by Supreme Court dicta did not resolve the issue; it was simply too deeply ingrained in the political psyche of the states' rights advocates. As delineated in *Cohens* v. *Virginia* (1821), the status of the state courts in the federal system was crucial for the states' rights advocates.[25] And as *Cohens* v. *Virginia* makes evident, there existed within the substratum of the federal system support for parity between the national and state courts, which subsequently found official sanction within the Confederacy.

The significant issue in *Cohens* v. *Virginia* was jurisdiction. Cohens was convicted in Virginia for selling lottery tickets, an activity legal in the District of Columbia but illegal in Virginia. He appealed his conviction to the federal courts. Virginia denied that the federal courts had jurisdiction in the case. They argued that the federal and state courts had concurrent jurisdiction in most cases, unless explicitly stated otherwise in the Constitution. The state courts retained jurisdiction in those areas in which they had it previous to the ratification of the U.S. Constitution, "unless taken away by the operation of that instrument," and not simply at the discretion of Congress, as Kent had maintained. Article III, section 2, does not deny such state jurisdiction. Furthermore, because "the judiciary of every government must be the judge of its own jurisdiction,"[26] there must be parity between the federal and state courts, otherwise the state courts are essentially extensions of the federal court system. To subject the state courts' determinations to an appellate process in which the U.S. courts have the last word would result in subordination for the states, which is inconsistent with state sovereignty as manifested in the Tenth Amendment to the U.S. Constitution. Thus, the U.S. courts are not paramount to the state high courts; rather, they are equals in the federal judicial system. Virginia maintained that Article III, section 2, of the U.S. Constitution extends the judicial power of the federal courts to cases in law and equity. This extension of federal jurisdiction should not be misinterpreted to mean exclusive jurisdiction; rather, the extension is to concurrent jurisdiction in the specified cases. Consequently, the final and authoritative resolution of an issue is not necessarily the product of an appellate process from the states to the U.S. Supreme

Court. Because of the parity between the federal and state courts in the realm of concurrent jurisdiction, appeals from the latter to the former are all but eliminated. According to Virginia, "whichsoever judiciary gets possession of the case, should proceed to final judgement, from which there should be no appeal." (It was by no coincidence that state high court judges in the C.S.A. utilized the same exact formula.) Virginia maintained that "every government must possess within itself, and independently, the power to punish offenses against its laws. It would degrade the state governments, and divest them of every pretension to sovereignty, to determine that they cannot punish offenses without their decisions being liable to a re-examination, both as to law and fact (if Congress please), before the Supreme Court of the United States."[27]

Had the Supreme Court sided with Virginia on the issue of jurisdiction, the core of American jurisprudence would have been much more favorable to state sovereignty than to national. Chief Justice Marshall was aware of the implications of Virginia's claims. Echoing the concerns of Publius, Marshall's opinion maintained that "the mischievous construction contended for on the part of Virginia, is also entitled to great consideration. It would prostrate, it has been said, the government and its laws at the feet of every state in the Union."[28] This prostration would be the result of diversity—political, cultural, economic—among the various states. To allow the states to resolve legal controversies according to their own preferences could indeed prostrate the national government if that government was pursuing a course of action contrary to the policy preferences of one or more states. But the emerging American empire had neither the time for recalcitrant states nor the disposition to nurture their consent, that is, the concurrent majority. Concurrent jurisdiction among the national and state courts was antithetical to the emerging order of nationalism. Marshall insightfully reasoned that

> a constitution is framed for ages to come, and is designed to approach immortality as nearly as human institutions can approach it. Its course cannot always be tranquil. It is exposed to storms and tempests, and its framers must be unwise statesmen indeed, if they have not provided it, as far as its nature will permit, with the means of self-preservation from the perils it may be destined to encounter. No government ought to be so defective in its organization as not to contain within itself the means of securing the execution of its own laws against other dangers than those which occur every day. Courts of justice are the means usually employed; and it is reasonable to expect that a government should repose on its own courts, rather than on others.[29]

Marshall's rationale for national judicial supremacy is the same utilized by Virginia on behalf of the states: that is, no government ought to be so defective as not to be in control of its own destiny. The distinction between the two is that Marshall preferred national destiny over that of potentially divergent states.

Nevertheless, Virginia stressed that the states' continued participation in the affairs of the Union was premised upon their consent. If that consent should cease to exist and to be replaced by unabated hostility, the Union would disintegrate, as it well should, the U.S. Supreme Court, Congress, and the president notwithstanding. Constitutionally, it is the consent of the states which holds the Union together, not force. (Of course, the notion that the Union was the product of a compact dependent upon the consent of the states was a recurring theme in the antebellum South.) Thus the state courts can be trusted to maintain the integrity of the U.S. Constitution due to their inherent support for the principles embodied therein.[30]

Marshall conceded that hostility to the Union on the state level would be irresistible. But, recurring to his nationalistic fervor he denied that a state could make such resistance. He reiterated that the nation is superior to any of its parts (i.e., the states) and that only the American people acting collectively through their national institutions could challenge the existing order. Resistance on the part of a state is usurpation and "ought to be repelled by those to whom the people have delegated their power of repelling it."[31] In short, the Publian axiom that coercion is to be resorted to in the absence of consent was the underlying principle of national judicial supremacy.

This theoretical backdrop makes all the more interesting the Confederate repudiation of Marshall's dicta of national judicial supremacy. That repudiation makes unquestionably clear the Confederates' commitment to a national government premised upon the consent of the people within their respective states, without their abandoning the idea of an effective national government. But in the event that an effective national government is irreconcilable with the consent of a state(s), the former must give way to the latter.

Confederate state judicial supremacy

The conscription acts of 1862 raised the issue of jurisdiction in every state of the Confederacy, although the procedures utilized varied. The constitutional question centered on whether a state could take jurisdiction by writs of habeas corpus in detention cases made under the authority of C.S.A. laws. Not only did state courts claim jurisdiction over these cases, they functioned as high courts of last resort for the people under their jurisdiction and passed judgment on the constitutionality of the act itself. This development in the states cannot be dismissed as the actions of activist state judges attempting to expand their powers at the expense of the Confederacy. Most state judges lacked the authority to issue writs of habeas corpus until the authority was granted by the various state legislatures responding to the C.S.A. conscription policies.[32] This is evidence of the popular support within the states for the state courts to check the augmented power of the C.S.A. secretary of war; otherwise the state legislatures would not have granted the courts the authority to issue the writs.[33]

The C.S.A. conscription acts provided the state high courts with the opportunity to procedurally and substantively delineate the Confederate variant of a limited constitution. Procedurally they accepted the responsibility of state judicial review over national laws without hesitation. In case after case the state high court judges functioned as the expounders of the C.S.A. Constitution without bemoaning the failure of the Confederate Congress to organize the Supreme Court. They reasoned that as the agents of the sovereign states, the state judiciaries were entitled to interpret those laws. Interestingly, state judicial review did not result in the chaos anticipated by Publius, Marshall, Kent, Story, and others. Rather, it occasioned the people within their respective states to reaffirm, through their state judiciaries, their obligatory compliance to laws premised upon the federal compact. This, indeed, is government based upon the consent of the governed, united by a compact (covenant) and not by coercion.

Because controversies about the terms of the compact were subject to resolution in state courts, state supremacy replaced the national supremacy of the Marshall Court.[34] State supremacy did not necessarily impugn the supremacy clause of Article VI, which was absolutely fundamental to the Confederacy.[35] Where Confederate state judicial supremacy deviated from the national supremacy of Marshall was the procedural question of jurisdiction. The states claimed that they possessed the prerogatives to determine the meaning of the C.S.A. Constitution and which statutes contravened it; in other words, the C.S.A. Constitution and those laws in pursuance thereof were supreme, with the qualification that the state courts would function as the preeminent interpreter of both fundamental and statutory laws within their respective jurisdictions. This is a significant prerogative, one that placed within the states the control of their own political destinies.

As the state courts reviewed the conscription acts, they willingly positioned themselves to declare the acts of the C.S.A. Congress unconstitutional. The issues they addressed were: Are the conscription acts constitutional? and, do the state courts have the authority to issue writs of habeas corpus to Confederate officials?

State high courts answered the first question in the affirmative. Not surprisingly they selectively cited authorities that supported their opinions, such as Publius, Marshall, Kent, Story, and John Codman Hurd. Due to the nature of the constitutional question involved—incrementally increasing the power of the Confederate government to conduct the war—state judges with objective views regarding Confederate powers as enumerated in Article I, section 8, helped to avoid a crisis between the two governments. Besides, the argument that the compulsory draft was constitutional was persuasive. Collectively, the state judges found in the enumerated powers of Article I, section 8—to declare war; raise and support armies; call forth the militia of the states; provide for, organize, arm, and discipline the militia; and make laws as per the necessary and proper clause—an implicit power authorizing a compulsory draft.[36]

But this power was not absolute and indefinite. Unlike in the judicial national supremacy of Marshall, the state judges consistently reserved the right of the states to interpose on behalf of their citizens. State judges, acknowledging the requirements of armed conflict with a formidable foe and the responsibility of the Confederate government to place in the field an effective army, reiterated the status of states' rights and the prerogative of the state high courts to curtail the Confederate war powers if they were to be used oppressively. Judge Moore of Texas concluded that although "a necessity exists today, and the law is therefore constitutional, if tomorrow that necessity should cease, its continuance would be as clearly unconstitutional." Judge Robertson of Virginia prefaced his major opinion on the subject stating that "considerations of expediency and policy cannot be permitted to control our judgement. We must expound the constitution according to what appears to be its true meaning . . . however disastrous may be the consequences of our decisions." He concluded that conscription was constitutional, but since it was a potential tool for oppression, as is the case with any power delegated to the government, the state courts must be prepared to intervene on behalf of its citizens. Security from such oppression was contingent upon the electoral accountability of the congressmen to their constituents, but more significantly upon "the reserved right of each state to resume the powers delegated to the Confederate government, whenever, in her judgement, they are perverted to the injury or oppression of her people."[37] In short, the Confederate power of conscription was exercised at the pleasure of the states.

The impressment policies of the Confederacy were also flash points of controversy between the Confederate and state authorities. Article I, section 9, clause sixteen, of the C.S.A. Constitution stipulates, "nor shall private property be taken for public use without compensation." Both Confederate and state authorities acknowledged the necessity of eminent domain, of which impressment was a variant. So the prerogative of the C.S.A. government to take private property in the tumultuous process of arming, feeding, clothing, and transporting their war machine was not questioned. Within the state courts, the controversy centered on what constituted "just compensation" and by what process that determination should be made.

The proposed impressment bills in the Congress were extensively debated. The congressmen were confronted with a twofold problem. First, they had to ascertain which type of impressment legislation was most conducive to maximizing the economic reality of supply and demand. An impressment policy too favorable to the government would diminish the incentive of the entrepreneurial community to produce. Furthermore, the war-torn economy of the South was plagued by speculators disrupting the normal flow of resources. In the first instance the supplies would be lacking, while in the second the costs would be prohibitive. Second, the Congress was cognizant of the need to satisfy the state high courts regarding the constitutionality of C.S.A. legislation, which in itself limited the options open to the C.S.A. Congress. In the course of one debate on the subject, Senator Yancey cautioned that "the right to property is one of the most sacred known to the Constitution."[38] The Confederate policymakers realized that their version of "just compensation" would be subjected to strict constitutional tests within the state judiciaries that had the responsibility of securing this sacred right against violations by the C.S.A.

Consequently, the Congressional debates paid particularly close attention to the Constitution's stipulation that those whose property had been taken were entitled to "just compensation." The C.S.A.

attorney general interpreted the stipulation to mean the market value of the property at the time and place of seizure.[39] Senator Allen T. Caperton of Virginia expressed the reasoning behind this interpretation.

> Our people had been accustomed to look to the Constitution as the great shield of their liberty and property, and notwithstanding the dreadful and devastating war in which the country was involved they could not realize, and he [Caperton] hoped they would never realize that the Constitutional safeguards, providing that no man's property could be taken for public use without just compensation, had been swept away. There might be ignorant men who knew nothing of the Constitution, but anyone had sense enough to see the gross injustice of taking his property at less than its real value while the property of his fellow citizens was left untouched. When the Government, for instance, took a barrel of flour, the market value of which was thirty dollars, giving the owner fifteen dollars for it, it obliged him to contribute out of his own pocket fifteen dollars towards the support of the Government. At the same time the cotton and tobacco planters, their property not being wanted by the Government, contributed nothing to its support. The terms of the Constitution should be strictly followed and full value given by Government for property impressed. Then should the Government take the barrel of flour valued at thirty dollars, giving for it the market value, when the taxes, which are levied alike upon the producer of grain and the cotton and tobacco planter, come to be paid, the equality contributed by all to the support of the Government be restored. In no other way could it be attained. By any other course the owner of property impressed would be compelled to contribute to the support of the Government the difference between the actual market value of that property and the price allowed him at the time of impressment.—Just compensation was the actual market value or price at the time and place of impressment. It had been so decided by the Attorney General, and for his life he could see no better or more just compensation.[40]

Caperton's position embodies three political principles that were fundamental to the Confederacy: (1) the constitutional sanctity of the citizens' liberties and properties, (2) the integral relationship between private property and the public welfare, the latter being a legitimate concern, and (3) an impressment policy that evenly distributes the burden of supplying the government by paying market value for the property impressed. Caperton and his supporters maintained that anything other than an impressment policy premised upon market-value compensation would be unjust, unconstitutional, and politically destabilizing.

Opponents of the market-value approach favored a process through which commissioners would establish fixed prices for a period of sixty days, after which the prices would be adjusted to reflect market realities. In response to Senator Caperton, Senator Benjamin Hill of Georgia "denied that the market price was just compensation. The market price might be temporary, fluctuating, and factitious. Speculators in any grain neighborhood knowing that the Government was about to make impressments there might combine to put up the 'market price' for the occasion." Senator Gustavus A. Henry of Tennessee "thought that the market price was of all standards the most fallacious. As an instance, Richard III, when down in the dust and blood at Bosworth field, offered his kingdom for a horse."[41]

In March of 1863 the Act to Regulate Impressments was finally passed. The legislation favored the market-value approach regarding just compensation, with the qualification that property in the possession of speculators was subject to a price schedule predetermined by a commission. Its basic provisions are: (a) impressments can only be exercised in cases of absolute necessity; (b) in the event that the impressing officer and the property owner fail to agree on the market value of the impressed property, two disinterested and loyal citizens, one chosen by the owner and the other by the officer, are to determine the market value. If these two fail to agree, then an umpire chosen by them will make the final decision; and (c) if the property in question is in the hands of speculators, the value of the property is predetermined by two commissioners, one appointed by the president and the other by the state's governor, according to a fixed schedule of prices.[42]

The Congress attempted to maintain the constitutional status of private property even in the face of the juggernaut of military necessity. The expectation was that by securing the rights of property, the engines of capitalism would provide the supplies to meet the military's ever-increasing demands. Speculation was not prohibited, but rather it was kept in check by the commission.

With the exception of Georgia, state high courts upheld the constitutionality of the act.[43] The high court in Georgia decided that disinterested citizens and the price schedules of the commissioners were not necessarily compatible with the constitutional stipulation requiring just compensation. Consequently, they declared sections five and six of the act as unconstitutional and void within the state. Such processes, Judge Charles J. Jenkins wrote in 1863, echoing the concerns of Senator Caperton, were arbitrary, and they subjected those owners of impressed property to an unconstitutional burden.

> The impressment authorized by the Constitution, is not designed
> to cheapen commodities for the Government, but to insure sup-
> plies at fair prices. Unless the Government pay prices which cit-
> izen consumers pay, the result will be that it levies contributions
> from one portion of the people in support of the war, from which
> all others escape. The difference in price paid by the citizen, on
> purchase, to one dealer, and the price paid by the Government on
> impressment, to another, will be the measure of contribution un-
> justly wrested from the latter.

Accordingly, the only reliable constitutional process for determining just compensation was through the market forces of supply and
demand, including just compensation for property in the possession of speculators. "That legislation can not do this, the principles
of political economy, based upon observations carefully made, and
collated, in the course of time, warrant us in affirming."[44]

The response of the Congress to Georgia's supreme court was
conciliatory. There was no support for force bills authorizing the
C.S.A. president to coerce compliance with the Confederate law. If
impressment was to be effected in Georgia, it would be with the
consent of the citizens of Georgia. Congressmen took Georgia's
objections so seriously that the Senate and House judiciary committees immediately went to work on considering amendments to the
original legislation.[45] In their revisions, the House and Senate differed over the central issue of Georgia's supreme court decision.
The Senate maintained the restrictions on speculators, whereas the
House removed them.[46] Even though the subject of impressment
was debated on numerous occasions during the ensuing weeks
following the Georgia Supreme Court decision, the legislative impasse was not to be resolved before time expired on the Confederacy.

The state courts in the Confederacy procedurally functioned according to the same standards from 1861 to 1865 as they did in the
antebellum period. There was not a deviation from the rule of law
and the republican ideals; as a citizen of the Confederacy could not
be arbitrarily deprived of his life, liberty, or property without due
process of law. The rights guaranteed by the U.S. Constitution were
recognizably prevalent in the Confederacy, the qualification being
that the state courts were responsible for securing those rights.

However, what was unique about the Confederacy was the unambiguous determination to uphold the integrity of state sovereignty
within the confines of an association of states under the jurisdiction
of a central government. Because both the central and the state
governments had specified policy responsibilities, disputes between

them were inevitable. In the event of such conflict, the states of the Confederacy reserved the right to adjudicate a settlement. There was no national supremacy in the sense that the state courts were obliged to accept a position subordinate to that of the Confederate courts. In the words of Judge Robertson of Virginia, "The state governments are an essential part of our political system; upon the separate and independent sovereignty of the states the foundation of our confederacy rests." Furthermore, "It is absurd to suppose that the government of the Confederate States can rightfully destroy the governments of the states which created it; and all the powers conferred on it must be understood to have been given with limitation that, in executing them, nothing shall be done to interfere with the independent exercise of its sovereign powers by each state."[47] The full significance of Robertson's words cannot be appreciated until one takes into account the fact that it was primarily the state courts, and subordinately the Confederate judiciary, which were to decide the nature of the limitations to be placed upon the powers of the Confederate government.

Significantly, state high court judges overwhelmingly upheld the constitutionality of Confederate legislation. Of course, the prospect of state judicial review did influence the course of Confederate legislation, as bills were modified to meet the anticipated standards of state sovereignty as defined by the states. This additional check on the Confederate government's policies was the concurrent majority of Calhoun, which aimed at national policies premised upon the consent of the governed within the respective states.

Chapter Seven

The American Origins of the Confederate Order

In the wake of the English Civil War (1642–1648), Thomas Hobbes made an analysis applicable to the dissolution of the Union in 1861.

> Though nothing can be immortal, which mortals make; yet, if men had the use of reason they pretend to, their common-wealths might be secured, at least, from perishing from internal diseases. For by the nature of their Institution, they are designed to live, as long as Man-kind, or as the Laws of Nature, or as Justice itself, which gives them life. Therefore, when they come to be dissolved, not by external violence, but by intestine disorder, the fault is not in men, as they are the *Matter*; but as they are the *Makers*, and orderers of them. For men, as they become at last wary of irregular justling and hewing one another, and desire with all their hearts, to conform themselves into one firm and lasting edifice; so for want, both of the art of making fit Laws, to square their actions by, and also of humility and patience, to suffer the rude and cumbersome points of their present greatness to be taken off, they cannot without the help of a very able Architect, be compiled, into any other than a crazy building, such as hardly lasting out of their own time, must assuredly fall upon the heads of their posterity.[1]

As the English Civil War was a struggle between Crown and Parliament over sovereignty, the dissolution of the United States into two nations, North and South was, to a significant extent, the consequence of the *Makers* who left indeterminate the locus of sovereignty. The deficiency regarding the locus of sovereignty was not the result of an oversight on the part of the framers, but rather it was the product of a bargaining process between the Antifederalists and Federalists in which neither side was willing to capitulate their preference as to where sovereignty was to reside. Initially this did not present an insurmountable problem, for the "majestic vagueness" of the U.S. Constitution facilitated the accommodation of both preferences. Because the Antifederalist and Federalist assumptions about sovereignty were mutually exclusive, the tenuous Union was certain to be tested as the national and state governments' public policy objectives clashed. Anticipation of "the tug" against the Union (to use Lincoln phraseology) was implicit in much of the 1787–1791 convention and ratification processes. In 1788 the Federal Farmer expressed the Antifederalists' sentiment regarding the impact of the proposed Constitution on the states when he wrote that "it appears to be a plan retaining some federal features, but to be the first important step, and to aim strongly, to one consolidated government of the United States."[2] The consolidated government of the United States could only be achieved when the respective sovereignties of the states were merged into a unitary national sovereign, the American people in contradistinction to the sovereign peoples of Virginia, Pennsylvania, New York, and so on. By definition, sovereignty is indivisible; therefore, any attempt to establish a federal system in which the national and state communities have mutually exclusive public policy objectives, while simultaneously having sovereignty within a specified area of public policy, is indeed a crazy structure.

The fundamental constitutional principle that distinguishes the C.S.A. Constitution from the U.S. Constitution is the locus of sovereignty. The former attempted to make conclusive what the latter left ambiguous. The Confederate framers' notion of sovereignty within a federal framework was not novel, but rather it was premised upon the eighteenth-century American Antifederalist interpretation of federalism—an interpretation antebellum Southern Democrats believed was embodied in the U.S. document, Publius and Northern Republicans notwithstanding.

Accordingly, the Southern leaders who produced the Permanent Confederate Constitution of 1861 were convinced that their document was a restoration of the original federal order that had gone awry as a consequence of misconstruction and intentional disregard for the constitutional federalism established in 1789. This does not mean that the Confederates were opposed to the U.S. Constitution in principle. To the contrary, they were convinced that their actions were in its defense and essential for a restoration of the original federal arrangement. The Alabamian "Fire Eater" William Yancey declared, "If then, my friends, you have heard that I am a disunion man, and if there is an apparent foundation for it, or any truth in it, it is because my life has been devoted to opposing those who would destroy the 'more perfect Union' of the constitution, and build up an usurping union or a law higher than the constitution."[3] The Confederate defense of American federalism was premised upon Antifederalist assumptions about the U.S. Constitution rather than upon the preponderant Federalist assumptions. The ambiguity as to which construction was historically correct centered on the sovereignty question—a question that was left begging from 1787 through 1865. An explication of the issue of federalism as debated in the 1787 convention makes evident that the formation of the C.S.A. Constitution had deep roots in American constitutionalism.

As was the case between antebellum Southern Democrats and Northern Republicans, the fundamental distinction between the Antifederalist and Federalist constructions of the document centered on the issue of sovereignty. This distinction emanated from their respective commitments as to the manner and extent to which the people were to be self-governing. The 1787 Constitutional Convention failed to resolve conclusively this issue within the context of a compound republic. This failure was due in large measure to the practical political problem of securing ratification of the document. The Antifederalists, in all probability, would not have supported a national constitution that explicitly deprived the states of their sovereignty. The Federalists, on the other hand, did not draft a document that left the sovereignty of the states intact; to do so would have defeated the purpose of supplanting the Articles of Confederation. The end result was a document that was indeterminate about sovereignty and, furthermore, a document that legitimately meant different things to different constructionists (such as the Antifederalists, the Federalists, the Jeffersonians, the Jacksonian Democrats, the Calhounian Democrats, and the Sewardian Republicans). As a consequence of this ambiguity regarding the locus of sovereignty, the U.S. Constitution facilitated the emergence of a scheme of government through which the national community could (and would) dominate the various state communities. The leading Federalists were aware of this eventuality. But the transformation from the confederacy established under the Articles of Confederation to national supremacy did not come easily; in fact, it did not come determinatively until Appomattox, in 1865. The reactionary Confederate framers were cognizant of this ongoing transformation and aimed at a restoration of Antifederalists' constitutional principles regarding the nature of American federalism.

To delineate the basic distinguishing characteristics between the Antifederalists and the Federalists as they vied for dominance in the 1787 convention, an analysis of their perspectives on political communities will be utilized, thereby providing insight into the Antifederalists commitment to their states, first and foremost, a commitment subsequently emulated by the Confederate framers of 1861.

The primary issue consistently raised by the Antifederalists in their declamations against ratification of the U.S. Constitution concerned the status of the states. They disconcertingly anticipated the consolidation of the states into a centralized national government. Consolidation, for all intents and purposes, denoted the absorption of the states into the national sphere of influence to the extent that they would be precluded from functioning as viable self-governing political units. The objections made by the Antifederalists of the Pennsylvania delegation to the convention typify the rationale behind opposition to ratification.

> We dissent, first because it is the opinion of the most celebrated writers on, and confirmed by uniform experience, that a very extensive territory cannot be governed on the principles of freedom, otherwise than by a confederation of republics, possessing all the powers of internal government, but united in their general, and foreign concerns. . . . We dissent, secondly, because the powers vested in Congress by this constitution, must necessarily annihilate and absorb the legislative, executive, and judicial powers of the several states, and produce from their ruins one consolidated government, which from the nature of things will be an **iron-handed despotism,** as nothing short of the supremacy of despotic sway could connect and govern these United States under one government.[4]

Underlying the Antifederalists' objection to the Federalists' plan was the expectation that it relinquished the sovereign prerogatives of the states in the attempt to achieve a more effective national government. An effective national government would in essence be a consolidated government—consolidated in the sense that sovereignty would be a national phenomenon, not an association of sovereign states. A transfer of sovereignty from the states to the national government was unacceptable for the Antifederalists. As the Antifederalist Federal Farmer maintained, based upon the principles of federalism, "each state must be known as a sovereign body."[5]

The subject of the locus of sovereignty was an issue because the basic assumptions and commitments of the Antifederalists and Federalists with respect to national and state communities differed. The former emphasized the homogeneity of interests at the state level, while the Federalists emphasized the absence of homogeneous communities and the need for a centralized government with the capacity to mediate the conflicts between diverse groups pursuing varying interests in both national and state communities. It is the degree of confidence in homogeneity (the extent that the members of a community are cognizant that their individual and group interests are inextricably linked to the general interests of the community and act accordingly) that is the basis of the similarities and dissimilarities between the Antifederalists' and Federalists' theories about federalism. Their respective commitments to a dominant nation or to states within a federal framework stemmed from their opinions about which level of government could be trusted to exercise power effectively and judiciously. Because the Federalists distrusted majority rule of each respective state, they preferred the transfer of sovereignty from the state to the national community, thereby diminishing majority rule by advancing national supremacy over the states.

Their divergent commitments to national versus state supremacy notwithstanding, the Antifederalist and Federalist shared the overall commitments to republicanism and to a scheme of federalism that secures the collective interests of the states. These commitments tenuously bridged the gap caused by the controversy over sovereignty, and for the most part permitted the Antifederalists and Federalists to leave the question of sovereignty begging and to move on to more negotiable topics. Both the Antifederalists and the Federalists were committed to devising a scheme of government that had as its *raison d'être* the general welfare, and it was this commitment to the general welfare that served as the common ground upon which they stood, convinced as they were that the general welfare could only be realized through republican principles and some sort of association of the states. In short, both were committed to a republican form of federalism, believing that it was most conducive to the general welfare in contradistinction to a scheme of government by the one or few that favored an entrenched privileged class. This shared commitment was significant, especially when placed in the context of the eighteenth century.

Which model of federalism constituted the best association for the states was variously interpreted. The Federalists were persuaded that republicanism was best served by strengthening the national government at the expense of the states' autonomy, whereas the Antifederalists were not prepared to accept Publius's claim that "the vigor of government is essential to the security of liberty," especially if that vigor were to be lodged in the hands of a distant national government.[6] Rather, for them popular consent to government policies, within a federal framework, was contingent upon popular control, and reliable popular control was contingent upon the proximity of the rulers to the ruled. As stated by the Federal Farmer, "It has been observed that the people in extensive territories have more power, compared with that of their rulers, than in small states. Is not directly the opposite true? The people in a small state can unite and act in concert and with vigor, but in large territories, the men who govern find it more easy to unite, while people cannot; while they cannot collect the opinions of each part, while they move to different points, and one part is often played off against the other."[7] Accordingly, the Antifederalists placed greater confidence in state governments, because these communities were more homogeneous and more susceptible to popular control than was the heterogeneously based and distant national government.

Publius stated that "the aim of every political constitution is, or ought to be, first to obtain for rulers men who possess most wisdom to discern, and most virtue to pursue, the common good of society; and in the next place, to take the most effectual precautions for keeping them virtuous while they continue to hold their public trust." This the Antifederalists would have had no difficulty in accepting; however, a divergence of theory emerges when "the most effectual precautions for keeping them virtuous while they continue to hold their public trust" are applied to a government with expanded jurisdiction over an association of states. The Antifederalists were not persuaded that the extended republic was the panacea the Federalists claimed it be; to the contrary, they feared that such a government presented a formidable threat to their liberties.[8]

From the Antifederalists' perspective of state government, a strong attachment exists between citizens and their respective local communities—an attachment in which individual wills combine into a Rousseauean "general will." Through this general will, community interests emerge and reign supreme to the extent that "community interests were considered superior to those of individuals. The community could expropriate land and property to pay debts or for community purposes. Virtually all those rights to which we now attach such great importance could be abridged by the local or colonial legislature for the good of the community."[9] Operating from the theoretical premise of community homogeneity within the states and diversity throughout the nation, the Antifederalists were obliged to devise a scheme of national government simultaneously commensurate with state autonomy (to protect the homogeneous interests of the respective states vis-à-vis the more heterogeneous national community) and collective state decision making (to secure the collective interests of the states). These two objectives are not irreconcilable provided that the national government to be established is limited in its powers and public policy responsibilities, thereby leaving most of the governing to the sovereign states.

At the state level the Antifederalists supported republican models premised upon legislative supremacy. They contended that the "representatives of the people would not act as spokesmen for the private and partial interests, but would be disinterested men, who could have no interest of their own to seek, and would employ their whole time for the public good; then there would be but one interest, the good of the people at large."[10] In short, representatives were elevated to their positions of public trust via the consent of the community and were to function as the mouthpiece of the body politic, which was assumed to be unified and essentially at peace with itself. Accordingly, the effectual precautions for keeping government officials virtuous were grounded in popular control through frequent elections at the state level, a practice synonymous with majority rule within the state, through which the genuine interests of the community would prevail. Because of the anticipated limited scope of the national government's power and public policy responsibilities, the Antifederalists were satisfied that the same principles were applicable to the national model.

The Federalists, however, questioned the existence of the homogenous community and asserted that conflicting interests and factions permeated all communities, the causes of which are "sown in the nature of man." Publius wrote:

> So strong is this propensity of mankind to fall into mutual animosities that where no substantial occasion presents itself the most frivolous and fanciful distinctions have been sufficient to kindle their unfriendly passions and excite their most violent conflicts. But the most common and durable source of factions has been the verious [sic] and unequal distribution of property. Those who hold and those who are without property have ever formed distinct interests in society. Those who are creditors, and those who are debtors, fall under a like discrimination. A landed interest, a manufacturing interest, a mercantile interest, a moneyed interest, with many lesser interests, grow up of necessity in civilized nations, and divide themselves into different classes, actuated by different sentiments and views.

Unlike the Antifederalists, who believed that legislators would not pursue partial interests contrary to the interests of the community, the Federalists maintained that legislators are in effect representatives in the political forum of conflicting interests and are not concerned with "the good of the people at large." It is "the regulation of these various and interfering interests that forms the principal task of modern legislation and involves the spirit of party and faction in the necessary and ordinary operations of government."[11] In other words, the public good is coincidental to a legislative process that not only tolerates factious behavior in its legislators but is premised upon such factionalism to the extent that the territory of the republic was to be extended in order to include a greater number and variety of factions.

Both Antifederalists and Federalists were concerned with the extent of the territory that the proposed Union was to encompass. The Antifederalist concern stemmed from the reasoning that as the territorial extent of a government increases, the homogeneity of the individuals associated together under the jurisdiction of the government decreases, and that as the distance between rulers and ruled increases, the control of the latter over the former decreases. Accordingly, those associated together under the jurisdiction of a city are more homogeneous than those under the jurisdiction of a county, a county is more homogeneous than a state, and a state is more homogeneous than a nation. Consequently, the size and extent of the territory to be governed were the important issues in the late 1780s. The Antifederalists were convinced that it had been "demonstrated, historically and theoretically, that free republican governments could extend over only a relatively small territory with a homogeneous population, and even among states this rule was evident, for the largest states were the worst governed."[12] The greater the extent of the territory to be included under the administration of a particular government, the less homogeneous will be its jurisdiction, thereby increasing the probability that the republican government would deteriorate into an oppressive form. This position was articulated by the Antifederalist Brutus.

> In a republic, the manners, sentiments, and interests of the people should be similar. If this be not the case, there will be a constant clashing of opinions; and the representatives of one part will be continually striving against those of the other. This will retard the operations of the government, and prevent such conclusions as will promote the public good. If we apply this remark to the condition of the United States, we shall be convinced that it forbids that we should be one government. The United States includes a variety of climates. The productions of the different parts of the Union are very variant, and their interests diverse. Their manners and habits differ as much as their climates and productions; and their

sentiments are by no means coincident. The laws and customs of the several states are, in many respects, very diverse, and in some opposite; each would be in favor of its own interests and customs, and a legislature formed of representatives from the respective parts, would not only be too numerous to act with any care or decision, but would be composed of such heterogenous and discordant principles as would constantly be contending with each other. [13]

The Federalists took a more optimistic position regarding the extensiveness of the territory to be placed under the jurisdiction of the proposed Constitution. The Federalists viewed the increased extent of the territory to be governed as advantageous to republicanism for two reasons: First, "extend the sphere and you take in a greater variety of parties and interests, and make it less probable that a majority of the whole will have a common motive to invade the rights of other citizens; or if such a common motive exists, it will be more difficult for all who feel it to discover their own strength and to act in unison with each other." And second, "as each representative will be chosen by a greater number of citizens in the large than in the small republic, it will be more difficult for unworthy candidates to practice with success the vicious arts by which elections are too often carried; and the suffrages of the people being more free, will be more likely to center on men who possess the most attractive merit and the most diffusive and established characters." [14] The extended American republic satisfies the criteria Publius utilized for effective government: (a) internal checks on majority rule, because as factions competed against one another, they minimized the chance that a monolithic majority would form, or if it did, it could not be sustained, and (b) qualitatively superior public officials, who would be attracted away from the states and into the service of the national government. The states fell short in both areas: too few factions to check the emergence of a majority and inferior public officials. Hence, for the very reason that the Antifederalists opposed an extensive territory—it would put distance between the elected and the electorate by diminishing the impact of majorities—the Federalists favored the extensive territory; furthermore, the Federalists' claim that candidates elected to public office in the extensive national republic would be better qualified than those elected in smaller state republics was contingent upon an assumption that the state legislatures were dominated by "unworthy" men concerned not with the public good but rather with the interests of a majority acting in "unison"; the Antifederalists did not make such a distinction.

The Antifederalists' less territorially extensive political community should not be interpreted to denote a community lacking diversities of people and interests. Rather, it denoted a community in many respects diverse—for example, in professions, talents, and wealth—and yet so interdependent that the welfare of any particular part is inextricably linked to the good of the whole, and any group not so linked is in effect outside of the community. They reasoned that the interdependent divisions in the community were the sine qua non of its viability because of the natural aristocracy and its role in the community—a role not unlike that given to it by the Federalists. The Antifederalists contended that each community—towns, counties, and states—was capable of discerning and pursuing community interests without outside interference. The *Essex Result*, a prominent Antifederalist document, states their understanding of the proper relationship between the government, the natural aristocracy, and the people at large, within the framework of republicanism.

> That among gentlemen of education, fortune, and leisure, we shall find the largest number of men, possessed of wisdom, learning, and a firmness and consistency of character. That among the bulk of the people, we shall find the greatest share of political honesty, probity, and a regard to the interests of the whole, of which they compose the majority. That wisdom and firmness are not sufficient without good intentions, nor the latter without the former. The conclusion is, let the legislative body unite them all. The former are called the excellencies that result from an aristocracy; the latter those that result from a democracy.[15]

For the Antifederalists there was a concordant relationship between the natural aristocracy and the people at large; whereas Publius, as noted above, insisted that "the most common and durable source of factions has been the various and unequal distribution of property," resulting in the incessant competition among factions within the states, especially between the aristocratic and democratic elements (i.e., the haves and have-nots, respectively).[16] Hence, the Federalists' counteraction to misrule in the states was to diminish state autonomy by shifting the decision-making process away from state majorities and into the hands of a less popularly engaged centralized authority.

The Antifederalists conceded that some form of stable republican government at the national level was necessary. Their aim was to

limit that government while reserving to the states as much autonomy as feasible; the Federalists, however, were primarily concerned
with "combining the requisite stability and energy in the national
government" while preserving "liberty and the republican form,"
that is, transferring significant portions of the public policy prerogatives of the states to the national government to enable it to do
whatever was necessary and proper to promote the general welfare.[17] Regarding the "republican form," both acknowledged the
need for a separation of powers, but for different reasons. The
Antifederalists favored a separation of powers in order to diminish
the power of the national government; the Federalists advocated a
separation of powers in order to diminish the political power of
national and state majorities, particularly the latter. For example,
concerning the legislative, executive, and judicial branches of government, *The Essex Result* maintains that "each having a check upon
the other, . . . that their independence shall be preserved—If the
three powers are united, the government will be absolute, whether
these powers are in the hands of one or a large number. The same
party will be the legislator, accusor, judge and executioner; and
what probability will an accused person have of an acquittal, however innocent he may be, when his judge will be also a party."[18] This
quotation is consistent with the Federalists' claim that "the accumulation of all powers, legislative, executive and judiciary, in the same
hands, whether of one, a few, or many and whether hereditary, self-
appointed or elective, may justly be pronounced the very definition
of tyranny." But the admonition "In Republican government the
legislative authority necessarily predominates" was meant to guard
against the legislative branch particularly, because it is the most
democratic and therefore the most threatening.[19] To reiterate, both
Antifederalists and Federalists favored some form of a separation of
powers, but for different reasons: the former to check the national
government, and the latter to check national and state majorities.

For the Antifederalists the balance of powers, which included a
balance of functions between the national and state governments,
was to serve as an obstacle to potential abuses of public trust by
government officials. It was for this reason that officials could not
hold dual positions in the various branches; for example, a legislator
could not hold a position in the executive branch, for in doing so, he
might thereby reduce the ease a factious group would have in gain-
ing the control of the government. And, because the legislature is
supposed to be the branch most directly representing distinct communities, the Antifederalists favored legislative supremacy. In short,

popular control through majority rule (expressed through the electoral and legislative processes) and the divisions of functions between the legislative, executive, and judicial branches (within the context of legislative supremacy) were the checks and balances between the states and the central government through which the Antifederalists attempted to utilize checks on arbitrary national policies.

As a consequence of the Federalists' lack of confidence in the notion of the homogeneous community, and their own views of communities as conglomerations of competing interests producing effects that if not mitigated by a strong central government will result in instability and the demise of just and efficient government, their scheme of checks and balances took on a different significance from what it had for the Antifederalists. Both aimed at the prevention of arbitrary government, and not unlike the Antifederalists, the Federalists believed that legislative, executive, and judiciary functions should not be lodged in the same hands; however, unlike the Antifederalists, the Federalists' exclusion of the accumulation of powers in the same hands included those powers of ominous state majorities acting through their legislators. Majority rule no longer represented the expression of community interests. Publius reasoned: "Complaints are everywhere heard from our most considerate and virtuous citizens, equally the friends of public and private faith and of public and personal liberty, that our governments [i.e., the states] are too unstable, that the public good is disregarded in the conflict of rival parties, and that measures are too often decided, not according to the rules of justice, but by the superior force of an interested and overbearing majority."[20] Thus, innovations made by the Federalists on the Antifederalists' scheme of government attempted to mitigate the destablilizing effects of democratic majorities in the states. Essentially, they attempted to achieve this in two ways: First, as previously mentioned, they increased the "extent of the country and the number of the people comprehended under the same government, so that the society will be broken into so many parts, interests and classes of citizens, that the rights of individuals, or of the minority, will be in little danger from interested combinations of the majority."[21] And second, the Federalists advocated a system of checks and balances between the legislative, executive, and judicial branches, giving each branch separate wills and specific functions. The merits of such a system, according to the Federalists, is that it induces delay in the political process, thereby deferring or canceling the impetus of majority rule. This built-in mechanism for delay enhances stability and protects numerical minorities.

Stemming from their different perspectives regarding the homogeneity of the community, the fundamental difference between the Antifederalists and Federalists was that for the former, the states exemplified the embodiment of the various community wills and were the bulwarks of republicanism, whereas for the latter, the states were considered to be politically unstable and obstacles to good government. This is not to say that their differences significantly outweighed their similarities, because in the final analysis the proposed Constitution was adopted and most Antifederalists seemed to have been satisfied with the Federalists' assurances aimed at appeasing concerns about an encroaching national government. Nevertheless, the national government established by the U.S. Constitution left the nation and states at such a variance regarding the locus of sovereignty that the issue would have to wait for judicial and military remedies.[22]

Notably, the Antifederalists' postulates regarding the homogeneous state, extensive republics, the natural aristocracy within a state, institutional checks and balances, and, most important, sovereignty are basically the same that distinguish the C.S.A. Constitution from the U.S. Constitution of antebellum America. The inevitable conclusion is that while the U.S. Constitution has fulfilled the designs of its Federalist framers, the C.S.A. Constitution is essentially a traditional Whig-Antifederalist document, designed not to thwart republicanism (government premised upon the consent of its citizenry) but to secure the states from uncontrollable and perhaps authoritarian central government.

In summary, the C.S.A. Constitution was based upon the retention of sovereignty by the states, an arrangement that would provide the states with the constitutional resources to check arbitrary policies of the Confederate government, as such policies were defined by the states—the same constitutional arrangement favored by the Antifederalists in the 1787 Constitutional Convention. This is not to imply that the C.S.A. Constitution established a more efficiently administered, a more active, and a grander central government than did the U.S. Constitution. Such was not the intention of the C.S.A. framers. Their intention was to establish a federal system of government that was more amenable to the consent of the states within a federal framework. Their model of federalism was in essence a reaction to the consolidation of economic, social, and political powers into the hands of a national elite. To put it otherwise, they preferred their state elites over a less accountable national elite.

When the serious student of American constitutionalism takes into consideration the substantive distinctions between the C.S.A. and U.S. constitutions, certain conclusions become compelling. However, before addressing those conclusions a few brief comments about the C.S.A. innovations are in order. Those innovations can be organized into two categories: The first is the recommitment to state sovereignty. That commitment permeates every aspect of C.S.A. constitutionalism. This does not mean that the Confederates' attempts at nationhood were insincere or trivial. The attachment to their Confederate nation was genuine. Four terrible years of war are evidence enough to dispel doubts to the contrary. Furthermore, their Confederate Constitution provided for the requisite national institutions (Articles I, II, and III), for full faith and credit between and among the states (Article IV), an amendment process to address the contingencies of changing political and social environments (Article V), and the supremacy of Confederate laws (Article VI). But support for nationhood was not synonymous with support for national sovereignty. Participation in and submission to Confederate affairs was premised upon consent, not coercion, and the bulwark of that consent was states' rights. Through states' rights, potential excesses of the Confederate government were to be constrained, while the states themselves were to be controlled by their respective citizenry. This is not meant to imply that state governments were considered to be the panacea for ideal government. The Confederates would readily denounce such wishful thinking. Government was a necessary evil; yes, some are better administered than others, but all systems of government are flawed to some degree. State governments are preferable to national governments because the former are more effectively controlled by the consent of their respective citizenries. Limited government was the Confederate ideal, and state sovereignty was more conducive to that Southern preference than was the alternative, national sovereignty.

The second category of Confederate innovations was designed to supplement state sovereignty by institutionally limiting the C.S.A. government. Some of those innovations include modifications of the budgetary and appropriations processes, such as the line-item veto, the elimination of legislative riders, the exclusion of industrial and agricultural protectionism, and drastic restrictions on internal improvements.

With that in mind, one should also take notice of the omissions, those provisions not included in the C.S.A. Constitution. Those omissions expose certain shibboleths, such as the specious contention that the Confederacy was designed exclusively or primarily to maintain a slavocracy. The Confederate Constitution does not mandate slavery; not only was slavery not constitutionally mandated, but certain constitutional provisions cleared the way for nonslave states to join the Confederacy. The C.S.A. constitution explicitly establishes a republican form of government and guarantees the same for its member states (Article IV, section 3, clause 4).

The Confederate Constitution can only be appreciated when considered in the context of the simplistic, specious declamations pronounced upon this extremely complex period of American constitutional development. In light of the principles of limited government and the consent of the governed, there is much to be learned from the theories that gave life and death to this American constitution.

Appendix

Constitution of the Confederate States of America

WE, the People of the *Confederate* States, *each State acting in its sovereign and independent character,* in order to form a *permanent federal government,* establish justice, insure domestic tranquillity, and secure the blessings of liberty to ourselves and our posterity—*invoking the favor and guidance of Almighty God*—do ordain and establish this constitution for the *Confederate* States of America.

ARTICLE I.

Section 1.

All legislative powers herein *delegated* shall be vested in a Congress of the *Confederate* States, which shall consist of a Senate and House of Representatives.

Section 2.

1. The House of Representatives shall be composed of members chosen every second year by the people of the several States; and the electors in each State shall *be citizens of the Confederate States, and* have the qualifications requisite for electors of the most numerous branch of the State Legislature; *but no person of foreign birth, not a citizen of the Confederate States, shall be allowed to vote for any officer, civil or political, State or Federal.*

2. No person shall be a Representative who shall not have attained the age of twenty-five years, and *be a citizen of the Confeder-*

The text is taken from the *Journal of the Congress of the Confederate States of America, 1861–1865,* 1:909–24. Portions of the text have been italicized by the author in order to denote noteworthy deviations from the U.S. Constitution.

ate States, and who shall not, when elected, be an inhabitant of that State in which he shall be chosen.

3. Representatives and direct taxes shall be apportioned among the several States, which may be included within this *Confederacy,* according to their respective numbers, which shall be determined by adding to the whole number of free persons, including those bound to service for a term of years, and excluding Indians not taxed, three fifths of all *slaves.* The actual enumeration shall be made within three years after the first meeting of the Congress of the *Confederate* States, and within every subsequent term of ten years, in such manner as they shall by law direct. The number of Representatives shall not exceed one for every *fifty* thousand, but each State shall have at least one Representative; and until such enumeration shall be made, the State of *South Carolina* shall be entitled to choose *six, the State of Georgia ten, the State of Alabama nine, the State of Florida two, the State of Mississippi seven, the State of Louisiana six, and the State of Texas six.*

4. When vacancies happen in the representation from any State, the Executive authority thereof shall issue writs of election to fill such vacancies.

5. The House of Representatives shall choose their Speaker and other officers; and shall have the sole power of impeachment, *except that any judicial or other Federal officer, resident and acting solely within the limits of any State, may be impeached by a vote of two thirds of both branches of the Legislature thereof.*

Section 3.

1. The Senate of the *Confederate* States shall be composed of two Senators from each State, chosen for six years by the Legislature thereof, *at the regular session next immediately preceding the commencement of the term of service;* and each Senator shall have one vote.

2. Immediately after they shall be assembled, in consequence of the first election, they shall be divided as equally as may be into three classes. The seats of the Senators of the first class shall be vacated at the expiration of the second year; of the second class at the expiration of the fourth year; and of the third class at the expiration of the sixth year; so that one third may be chosen every second year; and if vacancies happen by resignation, or otherwise, during the recess of the Legislature of any State, the Executive thereof may make temporary appointments until the next meeting of the Legislature which shall then fill such vacancies.

3. No person shall be a Senator who shall not have attained the age of thirty years, and *be a citizen of the Confederate* States; and who shall not, when elected, be an inhabitant of *the* State for which he shall be chosen.

4. The Vice-President of the *Confederate* States shall be President of the Senate, but shall have no vote unless they be equally divided.

5. The Senate shall choose their other officers; and also a President pro tempore in the absence of the Vice-President, or when he shall exercise the office of President of the *Confederate* States.

6. The Senate shall have the sole power to try all impeachments. When sitting for that purpose, they shall be on oath or affirmation. When the President of the *Confederate* States is tried, the Chief Justice shall preside; and no person shall be convicted without the concurrence of two-thirds of the members present.

7. Judgement in cases of impeachment shall not extend further than to removal from office, and disqualification to hold and enjoy any office of honor, trust, or profit, under the *Confederate* States; but the party convicted shall, nevertheless, be liable and subject to indictment, trial, judgement and punishment according to law.

Section 4.

1. The times, places, and manner of holding elections for Senators and Representatives, shall be prescribed in each State by the Legislature thereof, *subject to the provisions of this Constitution;* but the Congress may, at any time, by law, make or alter such regulations, except as to the *times and* places of choosing Senators.

2. The Congress shall assemble at least once in every year; and such meeting shall be on the first Monday in December, unless they shall, by law, appoint a different day.

Section 5.

1. Each House shall be the judge of the elections, returns, and qualifications of its own members, and a majority of each shall constitute a quorum to do business; but a smaller number may adjourn from day to day, and may be authorized to compel the attendance of absent members, in such manner and under such penalties as each House may provide.

2. Each House may determine the rules of its proceedings, punish its members for disorderly behavior, and, with the concurrence of two-thirds of the whole number, expel a member.

3. Each House shall keep a journal of its proceedings, and from time to time publish the same, excepting such parts as may in their judgment require secrecy; and the yeas and nays of the members of either House, on any question, shall, at the desire of one-fifth of those present, be entered on the journal.

4. Neither House, during the session of Congress, shall, without the consent of the other, adjourn for more than three days, nor to any other place than that in which the two Houses shall be sitting.

Section 6.

1. The Senators and Representatives shall receive a compensation for their services, to be ascertained by law, and paid out of the Treasury of the *Confederate* States. They shall, in all cases, except treason, felony, and breach of the peace, be privileged from arrest during their attendance at the session of their respective Houses, and in going to and returning from the same; and, for any speech or debate in either House, they shall not be questioned in any other place.

2. No Senator or Representative shall, during the time for which he was elected, be appointed to any civil office under the authority of the *Confederate* States, which shall have been created, or the emoluments whereof shall have been increased during such time; and no person holding any office under the *Confederate* States shall be a member of either House during his continuance in office. *But Congress may, by law, grant to the principal officer in each of the executive departments a seat upon the floor of either House, with the privilege of discussing any measures appertaining to his department.*

Section 7.

1. All bills for raising revenue shall originate in the House of Representatives; but the Senate may propose or concur with amendments, as on other bills.

2. Every bill which shall have passed *both Houses,* shall, before it becomes a law, be presented to the President of the *Confederate* States; if he approve, he shall sign it; but if not, he shall return it, with his objections, to that House in which it shall have originated, who shall enter the objections at large on their journal, and proceed to reconsider it. If, after such reconsideration, two-thirds of that House shall agree to pass the bill, it shall be sent, together with the objections, to the other House, by which it shall likewise be recon-

sidered, and, if approved by two-thirds of that House, it shall become a law. But, in all such cases, the votes of both Houses shall be determined by yeas and nays, and the names of the persons voting for and against the bill shall be entered on the journal of each House respectively. If any bill shall not be returned by the President within ten days (Sunday excepted) after it shall have been presented to him, the same shall be a law, in like manner as if he had signed it, unless the Congress, by their adjournment, prevent its return; in which case it shall not be a law. *The President may approve any appropriation and disapprove any other appropriation in the same bill. In such case he shall, in signing the bill, designate the appropriations disapproved; and shall return a copy of such appropriations, with his objections, to the House in which the bill shall have originated; and the same proceedings shall then be had as in case of other bills disapproved by the President.*

3. Every order, resolution, or vote, to which the concurrence of *both Houses* may be necessary (except on a question of adjournment,) shall be presented to the President of the *Confederate* States; and, before the same shall take effect, shall be approved by him; or, being disapproved, shall be re-passed by two-thirds of *both Houses,* according to the rules and limitations prescribed in case of a bill.

Section 8.

The Congress shall have power—

1. To lay and collect taxes, duties, imposts, and excises, *for revenue necessary* to pay the debts, provide for the common defense, *and carry on the Government of the Confederate* States; *but no bounties shall be granted from the Treasury; nor shall any duties or taxes on importations from foreign nations be laid to promote or foster any branch of industry; and all duties, imposts, and excises shall be uniform throughout the Confederate States*:

2. To borrow money on the credit of the *Confederate* States:

3. To regulate commerce with foreign nations, and among the several States, and with the Indian tribes; *but neither this, nor any other clause contained in the Constitution, shall ever be construed to delegate the power to Congress to appropriate money for any internal improvement intended to facilitate commerce; except for the purpose of furnishing lights, beacons, and buoys, and other aid to navigation upon the coasts, and the improvement of harbors and the removing of obstructions in river navigation, in all which cases, such duties shall be laid on the navigation facilitated thereby, as may be necessary to pay the costs and expenses thereof*:

4. To establish uniform *laws* of naturalization, and uniform laws on the subject of bankruptcies, throughout the *Confederate* States; *but no law of Congress shall discharge any debt contracted before the passage of the same*:

5. To coin money, regulate the value thereof, and of foreign coin, and fix the standard of weights and measures:

6. To provide for the punishment of counterfeiting the securities and current coin of the *Confederate* States:

7. To establish post-offices and post *routes; but the expenses of the Post-office Department, after the first day of March, in the year of our Lord eighteen hundred and sixty-three, shall be paid out of its own revenue*:

8. To promote the progress of science and useful arts, by securing for limited times to authors and inventors the exclusive right to their respective writings and discoveries:

9. To constitute tribunals inferior to the Supreme Court:

10. To define and punish piracies and felonies committed on the high-seas, and offenses against the law of nations:

11. To declare war, grant letters of marque and reprisal, and make rules concerning captures on land and on water:

12. To raise and support armies, but no appropriation of money to that use shall be for a longer term than two years:

13. To provide and maintain a navy:

14. To make rules for the government and regulation of the land and naval forces:

15. To provide for calling forth the militia to execute the laws of the *Confederate* States, suppress insurrections, and repel invasions:

16. To provide for organizing, arming, and disciplining the militia, and for governing such part of them as may be employed in the service of the *Confederate* States; reserving to the States, respectively, the appointment of the officers, and the authority of training the militia according to the discipline prescribed by Congress:

17. To exercise exclusive legislation in all cases whatsoever, over such district (not exceeding ten miles square) as may, by cession of *one or more* States, and the acceptance of Congress, become the seat of the Government of the *Confederate* States: and to exercise like authority over all places purchased by the consent of the Legislature of the State in which the same shall be, for the erection of forts, magazines, arsenals, dockyards, and other needful buildings: and

18. To make all laws which shall be necessary and proper for carrying into execution the foregoing powers, and all other powers vested by this Constitution in the Government of the *Confederate* States, or in any department or officer thereof.

Section 9.

1. The importation of *negroes of the African race, from any foreign country other than the slaveholding States or Territories of the United States of America, is hereby forbidden; and Congress is required to pass such laws as shall effectually prevent the same.*

2. *Congress shall also have power to prohibit the introduction of slaves from any State not a member of, or Territory not belonging to, this Confederacy.*

3. The privilege of the writ of habeas corpus shall not be suspended, unless when in cases of rebellion or invasion the public safety may require it.

4. No bill of attainder, ex post facto law, *law denying or impairing the right of property in negro slaves shall be passed.*

5. No capitation or other direct tax shall be laid, unless in proportion to the census or enumeration herein before directed to be taken.

6. No tax or duty shall be laid on articles exported from any State *except by a vote of two thirds of both Houses.*

7. No preference shall be given by any regulation of commerce or revenue to the ports of one State over those of another.

8. No money shall be drawn from the Treasury, but in consequence of appropriations made by law; and a regular statement and account of the receipts and expenditures of all public money shall be published from time to time.

9. *Congress shall appropriate no money from the Treasury, except by a vote of two-thirds of both Houses, taken by yeas and nays, unless it be asked and estimated for by some one of the heads of departments, and submitted to Congress by the President; or for the purpose of paying its own expenses and contingencies; or for the payment of claims against the Confederate States, the justice of which shall have been judicially declared by a tribunal for the investigation of claims against the Government, which it is hereby made the duty of Congress to establish.*

10. *All bills appropriating money shall specify, in Federal currency, the exact amount of each appropriation, and the purposes for which it is made; and Congress shall grant no extra compensation to any public contractor, officer, agent, or servant, after such contract shall have been made or such service rendered.*

11. No title of nobility shall be granted by the *Confederate* States; and no person holding any office of profit or trust under them shall, without the consent of the Congress, accept of any present, emolument, office, or title of any kind whatever, from any king, prince, or foreign state.

12. Congress shall make no law respecting an establishment of religion, or prohibiting the free exercise thereof; or abridging the freedom of speech, or of the press; or the right of the people peaceably to assemble and petition the Government for a redress of grievances.

13. A well-regulated militia being necessary to the security of a free state, the right of the people to keep and bear arms shall not be infringed.

14. No soldier shall, in time of peace, be quartered in any house without the consent of the owner; nor in time of war, but in a manner to be prescribed by law.

15. The right of the people to be secure in their persons, houses, papers, and effects, against unreasonable searches and seizures, shall not be violated; and no warrants shall issue but upon probable cause, supported by oath or affirmation, and particularly describing the place to be searched, and the persons or things to be seized.

16. No person shall be held to answer for a capital or otherwise infamous crime, unless on a presentment or indictment of a grand jury, except in cases arising in the land or naval forces, or in the militia, when in actual service in time of war or public danger; nor shall any person be subject for the same offense, to be twice put in jeopardy of life or limb; nor be compelled, in any criminal case, to be a witness against himself; nor be deprived of life, liberty, or property without due process of law; nor shall private property be taken for public use without just compensation.

17. In all criminal prosecutions, the accused shall enjoy the right to a speedy and public trial, by an impartial jury of the State and district wherein the crime shall have been committed, which district shall have been previously ascertained by law, and to be informed of the nature and cause of the accusation; to be confronted with the witnesses against him; to have compulsory process for obtaining witnesses in his favor; and to have the assistance of counsel for his defense.

18. In suits at common law, where the value in controversy shall exceed twenty dollars, the right of trial by jury shall be preserved; and no fact so tried by a jury shall be otherwise re-examined in any court of the *Confederacy,* than according to the rules of the common law.

19. Excessive bail shall not be required, nor excessive fines imposed, nor cruel and unusual punishment inflicted.

20. *Every law, or resolution having the force of law, shall relate to but one subject, and that shall be expressed in the title.*

Section 10.

1. No State shall enter into any treaty, alliance, or confederation; grant letters of marque and reprisal; coin money; make anything but gold and silver coin a tender in payment of debts; pass any bill of attainder, or ex post facto law, or law impairing the obligation of contracts, or grant any title of nobility.

2. No State shall, without the consent of the Congress, lay any imposts or duties on imports or exports, except what may be absolutely necessary for executing its inspection laws; and the nett produce of all duties and imposts, laid by any State on imports or exports, shall be for the use of the Treasury of the *Confederate* States; and all such laws shall be subject to the revision and control of Congress.

3. No State shall, without the consent of Congress, lay any duty *on tonnage, except on sea-going vessels for the improvement of its rivers and harbors navigated by the said vessels; but such duties shall not conflict with any treaties of the Confederate States with foreign nations. And any surplus revenue thus derived shall, after making such improvement, be paid into the common Treasury;* nor shall any State keep troops or ships-of-war in time of peace, enter into any agreement or compact with another State, or with a foreign power, or engage in war unless actually invaded, or in such imminent danger as will not admit of delay. *But when any river divides or flows through two or more States, they may enter into compacts with each other to improve the navigation thereof.*

ARTICLE II.

Section 1.

1. The Executive power shall be vested in a President of the *Confederate* States of America. *He and the Vice President shall hold their offices for* the term of *six* years; *but the President shall not be reeligible. The President and the Vice-President* shall be elected as follows:

2. Each State shall appoint, in such manner as the Legislature thereof may direct, a number of electors equal to the whole number of Senators and Representatives to which the State may be entitled in the Congress; but no Senator or Representative or person holding an office of trust or profit under the *Confederate* States, shall be appointed an elector.

3. The electors shall meet in their respective States and vote by

ballot for President and Vice President, one of whom, at least, shall not be an inhabitant of the same State with themselves; they shall name in their ballots the person voted for as President, and in distinct ballots the person voted for as Vice-President, and they shall make distinct lists of all persons voted for as President, and of all persons voted for as Vice President, and of the number of votes for each, which list they shall sign and certify, and transmit, sealed, to the seat of the Government of the *Confederate* States, directed to the President of the Senate; the President of the Senate shall, in the presence of the Senate and House of Representatives, open all the certificates, and the votes shall then be counted; the person having the greatest number of votes for President shall be the President, if such number be a majority of the whole number of electors appointed; and if no person have such majority, then from the persons having the highest numbers, not exceeding three, on the list of those voted for as President, the House of Representatives shall choose immediately, by ballot, the President. But in choosing the President, the votes shall be taken by States—the representation from each State having one vote; a quorum for this purpose shall consist of a member or members from two-thirds of the States, and a majority of all the States shall be necessary to a choice. And if the House of Representatives shall not choose a President, whenever the right of choice shall devolve upon them, before the fourth day of March next following, then the Vice-President shall act as President, as in the case of the death, or other constitutional disability of the President.*

4. The person having the greatest number of votes as Vice President, shall be the Vice President, if such number be a majority of the whole number of electors appointed; and if no person have a majority, then from the two highest numbers on the list, the Senate shall choose the Vice President: a quorum for the purpose shall consist of two-thirds of the whole number of Senators, and a majority of the whole number shall be necessary to a choice.

5. But no person constitutionally ineligible to the office of President shall be eligible to that of Vice-President of the *Confederate* States.

6. The Congress may determine the time of choosing the electors, and the day on which they shall give their votes; which day shall be the same throughout the *Confederate* States.

*This section is identical to the Twelfth Amendment to the U.S. Constitution (1804).

7. No person except a natural born citizen of the *Confederate* States, or a citizen thereof at the time of the adoption of this Constitution, *or a citizen thereof born in the United States prior to the 20th of December, 1860,* shall be eligible to the office of President; neither shall any person be eligible to that office who shall not have attained the age of thirty-five years, and been fourteen years a resident within the *limits of the Confederate* States, *as they may exist at the time of his election.*

8. In case of the removal of the President from office, or of his death, resignation, or inability to discharge the powers and duties of the said office, the same shall devolve on the Vice President; and the Congress may, by law, provide for the case of removal, death, resignation, or inability, both of the President and Vice President, declaring what officer shall then act as President; and such officer shall act accordingly, until the disability be removed or a President shall be elected.

9. The President shall, at stated times, receive for his services a compensation, which shall neither be increased nor diminished during the period for which he shall have been elected; and he shall not receive within that period any other emolument from the *Confederate* States, or any of them.

10. Before he enters on the execution of his office, he shall take the following oath or affirmation:

"I do solemnly swear (or affirm) that I will faithfully execute the office of President of the *Confederate* States, and will to the best of my ability, preserve, protect, and defend the Constitution *thereof.*"

Section 2.

1. The President shall be commander-in-chief of the army and navy of the *Confederate* States, and of the militia of the several States, when called into the actual service of the *Confederate* States; he may require the opinion, in writing, of the principal officer in each of the executive departments, upon any subject relating to the duties of their respective offices, and he shall have power to grant reprieves and pardons for offenses against the *Confederate States,* except in cases of impeachment.

2. He shall have power, by and with the advice and consent of the Senate, to make treaties, provided two-thirds of the Senators present concur; and he shall nominate, and by and with the advice and consent of the Senate, shall appoint ambassadors, other public ministers and consuls, judges of the Supreme Court, and all other

officers of the *Confederate* States, whose appointments are not herein otherwise provided for, and which shall be established by law; but the Congress may, by law, vest the appointment of such inferior officers, as they think proper, in the President alone, in the courts of law, or in the heads of departments.

3. *The principal officer in each of the executive departments, and all persons connected with the diplomatic service, may be removed from office at the pleasure of the President. All other civil officers of the executive department may be removed at any time by the President, or other appointing power, when their services are unnecessary, or for dishonesty, incapacity, inefficiency, misconduct, or neglect of duty; and, when so removed, the removal shall be reported to the Senate, together with the reasons therefor.*

4. The President shall have power to fill up all vacancies that may happen during the recess of the Senate, by granting commissions which shall expire at the end of their next session. *But no person rejected by the Senate shall be reappointed to the same office during their ensuing recess.*

Section 3.

1. *The President* shall, from time to time, give to the Congress information of the state of the *Confederacy,* and recommend to their consideration such measures as he shall judge necessary and expedient; he may on extraordinary occasions, convene both Houses, or either of them; and in case of disagreement between them, with respect to the time of adjournment, he may adjourn them to such time as he shall think proper; he shall receive ambassadors and other public ministers; he shall take care that the laws be faithfully executed, and shall commission all the officers of the *Confederate* States.

Section 4.

1. The President, Vice President, and all civil officers of the *Confederate* States, shall be removed from office on impeachment for and conviction of, treason, bribery, or other high crimes and misdemeanors.

ARTICLE III.

Section 1.

1. The judicial power of the *Confederate* States shall be vested in one Supreme Court, and in such inferior courts as the Congress may, from time to time, ordain and establish. The Judges, both of the Supreme and inferior Courts, shall hold their offices during good behavior, and shall, at stated times, receive for their services a compensation which shall not be diminished during their continuance in office.

Section 2.

1. The judicial power shall extend to all cases arising under this Constitution, the laws of the *Confederate* States, and treaties made, or which shall be made, under their authority; to all cases affecting ambassadors, other public ministers and consuls; to all cases of admiralty and maritime jurisdiction; to controversies to which the *Confederate* States shall be a party; to controversies between two or more States; between a State and citizens of another State, *where the State is plaintiff;* between citizens claiming lands under grants of different States; and between a State or the citizens thereof, and foreign states, citizens, or subjects; *but no State shall be sued by a citizen or subject of any foreign state.*

2. In all cases affecting ambassadors, other public ministers and consuls, and those in which a State shall be party, the Supreme Court shall have original jurisdiction. In all the other cases before mentioned, the Supreme Court shall have appellate jurisdiction both as to law and fact, with such exceptions and under such regulations as the Congress shall make.

3. The trial of all crimes, except in cases of impeachment, shall be by jury, and such trial shall be held in the State where the said crimes shall have been committed; but when not committed within any State the trial shall be at such place or places as the Congress may by law have directed.

Section 3.

1. Treason against the *Confederate* States shall consist only in levying war against them, or in adhering to their enemies, giving them aid and comfort. No person shall be convicted of treason unless on

the testimony of two witnesses to the same overt act, or on confession in open court.

2. The Congress shall have power to declare the punishment of treason; but no attainder of treason shall work corruption of blood, or forfeiture, except during the life of the person attainted.

ARTICLE IV.

Section 1.

1. Full faith and credit shall be given in each State to the public acts, records, and judicial proceedings of every other State. And the Congress may, by general laws, prescribe the manner in which such acts, records, and proceedings shall be proved, and the effect thereof.

Section 2.

1. The citizens of each State shall be entitled to all the privileges and immunities of citizens in the several States, *and shall have the right of transit and sojourn in any State of this Confederacy, with their slaves and other property; and the right of property in said slaves shall not be thereby impaired.*

2. A person charged in any State with treason, felony, or other crime *against the laws of such State,* who shall flee from justice, and be found in another State, shall on demand of the executive authority of the State from which he fled, be delivered up, to be removed to the State having jurisdiction of the crime.

3. *No slave or other* person held to service or labor *in any State or Territory of the Confederate States,* under the laws-thereof, escaping *or lawfully carried* into another, shall, in consequence of any law or regulation therein, be discharged from such service or labor: but shall be delivered up on claim of the party *to whom such slave belongs, or* to whom such service or labor may be due.

Section 3.

1. *Other States may be admitted into this Confederacy by a vote of two thirds of the whole House of Representatives and two thirds of the Senate, the Senate voting by States;* but no new State shall be formed or erected within the jurisdiction of any other State; nor any State be formed by the junction of two or more States, or parts of States,

without the consent of the legislatures of the States concerned, as well as of the Congress.

2. The Congress shall have power to dispose of and make all needful rules and regulations *concerning* the *property of the Confederate* States, *including the lands thereof.*

3. *The Confederate States may acquire new territory; and Congress shall have power to legislate and provide governments for the inhabitants of all territory belonging to the Confederate States, lying without the limits of the several States; and may permit them, at such times, and in such manner as it may by law provide, to form States to be admitted into the Confederacy. In all such territory, the institution of negro slavery, as it now exists in the Confederate States, shall be recognized and protected by Congress and by the territorial government; and the inhabitants of the several Confederate States and Territories shall have the right to take to such Territory any slaves lawfully held by them in any of the States or Territories of the Confederate States.*

4. The *Confederate* States shall guarantee to every State *that now is, or hereafter may become, a member of this Confederacy,* a republican form of government; and shall protect each of them against invasion; and on application of the legislature (or of the Executive when the legislature *is not in session,*) against domestic violence.

ARTICLE V.

Section 1.

1. *Upon the demand of any three States, legally assembled in their several conventions, the Congress shall summon a Convention of all the States, to take into consideration such amendments to the Constitution as the said States shall concur in suggesting at the time when the said demand is made; and should any of the proposed amendments to the Constitution be agreed on by the said Convention—voting by States—and the same be ratified by the Legislatures of two thirds of the several States, or by conventions in two-thirds thereof*—as the one or the other mode of ratification may be proposed by the *general Convention—they shall thence forward form a part of this Constitution. But* no State shall, without its consent, be deprived of its equal *representation* in the Senate.

ARTICLE VI.

1. *The Government established by this Constitution is the successor of the Provisional Government of the Confederate States of America, and all*

the laws passed by the latter shall continue in force until the same shall be repealed or modified; and all the officers appointed by the same shall remain in office until their successors are appointed and qualified, or the offices abolished.

2. All debts contracted and engagements entered into before the adoption of this Constitution shall be as valid against the *Confederate* States under this Constitution, as under the *Provisional Government.*

3. This Constitution, and the laws of the *Confederate* States made in pursuance thereof, and all treaties made, or which shall be made, under the authority of the *Confederate* States, shall be the supreme law of the land; and the Judges in every State shall be bound thereby, anything in the Constitution or laws of any State to the contrary notwithstanding.

4. The Senators and Representatives before mentioned, and the members of the several State Legislatures, and all executive and judicial officers, both of the *Confederate* States and of the several States, shall be bound by oath or affirmation to support this Constitution; but no religious test shall ever be required as a qualification to any office or public trust under the *Confederate* States.

5. The enumeration, in the Constitution, of certain rights, shall not be construed to deny or disparage others retained by the people *of the several States.*

6. The powers not delegated to the *Confederate* States by the Constitution, nor prohibited by it to the States, are reserved to the States, respectively, or to the people *thereof.*

ARTICLE VII.

1. The ratification of the conventions of *five* States shall be sufficient for the establishment of this Constitution between the States so ratifying the same.

2. *When five States shall have ratified this Constitution, in the manner before specified, the Congress under the Provisional Constitution shall prescribe the time for holding the election of President and Vice President; and for the meeting of the Electoral College; and for counting the votes, and inaugurating the President. They shall, also, prescribe the time for holding the first election of members of Congress under this Constitution, and the time for assembling the same. Until the assembling of such Congress, the Congress under the Provisional Constitution shall continue to exercise the legislative powers granted them; not extending beyond the time limited by the Constitution of the Provisional Government.*

Adopted unanimously by the Congress of the Confederate States of South Carolina, Georgia, Florida, Alabama, Mississippi, Louisiana and Texas, sitting in Convention at the capitol, in the city of Montgomery, Alabama, on the Eleventh day of March, in the year Eighteen Hundred and Sixty-One.

Howell Cobb, President of the Congress.

South Carolina.—R. Barnwell Rhett, C. G. Memminger, Wm. Porcher Miles, James Chestnut, Jr., R. W. Barnwell, William W. Boyce, Lawrence M. Keitt, T. J. Withers.

Georgia.—Francis S. Bartow, Martin J. Crawford, Benjamin H. Hill, Thos. R. R. Cobb.

Florida.—Jackson Morton, J. Patton Anderson, Jas. B. Owens.

Alabama.—Richard W. Walker, Robt. H. Smith, Colin J. McRae, William P. Chilton, Stephen F. Hale, David P. Lewis, Tho. Fearn, Jno. Gill Shorter, J. L. M. Curry.

Mississippi.—Alex. M. Clayton, James T. Harrison, William S. Barry, W. S. Wilson, Walker Brooke, W. P. Harris, J. A. P. Campbell.

Louisiana.—Alex. De Clouet, C. M. Conrad, Duncan F. Kenner, Henry Marshall.

Texas.—John Hemphill, Thomas N. Waul, John H. Reagan, Williamson S. Oldham, Louis T. Wigfall, John Gregg, William Beck Ochiltree.

Notes

Introduction

1. Frank Moore, ed., *The Rebellion Record: A Diary of American Events* (New York: G. P. Putnam, 1866), 2:277. In the same speech, Stephens claimed that "soon after the Constitution was formed, a large party in the North commenced, as I have said, by construction, to torture and twist the Constitution from its proper and legitimate meaning. . . . It is enough to say it ripened within the last few years, and came to maturity under the organization of that party now in power—that party which now has the destiny of the United States in its hands—known as the Republican party."

2. 1st Confederate Congress, 1st sess., preamble to Resolution no. 2, March 11, 1862.

3. See Louis Hartz, *The Liberal Tradition in America: An Interpretation of American Political Thought Since the Revolution* (New York: Harcourt, Brace & World, 1955), 145–200.

4. Gettysburg Address, 1863.

5. Bernard Bailyn, *The Ordeal of Thomas Hutchinson* (Cambridge: Harvard University Press, 1974), viii–ix.

Chapter One. Deconstructing the Constitution

1. Publius makes the following distinction:

> In a single republic, all the power surrendered by the people is submitted to the administration of a single government; and the usurpations are guarded against by a division of the government into distinct and separate departments. In the compound republic of America, the power surrendered by the people is first divided between two distinct governments, and then the portion allotted to each subdivided among distinct and separate departments. Hence a double security arises to the rights of the people. The different governments will control each other, at the same time that each will be controlled by itself. (James Madison, Alexander Hamilton, and John Jay, *The Federalist Papers*, ed. Clinton Rossiter [New York: New American Library, 1961], 323; hereafter, Madison et al. will be referred to in the text by their collective pseudonym, Publius.)

2. Ibid., no. 37, p. 229.
3. *Congressional Globe*, 31st Cong., 1st sess., 1850, p. 452.
4. Ibid., 451–52.
5. Ibid., appendix: 264, 265, 269.
6. Ibid., appendix: 264.
7. Ibid., 262, 263, 265.
8. Ibid., 265; 34th Cong., 1st sess., 1856, appendix: 405.
9. See Benjamin Fletcher Wright, *American Interpretations of Natural Law: A Study in the History of Political Thought* (New York: Russell & Russell, 1962), 172, 210–41. Seward and other like-minded Republicans elevated the Declaration of Indepen-

dence to constitutional status. The elevation of the Declaration reached its apex in Lincoln's Gettysburg Address, which has been instrumental in derailing the principles of the Constitution. See Willmoore Kendall and George Carey, "The Declaration of Independence: A Derailment?" in *The Basic Symbols of the American Political Tradition* (Baton Rouge: Louisiana State University Press, 1970), 75–95.

10. At the Republican State Convention in 1858, Lincoln proclaimed that "A house divided against itself cannot stand. I believe this government cannot endure permanently half slave and half free. I do not expect the Union to be dissolved; I do not expect the house to fall; but I do expect that it will cease to be divided. It will become all one thing, or all the other. Either the opponents of slavery will arrest the spread of it, and place it where the public mind shall rest in the belief that it is in the course of ultimate extinction, or its advocates will push it forward till it shall become alike lawful in all of the States, old as well as new, North as well as South" (Henry Steele Commager, ed., *Documents of American History*, 2 vols., 8th ed. [New York: Appleton-Century-Crofts, 1968], 1:345).

The extent to which Northern congressional leaders were actually committed to the equality of blacks and whites is uncertain. There is ample evidence that Republican leaders were playing the "slavery card" as a means to gain political ascendancy over Northern Democrats and Whigs. Nevertheless, the fact that such ascendancy was achieved is evidence that inherent in Northern political culture at the general electorate level was the commitment to demolish the caste social system of the South and subsequently initiate some vague policy of equality between whites and blacks. For an insightful account of early antebellum social conditions see Alexis De Tocqueville, *Democracy in America*, 2 vols. (New York: Schocken Books, 1974), 1:1–47.

11. *Congressional Globe*, 34th Cong., 1st sess., p. 5. The constitutionality of the law of comity is expressed in Article IV, section 2, of the U.S. Constitution: "The citizens of each State shall be entitled to all Privileges and Immunities of Citizens in the several States." According to the circuit court case of *Corfield* v. *Coryell*, 1823, "privileges and immunities, and the enjoyment of them by citizens of each state, was manifestly calculated (to use the expressions of the preamble of the old Articles of Confederation) 'the better to secure and perpetuate mutual friendship and intercourse among the people of the different States of the Union'" (6 Fed. Cas. No. 3230, Circuit Court, E.D., 1823, p. 552). Such being the case, it is significant that the fugitive slave provision is found in the same section of Article IV; obviously, the framers of the Constitution were cognizant of the linkage.

12. *Congressional Globe*, 34th Cong., 1st sess., 1856, appendix: 401, 485.

13. See Kirk H. Porter and Donald Bruce Johnson, comps., *National Party Platforms, 1840–1956* (Urbana: University of Illinois Press, 1856), 27–28; *Congressional Globe*, 35th Cong., 1st sess., 1858, p. 148.

14. Ibid., 146; 31st Cong., 1st sess., 1850, appendix: 269.

15. Ibid., 36th Cong., 1st sess., 1860, pp. 910–14. Senator Stephen A. Douglas lost no time in bringing Seward's rhetorical maneuvering to the attention of the Senate (ibid., 914–16).

16. Ibid., 2d sess., 1861, p. 341.

17. Ibid., 486, 487.

18. Jesse T. Carpenter, *The South as a Conscious Minority, 1789–1861* (New York: New York University Press, 1930), 224.

Chapter Two. John C. Calhoun, the Confederate Phoenix

1. Aristotle, *The Politics of Aristotle*, trans. and ed. Ernest Barker (New York: Oxford University Press, 1978), 110.

2. See "South Carolina Ordinance of Nullification, November 24, 1832" and "Jackson's Proclamation to the People of South Carolina, December 10, 1832," in Henry Steele Commager, ed., *Documents of American History*, 2 vols., 8th ed. (New York: Appleton-Century-Crofts, 1968), 1:261–68.

3. "The Essays of 'Brutus' to the Citizens of the State of New York," in Michael Kammen, ed., *The Origins of the American Constitution: A Documentary History* (New York: Penguin Books, 1986), 340.

4. Baron De Montesquieu, *The Spirit of the Laws*, 2 vols., trans. Thomas Nugent (New York: Hafner, 1949), 1:316–30. Both the U.S. and the C.S.A. framers championed the establishment of commercial republics, which were to be fostered and secured by their respective governments. See James Madison, Alexander Hamilton, and John Jay, *The Federalist Papers*, ed. Clinton Rossiter (New York: New American Library, 1961), 11, 22, and 6. On the Confederate side, see T. R. R. Cobb, *Substance of an Address of T. R. R. Cobb, to His Constituents of Clark County, April 6th, 1861*, and Jefferson Davis's *Inaugural Address of the President of the Provisional Government*, in James D. Richardson, ed., *A Compilation of the Messages and Papers of the Confederacy* (Nashville: United States Publishing Company, 1906), 1:32–36. In reference to the admission of California into the Union, Senator William Seward maintained that "commerce is the god of boundaries, and no man living can foretell his ultimate decree" (*Congressional Globe*, 31st Cong., 1st sess., 1850, appendix: 262).

5. *Federalist Papers*, no. 10, p. 79.

6. A. L. Hull, "The Making of the Confederate Constitution," *Southern Historical Society Papers* 28 (1900): 291.

7. "Kentucky Resolutions, November 16, 1798," in *Documents of American History*, 1:178–79. Dissatisfied with state responses to their statement of principles, the Kentucky legislature issued a reiteration in 1799 with the qualification that nullification was a state option in redressing transgressions against the U.S. Constitution (183–84).

8. See Article VI, section 3, C.S.A. Constitution, and Article VI, section 2, U.S. Constitution.

9. See appendix, herein.

10. Calhoun is justifiably utilized in this manner; he was the recognized theoretical leader of the South generally, and the vindicator of states' rights particularly. To wit:

> Mr. Calhoun held that it (the Union) could be maintained and perpetuated consistently with the preservation of Constitutional liberty only on the principle of the recognition of the ultimate sovereign rights of the States. These doctrines he advocated with an earnestness which showed the sound convictions of his judgement as well as his fearful apprehensions from the ascendancy of opposite principles. . . . Amongst the many great men with whom he was associated, Mr. Calhoun was by far the most philosophical statesman of them all. Indeed, with the exception of Mr. Jefferson, it may be questioned if in this respect the United States has ever produced his superior. Government he considered a science, and in its study his whole soul was absorbed. His treatise on the Constitution of the United States is the best that was ever penned on that subject, and his *Disquisition on Government* generally is one of the few books of this age, that will outlive the language in which it was written. (Alexander H. Stephens, *The War between the States*, 2 vols. [Philadelphia: National Publishing Company, 1868], 1:340–41)

According to Jefferson Davis:

> It was during the progress of these memorable controversies that the South lost its most trusted leader, and the Senate its purest and greatest statesman. He

was taken from us 'Like a summer dried fountain, when our need was the sorest'; when his intellectual power, and his devotion to the Constitution, might have diverted collision; or, failing in that, he might have been to the South the Palinurus to steer the bark in safety over the perilous sea. Truly did Mr. Webster—his personal friend, although his greatest political rival—say of him in his obituary address, 'There was nothing groveling, or low, or meanly selfish, that came near the head or heart of Mr. Calhoun.' His prophetic warnings speak from the grave with the wisdom of inspiration. Would that they could have been appreciated by his countrymen while yet he lived. (Jefferson Davis, *The Rise and Fall of the Confederate Government*, 2 vols. [New York: D. Appleton and Company, 1881], 1:17)

From a Northern perspective, John Motley wrote:

And yet, with hardly a superficial examination of our history and our Constitution, men talk glibly about a confederacy, a compact, a co-partnership, and the right of a State to secede at pleasure, not knowing that, by admitting such loose phraseology and such imaginary rights, we should violate the first principles of our political organization, should fly in the face of our history, should trample underfoot the teachings of Jay, Hamilton, Washington, Marshall, Madison, Dane, Kent, Story, and Webster, and accepting only the dogmas of Mr. Calhoun as infallible, surrender forever our national laws and our national existence. (Frank Moore, ed., *The Rebellion Record: A Diary of American Events* [New York: G. P. Putnam, 1861], 1:214)

And on May 29, 1860, Congressman James M. Ashley of Ohio remarked that the South was "trained in the disunion school of Calhoun," in a speech titled "The Success of the Calhoun Revolution" (*Congressional Globe*, 36th Cong., 1st sess., 1860, pp. 365–78); also see Senator James R. Doolittle's speech of January 3, 1869, titled "The Calhoun Revolution: Its Basis and Its Progress" (97). The relevance of *The Federalist Papers* in American constitutional theory is well known and need not be repeated here.

11. See Max Farrand, ed., *The Records of the Federal Convention of 1787*, 4 vols. (New Haven: Yale University Press, 1911), 3:195; and Herbert J. Storing, *What the Anti-Federalists Were For* (Chicago: University of Chicago Press, 1981).

12. *Federalist Papers*, no. 22, pp. 147–48.

13. Ibid., no. 10, p. 83; no. 33, p. 205.

14. John C. Calhoun, "A Disquisition On Government," in *Calhoun: Basic Documents*, ed. John M. Anderson (State College, Pa.: Bald Eagle Press, 1952), 29–30.

15. *Politics of Aristotle*, 6–7. As the slavery controversy intensified, Calhoun was on a regular basis derisively referred to as an Aristotelian by the opponents of slavery and advocates of the natural rights of all men, white and black.

16. Calhoun, *Calhoun: Basic Documents*, 31. Calhoun's refutation of the state of nature is contrary to Publius's acknowledgment of its validity (See *Federalist Papers*, no. 51, pp. 324–25).

17. Calhoun, *Calhoun: Basic Documents*, 31. Calhoun's conceptualization of government's function is Lockean. Admittedly, Calhoun rejected Locke's concocted state of nature, but Calhoun would have no difficulty with Locke's conclusion that "the great and chief end, therefore, of men's uniting into commonwealths and putting themselves under government is the preservation of their property. To which in the state of nature there are many things wanting" (see John Locke, "The Second Treatise of Civil Government," in *Two Treatises of Government*, ed. Thomas I. Cook [New York: Hafner Press, 1947], 184).

18. Calhoun, *Calhoun: Basic Documents*, 63.

19. Ibid., 63, 36.

20. *Federalist Papers*, no. 11, p. 87; Calhoun, *Calhoun: Basic Documents*, 84, 86. Calhoun maintained:

> When the causes now in operation have produced their full effect, and inventions and discoveries shall have been exhausted—if that ever may be,—they will give a force to public opinion, and cause changes, political and social, difficult to be anticipated. What will be their final bearing, time can only decide with any certainty. That they will, however, greatly improve the condition of man ultimately,—it would be impious to doubt. It would be to suppose, that the all-wise and beneficent Being,—the Creator of all—had so constituted man, as that the employment of high intellectual faculties, with which He has been pleased to endow him, in order that he might develop the laws that control the great agents of the material world, and make them subservient to his use—would prove to him the cause of permanent evil, —and not of permanent good. If, then, such a supposition be inadmissible, they must in their orderly and full development, end in his permanent good. (85–86)

21. Calhoun, *Calhoun: Basic Documents*, 61, 35; *Federalist Papers*, no. 7, p. 62.

22. Ibid., no. 9, p. 73; no. 8, p. 71; no. 9, p. 76;

23. Ibid., no. 6, p. 54; no. 9, p. 71; no. 11, p. 9; Publius unequivocally states his intention to establish an American commercial empire. See no. 14, p. 103; no. 22, p. 152; no. 23, p. 157, and no. 28, p. 182.

24. Ibid., no. 15, p. 110.

25. Ibid., no. 15, pp. 110, 109, 108.

26. Commager, ed., *Documents of American History*, 268.

27. Calhoun, *Calhoun: Basic Documents*, 20, 36, 44. For Calhoun, the states were the organisms that could effectively protect the ruled (i.e., citizens within their respective states) from oppressive national rulers (36).

28. *Federalist Papers*, no. 51, p. 322.

29. Calhoun, *Calhoun: Basic Documents*, 48, 36.

30. *Federalist Papers*, no. 10, p. 79.

31. Calhoun, *Calhoun: Basic Documents*, 40–41. By 1833, Calhoun was speaking in terms of two great sections, Northern and Southern. See Calhoun's speech on the Force Bill, February 15–16, 1833. Concerning this Senate speech, Jefferson Davis wrote, "If a young man should ask me where he could in condensed form, get the best understanding of the institutions and duties of an American patriot, I would answer in Calhoun's speech in the Senate on what is known as The Force Bill" (Jefferson Davis, *The Life and Character of the Honorable John Caldwell Calhoun*).

32. *Rebellion Record*, 1:4.

33. John C. Calhoun, "A Discourse on the Constitution and Government of the United States," in *The Works of John C. Calhoun*, ed. Richard K. Cralle (New York: D. Appleton and Co., 1851–1856), 1:187.

34. Two excellent books about this critical period are Gordon S. Wood's *The Creation of the American Republic, 1776–1787* (New York: The Norton Library, 1969) and Forrest McDonald's *Novus Ordo Seclorum* (Lawrence: University Press of Kansas, 1985).

35. Farrand, ed., *Records of the Federal Convention of 1787*, 1:249. The significant difference between the two plans were concisely stated by James Wilson.

> Virginia Plan proposes two branches in the legislature. Jersey a single legislative body. Virginia, the legislative powers derived from the people. Jersey, from the states. Virginia, a single executive. Jersey, more than one. Virginia, a majority of the legislature can act. Jersey, a small minority can control. Virginia, the legislature can legislate on all national concerns. Jersey, only on limited objects. Virginia, can negative all state laws. Jersey, giving power to the executive to compel obedience by force. Virginia, to remove the executive by

impeachment. Jersey, on application of a majority of states. Virginia, for the establishment of inferior judiciary tribunals. Jersey, no provision. (1:260)

36. Ibid., 1:291–93. Hamilton did not specify the procedure for selecting the justices; obviously, they were not to be elected officials.

37. Ibid., 1:286; *Federalist Papers*, no. 3, p. 41.

38. Calhoun, "A Discourse," in *Works of John C. Calhoun*, ed. Cralle, 1:340–41.

39. *Federalist Papers*, no. 15, p. 108; no. 39, passim.

40. Calhoun, "A Discourse," in *Works of John C. Calhoun*, ed. Cralle, 1:146. Calhoun referred to *The Federalist* (i.e., Publius) as "contradictory throughout" and specifically singled out *Federalist Papers*, nos. 39 and 40 (see ibid., 1:150–52).

Chapter Three. Federalism and Popular Sovereignty

1. Italics added. See appendix, herein. Of course, the Ninth and Tenth amendments to the U.S. Constitution were not originally a part of the document. But the Constitution was ratified with the expectation that amendments such as these would be added within the not too distant future. (Publius's arguments against the inclusion of a bill of rights is addressed in chap. 4, herein).

2. John C. Calhoun, "A Discourse on the Constitution and Government of the United States," in *The Works of John C. Calhoun*, ed. Richard Cralle (New York: D. Appleton and Company, 1856), 1:130.

3. Frank Moore, ed., *The Rebellion Record: A Diary of American Events* (New York: G. P. Putnam, 1861–1866), 1:3.

4. *Journal of the Congress of the Confederate States of America, 1861–1865*, 7 vols. (Washington, D.C.: Government Printing Office, 1904–1905), 1:888.

5. *Congressional Globe*, 36th Congress, 1st Sess., appendix: 67. As early as 1798, the phrase "several States" did not connote a consolidation of states. As mentioned earlier, the Kentucky and Virginia resolutions stated that "the several States composing the United States, are not united on the principles of unlimited submission to the General Government."

6. James Madison, Alexander Hamilton, and John Jay, *The Federalist Papers*, ed. Clinton Rossiter (New York: New American Library, 1961), no. 11, p. 90.

7. "Each state retains its sovereignty, freedom and independence, and every Power, Jurisdiction and rights, which is not by this confederation expressly delegated to the United States, in Congress assembled" (Article II, Articles of Confederation, ratified and in force on March 1, 1781. In Henry Steele Commager, ed., *Documents of American History*, 2 vols., 8th ed. [New York: Appleton-Century-Crofts, 1968], 1:111).

8. *Federalist Papers*, no. 21, pp. 138–39; no. 11, p. 91.

9. *Journal of the Congress of the Confederate States* 1:7.

10. Calhoun, "A Discourse," in *Works of John C. Calhoun*, ed. Cralle, 1:276.

11. See appendix, herein.

12. Moore, ed., *Rebellion Record*, 1:3. Once again, compare this to the Kentucky and Virginia resolutions, which state that "the Government created by this compact was not made the exclusive or final judge of the extent of the powers delegated to itself; . . . but in all other cases of compact among parties having no common Judge, each party has an equal right to judge for itself, as well of infractions as of the mode and measure of redress" (Commager, ed., *Documents of American History*, 1:178–79).

13. *Federalist Papers*, no. 44, p. 287.

14. In his speech on the Revenue Collection Bill (known as the Force Bill), February, 1833, Calhoun analyzed the various interests and how they are organized. His reference to "sovereign political bodies" is synonymous with states (see John C.

Calhoun, *Calhoun: Basic Documents*, ed. John M. Anderson [State College, Pa.: Bald Eagle Press, 1952], 155).

15. Ibid., 45.

16. Ibid., 29.

17. "By a faction I understand a number of citizens, whether amounting to a majority or minority of the whole, who are united and actuated by some common impulse of passion, or of interests, adverse to the rights of other citizens, or to the permanent and aggregate interests of the community" (*Federalist Papers*, no. 10, p. 78, which also provides a concise explication of the extended republic).

18. Ibid., no. 10, p. 83; Calhoun, *Calhoun: Basic Documents*, 38–39.

19. Ibid., 39. Regarding the homogeneous community, Calhoun contended:

> However small the community may be, and however homogeneous its interests, the moment the Government is put into operation, as soon as it begins to collect taxes, and to make appropriations, the different portions of the community must, of necessity, bear different and opposing relations in reference to the action of the Government. There must inevitably spring up two interests— a direction and stockholder interest; an interest profiting by the action of the Government, and interested in increasing its powers and action; and another at whose expense the political machine is kept in motion. (ibid., 176)

The states are also subject to this basic division into "two interests," but the division is aggravated at the national level because of its increased heterogeneity. Publius acknowledged this distinction when he wrote, "Extend the sphere and you take in a greater variety of parties and interests" (*Federalist Papers*, no. 10, p. 83).

20. *Federalist Papers*, no. 10, p. 80; Calhoun, *Calhoun: Basic Documents*, 48.

21. Ibid., 48–50; *Federalist Papers*, no. 45, pp. 292–93.

22. Ibid., no. 33, p. 204. Within the context of no. 33, Hamilton was obviously using "political societies" synonymously with states, and "political society" with national government (201–5). In the convention debates, Edmund Randolph advocated that "all laws to the particular States contrary to the Constitution or laws of the United States to be utterly void; and the better to prevent such laws from being passed, the Governor or President of each State shall be appointed by the General Government and shall have a negative upon the laws about to be passed in the State of which he is Governor or President" (Max Farrand, ed., *The Records of the Federal Convention of 1787*, 4 vols. [New Haven: Yale University Press, 1911], 1:293).

23. Calhoun, *The Works of John C. Calhoun*, ed. Cralle, 1:124, 145.

24. *Federalist Papers*, no. 51, 321–22.

25. Ibid., no. 10, pp. 78, 79, and passim.

26. This is similar to Adam Smith's notion of the "invisible hand" in the distribution of resources.

> As every individual, therefore, endeavors as much as he can both to employ his capital in the support of his domestic industry, and so to direct that industry that its produce may be of the greatest value; as every individual necessarily labors to render the annual revenue of the society as great as he can. He generally, indeed, neither intends to promote the public interest, nor knows how much he is in this, as in many other cases, led by an invisible hand to promote an end which was no part of his intention. (Adam Smith, *An Inquiry into the Nature and Causes of the Wealth of Nations*, ed. Edwin Cannan [Chicago: The University of Chicago Press, 1976], 477–78)

27. *Federalist Papers*, no. 10, p. 79.

28. Calhoun, *Calhoun: Basic Documents*, 47, 48, 49. Northern declamations against the enforcement of the fugitive slave laws and their contentions against the *Dred Scott* v. *Sandford* Supreme Court decision, as well as the emergence in the 1850s of

the sectional two-party system, substantiated, from a Southern perspective, Calhoun's warnings.

29. Moore, ed., *Rebellion Record*, 1:37.

30. J. K. Paulding, *State Sovereignty and the Doctrine of Coercion*, Charleston, 1860, pp. 6, 28.

31. *Journal of the Congress of the Confederate States* 1:8. During the debates on the Constitution, there was a proposed amendment that would have made explicit the constitutionality of secession; however, the amendment was tabled with apparently little controversy.

32. Jefferson Davis, *The Rise and Fall of the Confederate Government*, 2 vols. (New York: D. Appleton and Company, 1881), 1:172–73.

33. Daniel J. Elazar and John Kincaid, eds., *Covenant, Polity, and Constitutionalism* (New York: University Press of America, 1980), 11. At a crucial moment during the secession crisis, President-elect Lincoln chose to deemphasize this quality of the U.S. Constitution when, in his March 4, 1861, inaugural address, he confronted the South with the following challenge: "All profess to be content in the Union, if all constitutional rights can be maintained. Is it true, then, that any right, plainly written in the Constitution, has been denied? I think not. Happily the human mind is so constituted that no party can reach to the audacity of doing this. Think, if you can, of a single instance, in which a plainly written provision of the Constitution has ever been denied" (*Congressional Globe*, Vol. 30, March 4, 1861, 1434). Of course, many secessionists would answer in the affirmative; nevertheless, what is significant is Lincoln's reliance upon "what is plainly written in the Constitution" in contradistinction to the implied constitutional powers that are more closely linked to the good faith of the parties as embodied in the unwritten assumptions implicit in the document.

34. See appendix herein. A. L. Hull, "The Making of the Confederate Constitution," *Southern Historical Society Papers* 28 (1900): 291.

35. Cf. *Federalist Papers*, no. 10, p. 79.

36. Ibid., no. 51, p. 324; no. 10, p. 78. Publius was reiterating the Lockean position:

> The commonwealth seems to me to be a society of men constituted only for the procuring, preserving, and advancing their own civil interests. Civil interests I call life, liberty, health, and indolency of body; the possession of outward things, such as money, lands, houses, furniture, and the like. . . . Now that the whole jurisdiction of the magistrate reaches only to these civil concernments, and that all civil power, right, and dominion, is bounded and confined to the only care of promoting these things; and that it neither can nor ought in any manner to be extended to the salvation of souls. (John Locke, "A Letter Concerning Toleration," in *"The Second Treatise of Civil Government" and "A Letter Concerning Toleration,"* ed. J. W. Gough [Oxford: Basil Blackwell, 1946], 126–27).

37. Clement Eaton, *The Mind of the Old South* (Baton Rouge: Louisiana State University Press, 1964), 158–80.

38. T. R. R. Cobb, *Substance of an Address of T. R. R. Cobb, to His Constituents of Clark County, April 6th. 1861*, in James D. Richardson, ed., *A Compilation of the Messages and Papers of the Confederacy* (Nashville: United States Publishing Company, 1906), 1:32, 34, 36, 4, 7.

39. Ulrich Bonnell Phillips, ed., *The Correspondence of Robert Toombs, Alexander H. Stephens, and Howell Cobb* (New York: Da Capo Press, 1970), 555.

40. Richardson, ed., *Compilation*, 1:32, 34, 36.

41. This is not to imply that the Northern states were not experiencing a similar religious awakening during the same period. Their dogmatic denunciations of slav-

ery and adherence to "higher law" doctrine are two manifestations of a similar experience.

42. *Federalist Papers*, no. 33, p. 204.

Chapter Four. The Bill of Rights

1. See Irving Brant, *The Bill of Rights: Its Origin and Meaning* (New York: New American Library, 1965), 11–22.

2. Rhode Island was, nevertheless, committed to a declaration of rights applicable to the national government. As a matter of fact, in its document of ratification it proposed twenty-one amendments to the U.S. Constitution (see Jonathan Elliot, ed., *The Debates in the Several State Conventions on the Adoption of the Federal Constitution*, 5 vols. [Washington, D.C.: Taylor and Maury, 1854], 1:336–37). In 1787, the Charter of 1663 was Rhode Island's fundamental document. It was later superseded by the Rhode Island Constitution of 1842, which did contain a declaration of rights (see Benjamin P. Poore, ed., *The Federal and State Constitutions, Colonial Charters, and Other Organic Laws of the United States*, 2 vols. (Washington, D.C.: Government Printing Office, 1877), 1594–1614.

3. Those states are Massachusetts, New Hampshire, New York, and Rhode Island. See Elliot, ed., *Debates*, 1:322–37.

4. Poore, *Federal and State Constitutions*, 1908–9.

5. James Madison, Alexander Hamilton, and John Jay, *The Federalist Papers*, ed. Clinton Rossiter (New York: New American Library, 1961), no. 84, pp. 513–14.

6. W. B. Allen, ed., *The Essential Antifederalist* (New York: University Press of America, 1985), 60–62.

7. Ibid., 55, 47–48.

8. Elliot, ed., *Debates*, 1:334. New York's ratification document copied verbatim this statement by Rhode Island (see 1:327).

9. Ibid., New York's ratification document, 1:331, and Massachusetts's ratification document, 1:322.

10. *Annals of The Congress of the United States* (Washington, D.C.: Gales and Seaton, 1834), 1:458.

11. The same was constitutionally realized by the postbellum Fourteenth Amendment to the U.S. Constitution, as interpreted by the U.S. Supreme Court in the course of developing its theory of selective incorporation.

12. *Annals of the Congress*, 1:800–801.

13. The importance of property should not be underestimated. Publius conceded that "the most common and durable source of factions has been the verious [*sic*] and unequal distribution of property. Those who hold and those who are without property have ever formed distinct interests in society" (*Federalist Papers*, no. 10, p. 79).

14. *Annals of the Congress*, 1:452; Elliot, ed., *Debates*, 3:330.

15. John C. Calhoun, *Calhoun: Basic Documents*, ed. John M. Anderson (State College, Pa.: Bald Eagle Press, 1952), 63–64.

16. Edmund Ruffin, *African Colonisation Unveiled*, Virginia, 1860, pp. 1–2. Moreover, "the right, would have been destructive to the form of pure democracy at the North. The principle that all men are equal and equally right, would have been destructive of slavery in the South" (Hon. L. W. Spratt, *Philosophy of Secession: A Southern View*, Montgomery, Ala., 1861, p. 2).

17. Albert Taylor Bledsoe, LL.D., "Liberty and Slavery," in E. N. Elliott, ed., *"Cotton Is King" and Pro-Slavery Arguments, Comprising the Writings of Hammond, Harper, Christy, Strungfellow, Hodge, Bledsoe, and Cartwright* (Augusta, Ga.: Pritchard, Abbott & Loomis, 1860), 273.

18. Hon. Robert H. Smith, *An Address to the Citizens of Alabama on the Constitution and Laws of the Confederate States of America*, Mobile, Ala., 1861, p. 19. The "euphony" to which Smith refers is "persons held to service" of Article IV, section 2, of the U.S. Constitution.

19. James D. Richardson, ed., *A Compilation of the Messages and Papers of the Confederacy*, 2 vols. (Nashville: United States Publishing Company, 1906), 1:493–94.

20. Bledsoe, "Liberty and Slavery," 275, 284, 285. Of course, Bledsoe is referring to state civil society. An association of states, such as the Union or Confederacy, would indeed be "things of compacts," whereas a state has its origin in the law of nature.

21. Ibid., 287–88. Aristotle's conception of the individual's relationship to the community, is analogous to the public good being the whole and individual civil liberties its parts, with the former preceding the latter in time and importance.

22. *The Messages and Papers of Jefferson Davis and the Confederacy: Including Diplomatic Correspondence, 1861–1865*, 2 vols. (New York: Chelsea House-Robert Hector Publishers, 1966), 1:496.

23. Indeed, this policy was considered as the need for manpower necessitated the consideration of Negro recruitment. See Albert Burton Moore, *Conscription and Conflict in the Confederacy* (New York: Hillary House Publishers, 1963), 344–50. Also see "Proceedings of the Second Confederate Congress," *Southern Historical Society Papers* 52:452–57.

24. *Congressional Globe*, 36th Cong., 1st sess., 1860, pp. 2149, 2148.

25. Ibid., 2149.

26. *Journal of the Congress of the Confederate States of America, 1861–1865*, 7 vols. (Washington, D.C.: Government Printing Office, 1904–1905), 1:883–85.

27. See appendix, Article IV, section 3, and *Journal of the Congress of the Confederate States*, 1:895.

28. *Congressional Globe*, 36th Cong., 1st sess., 1859, p. 1244.

29. Smith, *An Address to the Citizens of Alabama*, 20.

30. John C. Calhoun, *The Works of John C. Calhoun*, ed. Richard Cralle, 6 vols. (New York: D. Appleton and Company, 1851–1856), 3:179–80.

31. J. H. Hammond, "Slavery in the Light of Political Science," in Elliott, ed., *"Cotton Is King" and Pro-Slavery Arguments*, 638–39.

32. "Leisure is a necessity, both for growth in goodness and for the pursuit of political activities" (Aristotle, *The Politics of Aristotle*, trans. and ed. Ernest Barker [New York: Oxford University Press, 1930], bk. 6, chap. 9, p. 301). This is not to say that Aristotle would endorse the Southern institution of slavery, or that skin pigmentation is a sufficient criterion for enslaving an entire people. However, the Aristotelian tradition and the Southern institution of slavery are compatible insofar as both regarded slavery as a natural condition for some individuals. Senator Hammond (referred to by the antislavery Senator James R. Doolittle as "an eloquent disciple in the school of Calhoun," *Congressional Globe*, 36th Cong., 1st sess., January 3, 1860, p. 97) stated on the floor of the Senate the hard-line proslavery position.

> In all social systems there must be a class to do the mean duties, to perform the drudgery of life. That is, a class requiring but a low order of intelligence and but little skill. Its requisites are vigor, docility, fidelity. Such a class you must have, or you would not have that other class which leads progress, refinement, and civilization. It constitutes the very mudsills of society and of political government; and you might as well attempt to build a house in the air, as to build either the one or the other, except on the mudsills. Fortunately for the South, she found a race adapted to that purpose to her hand. A race inferior to herself, but eminently qualified in temper, in vigor, in docility, in capacity to stand the climate, to answer all her purposes. We use them for that purpose,

and call them slaves. We are old fashioned at the South yet; it is a word discarded now by ears polite; but I will not characterize that class at the North with that term; but you have it; it is there; it is everywhere; it is eternal. (Ibid., 35th Congress, 1st sess., March 4, 1858, p. 962)

33. Dred Scott v. John Sandford, 15 L.Ed. 692 (1857).

34. Smith, *An Address to the Citizens of Alabama*, 15.

35. "The citizen in the strict sense is best defined by one criterion, 'a man who shares in the administration of justice and in the holding of office'" (Aristotle, *Politics*, bk 3, chap. 1, p. 93).

36. Dred Scott v. John Sandford, 15 L.Ed. 706 (1857).

37. See Calhoun, *Calhoun: Basic Documents*, 62–63.

38. Smith, *An Address to the Citizens of Alabama*, 15. The motivating force behind this constitutional arrangement resembles several planks of the 1856 American party platform. For example, "A change in the laws of naturalization, make a continued residence of twenty-one years, of all not heretofore provided for, an indispensable requisite for citizenship hereafter, and excluding all paupers, and persons convicted of crime, from landing upon our shores; but no interference with the vested rights of foreigners" (Henry Steele Commager, ed., *Documents of American History*, 2 vols., 8th ed. [New York: Appleton-Century-Crofts, 1968], 1:337).

39. Frank Moore, ed., *The Rebellion Record: A Diary of American Events* (New York: G. P. Putnam, 1861–1866), vol. 1, doc. 3, p. 4.

40. *Journal of the Congress of the Confederate States*, 2:227.

41. The C.S.A. attorney general was the recognized Confederate expositor of the C.S.A. Constitution, in lieu of the Congress's refusal to pass an enabling act to organize the C.S.A. Supreme Court.

42. Rembert W. Patrick, ed., *The Opinions of the Confederate Attorneys General, 1861–1865*, (Buffalo, N.Y.: Dennis & Co., 1950), 258, 314.

43. Ibid., 530.

44. Cited in J. G. DeRoulhac Hamilton, "The State Courts and the Confederate Constitution", *Journal of Southern History* 4, no. 4 (November, 1938): 427.

45. As a case in point, in 1863 C.S.A. Attorney General Watts, the highest Confederate judicial authority, reiterated the right of secession (see Patrick, ed., *Opinions of the Confederate Attorneys General*, 239–40).

Chapter Five. Institutional Innovations

1. Usurpation is here referred to in the Lockean sense: "As conquest may be called a foreign usurpation, so usurpation is a kind of domestic conquest, with this difference, that no usurper can ever have right on his side, it being no usurpation but where one is got into the possession of what another has a right to" (John Locke, "The Second Treatise Of Civil Government," chap. 27, sec. 197, in *Two Treatises of Government*, ed. Thomas I. Cook [New York: Hafner Press, 1947], 221). One might add, as the Confederate framers certainly would, that the prevention of usurpation decreases the probability of tyranny. Locke maintained: "This, so far as it is usurpation, is a change only of persons, but not of the forms and rules of the government; for if the usurper extend his power beyond what of right belonged to the lawful princes or governors of the commonwealth, it is tyranny added to usurpation" (221–22).

2. Walter Bagehot, *The English Constitution and Other Political Essays* (New York: D. Appleton & Company, 1877), 47.

3. Hon. Robert H. Smith, *An Address to the Citizens of Alabama on the Constitution and Laws of the Confederate States of America*, Mobile, Ala., 1861, p. 9.

4. Ibid., 9; Bagehot, *The English Constitution*, 82.

5. Ibid., 84.

6. James Madison, *Notes of Debates in the Federal Convention of 1787*, ed. Adrienne Koch (Athens: Ohio University Press, 1966), 61–62.

7. Ibid., 62, 64.

8. See ibid., 66.

9. James Madison, Alexander Hamilton, and John Jay, *The Federalist Papers*, ed. Clinton Rossiter (New York: New American Library, 1961), no. 73, pp. 443, 446.

10. Smith, *An Address to the Citizens of Alabama*, 7–8.

11. Ibid., 8.

12. John C. Calhoun, *Calhoun: Basic Documents*, ed. John M. Anderson (State College, Pa.: Bald Eagle Press, 1952), 239, 52.

13. *Federalist Papers*, no. 71, pp. 431, 432.

14. Ibid., no. 72, pp. 437, 438.

15. Ibid., 439; no. 37, p. 227.

16. See Forrest McDonald, *Novus Ordo Seclorum: The Intellectual Origins of the Constitution* (Lawrence: University of Kansas Press, 1985), 82–83.

17. See Calhoun, *Calhoun: Basic Documents*, 54–56.

18. John C. Calhoun, "A Discourse on the Constitution," in *The Works of John C. Calhoun*, ed. Richard Cralle (New York: D. Appleton and Company, 1851–1856), 1:350–51.

19. Article I, section 8, U.S. Constitution; *Federalist Papers*, no. 44, p. 285; Article I, section 8, clause 18, C.S.A. Constitution.

20. Calhoun, *Calhoun: Basic Documents*, 42.

21. Calhoun, "A Discourse," in *Works of John C. Calhoun*, ed. Cralle, 174. Calhoun forewarned that "this system, if continued, must end, not only in subjecting the industry and property of the weaker section to the control of the stronger, but in proscription and political disfranchisement. It must finally control elections and appointments to offices, as well as acts of legislation, to the great increase of the feelings of animosity, and of the fatal tendency to complete alienation between the sections" (175).

22. *Congressional Globe*, 35th Cong., 2 sess., appendix: 190, 201, 86, 69.

23. J. T. Headley, *The Great Rebellion: A History of the Civil War in the United States*, 2 vols. (Hartford: Hurlbut, Williams & Company, 1863), preface.

24. Smith, *An Address to the Citizens of Alabama*, 11.

25. Madison, *Notes*, 449–550.

26. Ibid., 547, 550.

27. Cf. Article I, section 10, U.S. Constitution.

28. See Madison, *Notes*, 543–44.

29. *Federalist Papers*, no. 7, pp. 62–63.

30. *Congressional Globe*, 35th Cong., 2 sess., appendix: 188.

31. Ibid., 244.

32. *Federalist Papers*, no. 42, p. 271.

33. See Herbert Wender, "Southern Commercial Conventions, 1837–1859," in *Johns Hopkins University Studies in Historical and Political Science*, series 48, no. 4 (Baltimore: Johns Hopkins Press, 1930), 1–29.

34. See Ibid., passim. A circular announcing the 1837 commercial convention in Augusta, Georgia, exemplifies the intended function of these conventions.

> A crisis has arrived in the commercial affairs of the South and Southwest; a crisis the most favorable that has occurred since the formation of the American Government to attempt a new organization of our commercial relations with Europe. We ought to be our own importers and exporters, for the very best reason, that we furnish nearly all the articles of export in the great staples of cotton, rice, and tobacco. This is a singular advantage for any people to enjoy.

Yet, with all this in our favor by nature, we employ the merchants of the Northern cities as our agents in this business. . . . It has indeed, either directly or indirectly, made the whole of the North and Northwest what they are. It is time this unequal state of things should cease; that we should look to the natural advantages of our situation as Southern men, and take measures to secure to ourselves the full enjoyment of them. (Ibid., 11)

35. Smith, *An Address to the Citizens of Alabama*, 24.

Chapter Six. Judicial Review

1. See Charles Alan Wright, *Law of the Federal Courts* (St. Paul, Minn: West Publishing Co., 1976), 289–91.
2. William M. Robinson, *Justice in Grey: A History of the Judicial System of the Confederate States of America* (Cambridge: Harvard University Press, 1941), 45. Robinson's research is to date the most comprehensive account of the Confederate judicial systems.
3. See Wright, *Law of the Federal Courts*, 289–91.
4. James Madison, Alexander Hamilton, and John Jay, *The Federalist Papers*, ed. Clinton Rossiter (New York: New American Library, 1961), no. 80, p. 480.
5. John P. Kaminski and Richard Leffler, eds., *The Federalists and Antifederalists: The Debate over the Ratification of the Constitution* (Madison: Madison House, 1989), 124.
6. Quoted in Christopher Wolfe, *The Rise of Modern Judicial Review: From Constitutional Interpretation to Judge-Made Law* (New York: Basic Books, 1986), 19.
7. See Joseph Story, *Commentaries on Equity Jurisprudence as Administered in England and America*, 2 vols. (New York: Anno Press, 1972), 1:1–37.
8. See Chisholm v. Georgia, 2 U.S. (2 Dallas) 419 (1793).
9. The exceptions being North Carolina and South Carolina, where judges were appointed by both legislative chambers for life, that is, during good behavior, and Florida and Georgia, where judges were nominated by the executive and confirmed by the Senate (Robinson, *Justice in Grey*, 73). Even so, the Carolinians' processes were more democratic than the U.S. process because of the participation of the lower chamber of their legislatures.
10. See *Federalist Papers*, no. 78, pp. 464–72.
11. L. Q. Washington, among others, as a participant in a symposium titled "Why the Confederate States of America Had No Supreme Court," maintained that the contingencies of war prevented the C.S.A. Supreme Court from being organized (see *Publications of the Southern History Association* 4, no. 2 [March, 1900]: 100).
12. Albert Burton Moore, *Conscription and Conflict in the Confederacy* (New York: Hillary House Publishers, 1963), 166–67.
13. Ibid., 163.
14. 4 L.Ed. 579 (1819).
15. See *U.S. Statutes at Large* 1:73 ff.
16. 3 L.Ed. 162 (1810) and 4 L.Ed. 97 (1816).
17. *Acts and Resolutions of the First Session of the Provisional Congress of the Confederate States* (Richmond, 1861), no. 82, p. 128, as cited in J. G. De Roulhac Hamilton, "The State Courts and the Confederate Constitution," *Journal of Southern History* 4, no. 4 (November, 1938): 426.
18. Ibid., 427.
19. "Proceedings of the First Confederate Congress," *Southern Historical Society Papers* 48:4.

20. Ibid., 15.

21. Ibid., 50:68.

22. John Codman Hurd, *The Law of Freedom and Bondage in the United States*, 2 vols. (New York: D. Van Nostrand, 1858), 1:22.

23. *Federalist Papers*, no. 82, p. 495.

24. James Kent, *Commentaries on American Law*, 4 vols. (New York: E. B. Clayton, James Van Norden, Printers, 1836), 1:395.

25. 5 L.Ed. 257 (1821).

26. Ibid., 270–71, 272. Virginia reasoned that "the Constitution provides, that the judicial power of the United States shall 'extend to' certain enumerated cases. These words signify plainly, that the federal courts shall have jurisdiction in those cases; but this does not imply exclusive jurisdiction, except in those cases where the jurisdiction of the state courts would be contrary to the necessary effect of the provisions of the constitution. Civil suits, arising under the laws of the United States, may be brought and finally determined in the courts of foreign nations; and, consequently, may be brought and finally determined in the states courts" (272).

27. Ibid., 271.

28. Ibid., 286. Marshall acknowledged that "the opinion of the *Federalist* has always been considered of great authority. It is a complete commentary on our Constitution" (294). An axiom of that "great authority" was that "thirteen independent courts of final jurisdiction over the same causes, arising upon the same laws, is a hydra in government from which nothing but contradiction and confusion can proceed" (*Federalist Papers*, no. 80, p. 476).

29. 5 L.Ed. 287.

30. Ibid., 268.

31. Ibid., 287.

32. Robinson, *Justice in Grey*, 72. State legislatures were not averse to political entanglements regarding constitutional disputes. For example, not only did state judges by and large have the support of their respective executive and legislative branches, some of these branches, such as the state legislatures of Georgia, Mississippi, and North Carolina, pronounced as unconstitutional the C.S.A. policies that suspended the writ of habeas corpus (Sidney D. Brummer, "The Judicial Interpretation of the Confederate Constitution," in *Studies in Southern History and Politics* [New York: Columbia University Press, 1914], 129).

33. On behalf of the states' rights position, Senator Louis T. Wigfall of Texas attempted to bring some uniformity to the controversy at the national level when he introduced the following resolutions in the Senate:

> *Resolved*, That the Congress of the Confederate States has the undoubted right, during invasion or rebellion, and when the public safety requires it, to suspend the privilege of the writ of haveas corpus, and that while so suspended it is not competent for any Confederate judge to discharge from custody any person held under or by virtue of the authority of the Confederate States. *Resolved*, That the State courts being established by State authority, can in no manner be affected by Confederate legislation, and therefore that an act of the Confederate Congress suspending the privilege of the writ of habeas corpus does not apply to them, and in no wise prevents their exercising such jurisdiction, or issuing such writs, as by the laws of their States they are allowed to execute or issue. . . . *Resolved*, That the Constitution of the Confederate States is, as to the States and between them, a compact; and that each has, as in all cases of compacts between sovereigns, a perfect right to declare its true intent and meaning; and that the citizens of each State are bound by such decisions. (Hamilton, "The State Courts and the Confederate Constitution," 434)

34. See McCulloch v. Maryland, 4 L.Ed. 579 (1819).

35. "This Constitution, and the laws of the Confederate States made in pursuance thereof, and all treaties made or which shall be made under the authority of the Confederate States, shall be the supreme law of the land; and the Judges in every State shall be bound thereby, anything in the Constitution or laws of any State to the contrary notwithstanding" (Article VI).

36. The significant cases representing the rationale of the states are Jeffers v. Fair, 33 Georgia, 347; ex Parte Coupland, 26 Texas 386; Burroughs v. Peyton, 16 Virginia 470; in re Bryan, 60 North Carolina 1.

37. Ex parte Coupland, 404; Burroughs v. Peyton, 472, 481.

38. *Southern Historical Society Papers* 48:243.

39. See Rembert W. Patrick, ed., *The Opinions of the Confederate Attorneys General, 1861–1865* (Buffalo, N.Y.: Dennis & Co., 1950), 460.

40. *Southern Historical Society Papers* 48:253–54.

41. Ibid., 255.

42. Ibid., 49:12–17.

43. For example, a railroad company filed suit in Alabama on the grounds that impressment impaired the obligation of a contract to which it was a party. The high court ruled in favor of impressment on the grounds that contracts imply the potentiality of governmental policies such as impressment (Alabama and Florida Railroad Co. v. Kenney, 39 Ala. 307).

44. Cunningham v. Campbell et al., 33 G 635, 636.

45. *Southern Historical Society Papers* 50:29, 53.

46. Representative Lucius J. Gartrell spoke on behalf of the House version: "The whole principle of the bill was, that whenever the Government shall impress the property of an individual it shall pay the owner a fair and just compensation" (ibid., 90). The prevailing position of the Senate was expressed by Senator Benjamin Hill: "The power to fix prices should not be withdrawn from the commissioners, as no damage would result from the further exercise of that power. When prices were fixed by the commissioners there was a willingness, on the part of the producers, to submit to them. The machinery already existed" (ibid., 252).

47. Burroughs v. Peyton 16 Virginia 483 (1864), 484.

Chapter Seven. The American Origins of the Confederate Order

1. Thomas Hobbes, *Leviathan; or, The Matter, Forme, and Power of a Commonwealth, Ecclesiasticall and Civill*, ed. C. B. Macpherson (1651; reprint Baltimore: Penguin Books, 1968), 363.

2. W. B. Allen, ed., *The Essential Antifederalist* (New York: University Press of America, 1985), 56–57.

3. *Constitutional Rights Speech of the Hon. William L. Yancy of Alabama at Wieting Hall, Syracuse, N.Y., October 15, 1860*, 3. Alexander H. Stephens stated the Southern consensus: "I assume, in the outset, that the Government, as it exists, is worth preserving; nay, more, with all its errors and defects, with all its corruptions in administration, and short-comings of its officers, it is the best Government on earth, and ought to be sustained, if it can be, on the principles upon which it was founded" (*Speech of the Hon. Alexander H. Stephens, Delivered in the City Hall Park, Augusta, Georgia, on Saturday Evening, September 1, 1860*).

Furthermore, the 36th Congress abounds with Southern legislators admonishing their Northern colleagues to restore fundamental constitutional principles that allegedly had been set aside for political expediency. For example, Senator Toombs's speech in the Senate on January 24, 1860, in part stated that "the fundamental principles of the system or our social Union are assailed, invaded, and threatened with destruction; our ancient rights and liberties are in danger; the peace and tranquility of our homes have been invaded by lawless violence, and their further invasion is imminent; the instinct of self-preservation arouses society to their defense. These are the causes which are undermining, and which, if not soon arrested, will overthrow the Republic" (*Congressional Globe*, 36th Cong., 1st sess., appendix: p. 88). Moreover, the various state declarations, which served the dual purposes of announcing and justifying secession, never criticized the U.S. Constitution per se, but rather they condemned the Northern states for their failure to live up to their constitutional obligations. South Carolina's official statement contends that "an increasing hostility on the part of the non-slaveholding States to the Institution of Slavery has led to a disregard of their obligations, and the laws of the General Government have ceased to effect the objects of the Constitution. . . . Thus the constitutional compact has been deliberately broken and disregarded by the non-slaveholding States, and the consequence follows that South Carolina is released from her obligation" (*Causes Which Induce and Justify the Secession of South Carolina from the Federal Union: and the Ordinance of Secession,* official pamphlet, 1860, pp. 6–7).

4. Allen, ed., *Essential Antifederalist*, 56–57.

5. Ibid., 83.

6. James Madison, Alexander Hamilton, and John Jay, *The Federalist Papers*, ed. Clinton Rossiter (New York: New American Library, 1961), no. 1, p. 35.

7. Allen, ed., *Essential Antifederalist*, 92.

8. *Federalist Papers*, no. 57, p. 350; no. 9, pp. 64–76.

9. Donald S. Lutz, *Popular Consent and Popular Control* (Baton Rouge: Louisiana State University Press, 1979), 224.

10. Gordon S. Wood, *The Creation of the American Republic, 1776–1787* (New York: Norton Library, 1969), 57–58.

11. *Federalist Papers*, no. 10, p. 79.

12. Herbert J. Storing, *What the Anti-Federalists Were For* (Chicago: University of Chicago Press, 1981), 15.

13. Allen, ed., *Essential Antifederalist*, 109.

14. *Federalist Papers*, no. 10, pp. 82–83.

15. Theosophilus Parsons, "The Essex Result," in *American Political Writings during the Founding Era, 1760–1805,* ed. Charles Hyneman and Donald Lutz, 2 vols. (Indianapolis: Liberty Press, 1983), 1:491.

16. *Federalist Papers*, no. 10, p. 79.

17. Ibid., no. 37, p. 226.

18. Parsons, "The Essex Result," 1:494.

19. *Federalist Papers*, no. 47 p. 301; no. 51, p. 322.

20. Ibid., no. 10, p. 77.

21. Ibid., no. 51, cited in Wood, *Creation of the American Republic*, 605.

22. The destructiveness of the war between the states and U.S. Supreme Court's dicta attest to this fact.

Bibliography

Congressional Globe

The Congressional speeches and debates included in this bibliography serve a twofold purpose. First, they make manifest the development of the issues that split the Union. And second, the constitutional doctrine articulated by Southern congressmen, as they debated the issues with their Northern colleagues, finds its way into the C.S.A. Constitution; hence, the former provides invaluable insight into the latter. (The references with an asterisk [*] are to be found in the appendix of the *Congressional Globe* being cited.)

Congressional Globe. 46 vols. Washington, D.C., 1834–1873.

31st Congress, 1st Session

Senator Henry Clay, January 29, 1850, "The Slavery Question," 242–52.

Senator Jefferson Davis, February 13 and 14, 1850, "Slavery in the Territories," 149–57.

Senators Henry S. Foote and Henry Clay, February 14, 1850, "California," 365–69.

Senator John C. Calhoun, March 4, 1850, "The Compromise," 451–56.

Senator Daniel Webster, March 7, 1850, "Compromise Resolutions," 269–76.*

Senator William Seward, March 11, 1850, "California, Union, and Freedom," 260–69.*

Senator Stephen A. Douglas, March 13 and 14, "The Territorial Question," 364–75.*

Senator Robert M. T. Hunter, March 25, 1850, "The Territorial Question," 375–82.*

Senator James M. Mason, May 27, 1850, "The Compromise Bill," 650–55.*

Representative Williamson R. W. Cobb, June 3, 1850, "The Slavery Question," 646–49.*

34th Congress, 1st Session

Representative William R. Smith, March 10, 1856, "Kansas Contested Election," 156–60.*

Representative A. H. Stephens, March 11, 1856, "Kansas Contested Election,"179–83.*

Senator Lewis Cass, March 13 and 14, 1856, "Kansas—The Territories," 512–26.*

Senator Stephen A. Douglas, April 4, 1856, "Admission of Kansas," 358–64.*

Senator William Seward, April 9, 1856, "Admission of Kansas," 399–405.*

Senator Clement C. Clay, Jr., April 21, 1856, "Affairs of Kansas-Slavery Question," 481–90.*

Senator Albert G. Brown, April 28, 1856, "Admission of Kansas," 433–35.*

Representative John J. Perry, May 1, 1856, "Policy of the Republican Party," 456–76.*

Senators Charles Sumner, Stephen A. Douglas, and James M. Mason, May 19 and 20, 1856, "Kansas Affair," 529–44.*

Senator Andrew P. Butler, June 12 and 13, 1856, "Mr. Brooks and Sumner," 625–35.*

Senators Robert M. T. Hunter and William Seward, June 24, 1856, "Debate in the Senate," 656–63.*

Representative A. H. Stephens, June 28, 1856, "Admission of Kansas," 723–29.*

Senators Robert Toombs, John P. Hale, and John J. Crittenden, July 2, 1856, "Admission of Kansas," 767–72.*

Senators Benjamin Wade, Asa Biggs, Henry Wilson, and John J. Crittenden, July 2, 1856, "Debate in the Senate on the Admission of Kansas," 749–64.

Senator Robert Toombs, July 9, 1856, "Kansas Affairs," 869–72.*

Representative Howell Cobb, July 10, 1856, "Assault on Sumner," 809–12.*

35th Congress, 1st Session

Senators Albert G. Brown, Stephen A. Douglas, Jefferson Davis, James R. Doolittle, George E. Pugh, James S. Green, Robert M. T. Hunter, Charles E. Stuart, William Bigler, Thomas C. Clingman, John P. Hale, Daniel Clark, Lyman Trumbull, and John J.

Crittenden, February 23, 1859, "Territorial Question/Fugitive Slave Laws," 1241–75.

Senators James H. Hammond, Stephen A. Douglas, James M. Mason, Henry Wilson, and James R. Doolittle, March 4, 1858, "Lecompton Constitution—Admission of Kansas," 959–64.

Senator James H. Hammond, March 4, 1858, "Lecompton Constitution," 68–71.*

Senator James M. Mason, March 15, 1858, "Lecompton Constitution," 76–80.*

Senator Daniel Clark, March 15, 1858, "Lecompton Constitution," 84–95.*

Senator Robert Toombs, March 18, 1858, "Lecompton Constitution," 124–29.*

Senator John Bell, March 18, 1858, "Lecompton Constitution," 132–40.*

Senator Clement C. Clay, March 19, 1858, "Lecompton Constitution," 144–51.*

Senator Solomon Foot, March 20, 1858, "Lecompton Constitution," 153–58.*

Senator James F. Simmons, March 20, 1858, "Lecompton Constitution," 158–63.*

Senator Henry Wilson, March 20, 1858, "Lecompton Constitution," 167–74.*

Senator Charles E. Stuart, March 22, 1858, "Lecompton Constitution," 174–81.*

Senator James A. Bayard, March 22, 1858, "Lecompton Constitution," 181–91.*

Senator David C. Broderick, March 22, 1858, "Lecompton Constitution," 191–93.*

Senator Stephen A. Douglas, March 22, 1858, "Lecompton Constitution," 194–201.*

Senator Robert Toombs, March 22, 1858, "Lecompton Constitution," 201–4.*

Senator James S. Green, March 23, 1858, "Lecompton Constitution," 204–12.*

Senator John J. Crittenden, March 23, 1858, "Lecompton Constitution," 212–14.*

36th Congress, 1st Session

Representative Jabez L. M. Curry, December 10, 1859, "Progress of Anti-Slaveryism," 39–42.*

Senators Alfred Iverson, George E. Pugh, James A. Mason, Lyman
   Trumbull, Andrew Johnson, and James R. Doolittle, December
   12, 1859, "Invasion of Harper's Ferry," 98–107.
Senator James R. Doolittle, January 3, 1860, "The Calhoun Revolu-
   tion," 97–104.*
Senator Thomas C. Clingman, January 17, 1860, "Abolitionism,"
   449–56.
Senator Robert Toombs, January 24, 1860, "Invasion of the States,"
   88–92.*
Representative Laurence M. Keitt, January 25, 1860, "Organization
   of the House," 93–97.
Senator Robert M. T. Hunter, January 31, 1860, "Invasion of the
   States," 104–9.*
Representative James Wilson, May 1, 1860, "Slavery Question,"
   319–27.
Representative Henry C. Longnecker, May 4, 1860, "The Tariff,"
   344–48.*
Representative Horace Maynard, May 7, 1860, "The Tariff," 328–31.*
Senator Jefferson Davis, May 8, 1860, "Relations of the States,"
   1937–44.
Senator James M. Mason, May 18, 1860, "Property in the Territo-
   ries," 316–19.
Representative Williamson R. W. Cobb, May 19, 1860, "Slavery
   Question," 335–38.*
Representative Israel Washburn, May 19, 1860, "The Dred Scott
   Decision and Parties," 348–55.*
Senator Robert Toombs, May 21, 1860, "Property in the Territories,"
   338–45.*
Representative James M. Ashley, May 29, 1860, "Success of the
   Calhoun Revolution," 365–77.
Representative Reuben Davis, June 6, 1860, "Slavery Question,"
   384–87.*

36th Congress, 2d Session

Senator Alfred Iverson, December 11, 1860, "The State of the
   Union," 48–51.
Senator George E. Pugh, December 20, 1860, "State of the Union,"
   29–35.*
Senator Louis T. Wigfall, December 12, 1860, "Irrepressible Con-
   flict," 73–76.

Senator John J. Crittenden, December 18, 1860, "Compromise," 112–14.

Senator Andrew Johnson, December 18, 1860, "Amendment of the Constitution," 117–20.

Senator Judah P. Benjamin, December 31, 1860, "Amendments to the Constitution," 212–18.

Senator Jefferson Davis, January 10, 1861, "The Impending Crisis," 306–12.

Senator Robert M. T. Hunter, January 11, 1861, "State of the Union," 328–32.

Senator Trusten Polk, January 14, 1861, "The Momentous Crisis," 355–60.

Representative James M. Ashley, January 17, 1861, "The Union of the States," 61–70.*

Senators David Levy Yulee, Stephen R. Mallory, Clement C. Clay, Benjamin Fitzpatrick, and Jefferson Davis, January 21, 1861, "Withdrawal from the Senate," 484–87.

Senator Alfred Iverson, January 28, 1861, "Withdrawal from the Senate," 589.

Senator John Slidell, February 4, 1861, "Withdrawal from the Senate," 720–22.

Senator Thomas C. Clingman, February 4, 1861, "Seward's Speech," 723–28.

Representative Thomas Ruffin, February 20, 1861, "State Rights and State Equality," 225–28.*

Representative Clement L. Vallandigham, February 20, 1861, "The American Revolution of 1861," 235–43.*

President Abraham Lincoln, March 4, 1861, "Inaugural Address," 1433–35.

Senators Thomas C. Clingman, Stephen A. Douglas, Louis T. Wigfall, James M. Mason, March 6, 1861, "The Inaugural Address," 1436–46.

Pamphlets and Other Primary Sources

Through their publication and subsequent distribution, pamphlets served as vehicles for mobilizing and solidifying Southern public opinion for the "impending crisis." This public opinion, conducive to Southern nationhood, approached its apex during the framing of the C.S.A. Constitution. An excellent reference for locating archives holding these and other useful pamphlets and documents is Henry Putney Beers, *Guide to the Archives of the Government of the Confederate States of America* (Washington, D.C.: The National Archives, National Archives and Records Service General Service Administration, 1968).

Amor Patriae. *The Blasphemy of Abolitionism Exposed.* Ca. 1860, 24 pp.

"The Address of the People of South Carolina, Assembled in Convention, to the People of the Slaveholding States of the United States." Charleston, S.C., 1860, 16 pp.

The Bible or Atheism. Ca. 1861, 31 pp.

Calhoun, John C. *Calhoun: Basic Documents.* Edited by John M. Anderson. State College, Pa.: Bald Eagle Press, 1952.

———. "Disquisition on Government" and "A Discourse on the Constitution and Government of the United States." In *The Works of John C. Calhoun.* Edited by Richard Cralle. 6 vols. New York: D. Appleton and Company, 1856.

The Confederate Papers: I–XII. Ca. 1861, 96 pp.

The Correspondence between the Commissioners of the State of South Carolina to the Government at Washington and the President of the United States, Together with the Statement of Messrs. Miles and Keitt. Charleston, S.C., 1861.

Cobb, T. R. R. *Substance of an Address of T. R. R. Cobb, to His Constituents of Clark County,* April 6, 1861, 8 pp.

Davis, Jefferson. *The Life and Character of the Honorable John Caldwell Calhoun.* 15 pp.

———. *The Rise and Fall of the Confederate Government.* 2 vols. New York: D. Appleton and Company, 1881.

DeBow, James D. "The Interest in Slavery of the Non-Slaveholder." New York, 1860.

The Designs of Black-Republicanism, and the Issues of 1860, in Their Consequences to the South, the Constitution, and the Union. 1860.

Elliot, Jonathan, ed. *The Debates in the Several State Conventions on the Adoption of the Federal Constitution.* Washington, D.C.: Taylor and Maury, 1854.

Elliott, E. N., ed. *"Cotton Is King" and Pro-Slavery Arguments, Comprising the Writings of Hammond, Harper, Christy, Strungfellow, Hodge, Bledsoe, and Cartwright.* Augusta, Ga.: Pritchard, Abbott & Loomis, 1860.

Farrand, Max, ed. *The Records of the Federal Convention of 1787.* New Haven: Yale University Press, 1911.

Fitzhugh, George. *Sociology for the South; Or, the Failure of Free Society.* New York: Burt Franklin, 1855.

Fox, Dixon R., ed. *Documents of American History.* New York: F. S. Crofts & Company, 1943.

Gentleman of Mississippi. *Secession: Considered as a Right in the States Composing the Late American Union of States, and as to the*

Grounds of Justification of the Southern States in Exercising the Right. Jackson, Miss., 1863, 45 pp.

Hall, Rev. William A. *The Historic Significance of the Southern Revolution.* Petersburg, Va., 1864, 45 pp.

Headley, J. T. *The Great Rebellion: A History of the Civil War in the United States.* 2 vols. Hartford, Conn.: Hurlbut, Williams & Company, 1863.

Hughes, Henry. *Treatise on Sociology.* Philadelphia: Lippincott, Grambo & Co., 1854.

Hull, A. L. "The Making of the Confederate Constitution." 1861. Reprint. *Southern Historical Society Papers* 28 (1900): 272–92.

Hull, Augustus L., ed. "The Correspondence of Thomas Reade Rootes Cobb, 1860–1862." *Southern Historical Association, Publications,* 11:147–85, 233–60.

Hyneman, Charles, and Lutz, Donald, eds. *American Political Writings during the Founding Era, 1760–1805.* 2 vols. Indianapolis: Liberty Press, 1983.

Inexorable Logic: Congressional Sovereignty vs. Democratic Faith. St. Louis, Mo., 1860, 24 pp.

Johnson, Hon. Reverdy. *Popular Sovereignty, as Maintained and Denied Respectively by Judge Douglas and Attorney General Black.* 17 pp.

Journal of the Congress of the Confederate States of America, 1861–1865. Vols. 1–7. (Ser. doc. 234, 58th Congress, 2d sess.) Washington, D.C.: Government Printing Office, 1904–1905.

Letter of Governor Wise to The New York Tammany Society. Richmond, Va., 1857, 7 pp. *Review of a Review of Governor Wise's Tammany Letter, by an Eminent Virginia Statesman.* Richmond, Va., 1858, 11 pp. *Continuation of a Review of a Review of Governor Wise's Tammany Letter, by an Eminent Virginia Statesman.* Richmond, Va., 1858, 47 pp.

Madison, James. *Notes of Debates in the Federal Convention of 1787.* Edited by Adrienne Koch. Athens: Ohio University Press, 1966.

Madison, James, Alexander Hamilton, and John Jay. *The Federalist Papers.* New York: New American Library, 1961.

Miles, Rev. James W. *The Discourse on the Occasion of the Funeral of the Hon. John C. Calhoun, Delivered under the Appointment of the Joint Committee of the City Council and Citizens of Charleston, in St. Philip's Church, April 26, 1850.* 39 pp.

Moore, Frank, ed. *The Rebellion Record: A Diary of American Events,* Vols. 1–6. New York: G. P. Putnam, 1861–1863. Vols. 7–12. New York: D. Van Nostrand, 1864–1868.

Patrick, Rembert W., ed. *The Opinions of the Confederate Attorneys General, 1861–1865.* Buffalo, New York: Dennis & Co., 1950.

Paulding, J. K. *State Sovereignty and the Doctrine of Coercion.* Charleston, 1860, 29 pp.

Phillips, Ulrich B., ed. *The Correspondence of Robert Toombs, Alexander Stephens, and Howell Cobb.* New York: Da Capo Press, 1970.

Pollard, Edward A. *The Lost Cause: A New Southern History of the War of the Confederates.* New York: E. B. Treat & Co., 1867.

Poore, Benjamin P., ed. *The Federal and State Constitutions, Colonial Charters, and Other Organic Laws of the United States.* Washington, D.C.: Government Printing Office, 1877.

Preston, Hon. John S. *Address of Hon. John S. Preston, Commissioner from South Carolina, to the Convention of Virginia, February 19, 1861.* 22 pp.

Report on the Address of a Portion of the Members of the General Assembly of Georgia. Charleston, S.C., 1860, 6 pp.

Richardson, James D., ed. *A Compilation of the Messages and Papers of the Confederacy.* 2 vols. Nashville: United States Publishing Company, 1906.

The Right to Secede. Charleston, S.C., 1860, 9 pp.

Ruffin, Edmund. *African Colonization Unveiled.* Virginia, 1860, 32 pp.

―――. *The Political Economy of Slavery.* Washington, D.C., 1857, 31 pp.

Sledd, Rev. R. N. *A Sermon: Delivered in the Market Street M. E. Church, Petersburg, Virginia, before the Confederate Cadets on the Occasion of Their Departure for War, Sunday, September 22nd, 1861.* 23 pp.

Smith, Hon. Robert H. *An Address to the Citizens of Alabama, on the Constitution and Laws of the Confederate States of America.* Mobile, Ala., March 30, 1861, 24 pp.

Spratt, Hon. L. W. *Philosophy of Secession: A Southern View.* Montgomery, Ala., 1861, 16 pp.

State Sovereignty and the Doctrine of Coercion. Charleston, S.C., 1860, 29 pp.

Stephens, Alexander H. *Speech of the Hon. Alexander H. Stephens Delivered in the City Hall Park, Augusta, Georgia, on Saturday Evening, September 1, 1860.* 16 pp.

―――. *The War between the States.* Philadelphia: National Publishing Company, 1868.

Tucker, Hon. Beverly. *Southern Convention Remarks.* Virginia, 1860, 16 pp.

Vernor, Rev. W. H. *A Sermon, Delivered before the Marshall Guards No. 1.* Lewisburg, Tenn., 1861, 15 pp.

Van Deusen, John G. *The Ante-Bellum Southern Commercial Conventions.* Historical Papers Published by the Trinity College Historical Society, no. 16. Durham, N.C.: Duke University Press, 1926.

Virginia Commission on Constitutional Government. *We the States: An Anthology of Historic Documents and Commentaries.* Richmond, Va.: William Byrd Press, 1964.

Virginius. *The Right and Propriety of Southern States.* Richmond, Va., 1861, 56 pp.

Walker, R. J. *Inaugural Address of R. J. Walker, Governor of Kansas Territory.* Lecompton, Kans., 1857, 24 pp.

Wender, Herbert. "Southern Commercial Conventions: 1837–1859." *Johns Hopkins University Studies in Historical and Political Science,* series 48, no. 4. Baltimore: Johns Hopkins Press, 1930.

Yancey, William L. *An Address on the Life and Character of John C. Calhoun, Delivered before the Citizens of Montgomery, Alabama, on the Fourth of July, 1850, by William L. Yancey.*

———. *Constitutional Rights Speech.* New York, 1860, 39 pp.

———. *Speech of the Hon. William L. Yancey of Alabama, Delivered in the National Democratic Convention.* Charleston, S.C., 1860, 20 pp.

Index

American empire, 30, 157n
Amendment process, 43–44
Antifederalists, 23–24; support for a bill of rights, 60–61; and executive veto power, 83–84; and federal courts, 102; C.S.A. framers' relation to, 121, 122; 1787 convention debates, 124–34 *passim*; on the extended republic, 128–29
Appomattox, 122
Aristotle, 73, 162n; definition of constitution, 18; on state of nature, 26; definition of citizen, 163n
Articles of Confederation, 5, 13, 31, 35, 41, 60, 95, 122; Article II, 158n
Ashley, James: on the influence of Calhoun, 156n

Bagehot, Walter, 82
Bailyn, Bernard, 3–4
Bank of the United States, 38
Bedford, Gunning, 83
Bill of Rights: defined, 57; 1787 convention debate, 57–63; ratification documents in support of, 61; C.S.A. reserved rights, 63
Blackstone, Sir William, 102
Bledsoe, Albert Taylor, 162n; on slavery, 65; on natural rights, 67–68
Boyce, William W., 97
British Constitution, 59–60
Brown, Albert G.: on the status of slavery within the Confederacy, 71
Brutus: on the public good, 127; on the extended republic, 127–28

Cabinet government, 81
Calhoun, John C., 1–56 *passim*; nationally consolidated democracy, 10; slavery controversy, 9–10; rejection of state of nature, 26–27; basis of rights, 28–29; sectional interests, 33–34; federalism, 34–36; reference to *The Federalist*, 36, 158n; *imperium in imperio*, 37; compact theory, 44–45; concurrent majority, 46; critique of the ex-

tended republic, 47–48; sovereignty of the states, 49; written constitutions, 51; "several states," 54; entitlement to liberty, 64; theory on rights, 65; on slavery, 66; referred to by J. Davis, 71; legislative process, 86–87; executive powers, 89; general welfare, 90; fiscal policy, 91, 92; Fort Hill address, 92, 164n; Southern commercial conventions, 98; concurrent majority, 119; leader of the South, 155–56n; about progress, 157n; on the Force Bill, 158–59n; on the homogeneous community, 159n
Caperton, Allen T.: C.S.A. impressment policy, 116
Carey, George, 154n
Carpenter, Jesse T., 17
Checks and balances. *See* Separation of powers
Checks on government, 45–46
Chisholm v. *Georgia* (1793), 103
Citizenship, C.S.A., 74–75
Clay, Clement C.: higher law, 14–15; 1856 Republican party platform, 15; secession, 16; law of comity, 14; C.S.A. Supreme Court, 107
Clay, Henry, 9
Cobb, Thomas R. R., 54; on the status of slavery in the Confederacy, 71
Cohens v. *Virginia* (1821), 110, 111, 166n
Comity, law of, 14; defined in *Corfield* v. *Coryell* (1823), 154n
Commercial conventions, 98; 1837 circular, 164–65n
Commercial republic, 20–21; C.S.A. disposition toward, 72
Common good, 50, 125; Publius's and Calhoun's interpretation of, 50–51
Common-law tradition, 59–60
Community of individuals, 40; interpretations of, 125–27, 131
Compact theory of federalism, 44–45, 53–54; South Carolina's, 45
Concurrent majority, 25–37 *passim*; as

179